Liml Carley
'Worthing
2. iv. 97

ROSE:
My Life in Service

ROSE:
My Life in Service

ROSINA HARRISON

CASSELL · LONDON

CASSELL & COMPANY LIMITED
35 Red Lion Square, London WC1R 4SG
and at Sydney, Auckland, Toronto, Johannesburg
an affiliate of
Macmillan Publishing Co., Inc.,
New York

First published September 1975
First edition, second impression November 1975
First edition, third impression December 1975

ISBN 0 304 29470 5

*Printed in Great Britain by
The Camelot Press Ltd, Southampton*

1175

To Leigh 'Reggie' Crutchley, who made it possible

Good Luck

Rosina Harrison

Contents

Foreword   xi

1   Childhood   1

2   I Go into Service   15

3   Meeting the Astors   39

4   My Lady and My Duties   63

5   Coming to Terms with My Job   81

6   Entertaining in the Grand Manner   108

7   The Astor Family   144

8   A Family in Wartime   178

9   Achieving My Ambition   205

10   Religion and Politics   233

11   Last Years   248

Index   262

List of Illustrations

following page 84
My mother
My father
With my younger sisters and brother
Our home at Aldfield, near Ripon
Our kitchen in 1917: a drawing by Lt. O'Dowd
I had this picture taken for my parents
One of my first employers: Lady Cranborne dressed for a
    pageant
Phyllis Astor: 'Miss Wissie'
David, Lady Astor's second son
Lady Astor wearing the Astor tiara
The dining-room at 4 St James's Square
How the Cliveden menservants were dressed
Gordon Grimmett, footman, at Rest Harrow
Edwin Lee, butler, and Arthur Bushell, valet
A page from Mr Lee's 'black book', his record of
    Cliveden guests
Cliveden, Buckinghamshire (*Keystone Press*)
Lord and Lady Astor (*Weekly Illustrated*)

following page 180
At Lord Mildmay's. We had been out for a drive
This is when Lady Astor sent us fishing
With the ghillie at Jura, 1931
My sister Ann as 'Washing Day'
'Eliza Comes to Stay'
My brother-in-law Cyril Price as 'National Health'
My sister Olive as Nell Gwynn
At the Hotel Astor
In Tucson, Arizona

LIST OF ILLUSTRATIONS

Mirador, Virginia
At Georgetown, Bermuda
Lady Astor and Mr George Bernard Shaw
Lady Astor dancing with a sailor on Plymouth Hoe, 1942
  (*Wide World Photo*)
A page from my record of Lady Astor's jewellery
Charles Dean, the butler, Otto the chef, two French dailies
  and me in France, 1961
With Otto, the chef
Lady Astor in her last years ...
... and a few weeks before she died

Family Trees
The Langhorne Family *page* 42
The Astor Family *page* 43
The Astor Households, 1928 *pages* 110–11

Foreword

Although this book is about domestic service it is also about people, and apart from myself about one person in particular: Nancy, Lady Astor. There have been others who have written of my lady's personal and political life. Some have spoken highly of her, others have been savagely critical. I am not like any of them. To begin with I haven't the use of words that they have, nor have I their education or their kind of background, so I have kept away from the parts of Lady Astor's life that I was not able to understand and have written about those that I could. This may have given an uneven portrait of her, but everyone has to write from a position and mine was at least one that kept me in contact with her every day for thirty-five years. There were times and places where I was not able to observe her closely and to tell of these I have had to rely on the memories of those of her staff who were present. Always though they have been the servants' views of her, not the opinions of associates and friends in her own class.

My life with my lady was one of constant conflict and challenge, and despite occasional wounds on both sides, one that we enjoyed hugely. Although divided by rank and money we had similar natures and I think it is true to say that we always respected each other. I hope my writing will cause no hurt to anyone. None is intended and the last thing I wish to do is to spoil the image of a lady who over the years became the expression of my own life. Whatever else it is, this book is the truth as I saw it.

I am grateful to so many people for helping me to prepare it. To Cyril Price; to Frank and Ronald Lucas of Walton-on-Thames, to Edwin Lee, Charles Dean, Frank Copcutt, Noel Wiseman and Gordon Grimmett, who have filled in the gaps; to my sisters Olive and Ann, who always had faith and so gave me courage; to Desmond Elliott, my agent, Michael Legat, my publisher, and Mary Griffith, my editor; to Jenny Boreham who typed and retyped with unflagging energy, and finally to Leigh 'Reggie' Crutchley, to whom I dedicate this book.

ROSINA HARRISON

1 Childhood

I was born in 1899 in a pretty little village, Aldfield, near Ripon in Yorkshire. It's very near that famous old ruin Fountains Abbey. The village and the land surrounding it were owned then by the Marquess of Ripon who lived at Studley Royal. I suppose, though I was never conscious of it, that he dominated our lives and those of everybody who lived on his estate from the farmers downwards. He was a kind of benevolent dictator. The men would touch their forelocks or doff their caps to him and to her ladyship and the women would curtsy. It wouldn't have done to have offended him in the slightest way, but speaking for our family this was unlikely; we knew our place. By that I don't mean that we were subservient. Knowing your place was a kind of code of behaviour at that time and we followed it to the letter. In any case there wasn't time to think about the rights and wrongs of it; people were all too busy working and bringing up a family for that.

My father was employed as a stonemason by the Marquess of Ripon. It was a skilled trade, fashioning the stones or slates and repairing buildings on the estate. He also helped to preserve Fountains Abbey. His wage was £1 a week. He was also sexton and caretaker for our church at Aldfield and the one at Studley. This brought in another thirty shillings a year and it was augmented when there were weddings or funerals. He was also the gravedigger and earned a few extra shillings by tending the graves, weeding them and seeing to the flowers. He even made a little more in the summer by scything the grass in the church-yard, stooking it into a small hayrick and selling it to a nearby farmer.

Before she married, my mother was laundrymaid at

Tranby Croft and Studley Royal which was how she met my father. They must have been pleased with her work at the big house because when Dad and she set up home together she continued to do the household and personal laundry for the Marquess and Marchioness at our home. Clothes! I grew up hating the sight of them. The only time our kitchen was free of them was on Saturdays and Sundays. I must have seen more of ladies' and gentlemen's underwear than was good for me by the time I left home. We only saw the fire at weekends or when we were baking or cooking; at all other times there would be a clothes-horse surrounding it. Dad used to complain but he knew there was really no use his grumbling, it brought in the extra money that was so necessary. I never knew how much and I don't think Dad did, but Mum always seemed to have what was needed in a crisis.

There were four of us children: I was the eldest, then came my brother Francis William and sisters Suzanne and Olive, all at two-yearly intervals. I was christened Rosina, but since this was bound to be abbreviated to Rose, my mother's name, and since she was not going to have the distinction of 'Old' Rose, I have always been called 'Ena' by my family. It's the sort of situation that should have been thought about before I was christened, as it has caused a lot of confusion and irritation during my life.

People have often said to me how lucky I was to be brought up in a village in the beautiful countryside with the freedom of the fields and lanes, the simplicity of life among animals and above all in peace. It sounds lyrical as I write it and perhaps in a way it was, but people forget and sometimes I do that for the most part life was continual hard work even as a young child. From the time any of us can first remember we had to play our part in the running of the house. Mum and I would get up before six every morning. Dad had to set off for work at half-past. He walked to the lodge at Fountains Abbey to get his orders from the foreman and be told where he had to go to for the day. At one time he cycled but he had been struck by lightning which made him too nervous to ride a bicycle ever again.

My first job was to lay the kindling wood and to get the fire going. We burnt logs which Dad and I had to cut with a cross-cut saw from a load of timber he bought off the estate. We didn't use coal; it wasn't necessary and it cost money. Even the baking was done with wood, thin pieces cut to size which we poked under the oven to get it to the right heat. Then there was the water to be fetched in buckets from the pump outside or, if it was a fine summer and the well there had dried up, from the one farther down in the village. The small boiler in the fireplace had to be filled. This and the kettle were the only supplies of constant hot water. After that I helped Mum get Dad's breakfast and of course there were my brother and sisters to be got up, helped with their dressing and generally hurried up and shouted at.

It was a relief to get to school. I enjoyed learning. The building was typical of the time. There were two classrooms and we were taught by the headmaster and his wife, a Mr and Mrs Lister, just the three R's with a little geography, history, art and, for the girls, sewing and embroidery. Opposite the school there was a field where we used to play football. I used to keep goal at one end and Mr Lister at the other. I loved it. Apart from the fact that I was good at it and very few balls got past me, it gave me the opportunity to use my voice. I'd scream encouragement and advice from beginning to end of the game and I could be heard all over the village. When I went home my Mum would be angry with me and tell me off about my unladylike behaviour. It didn't make any difference – I'd be at it again the next time. The game used to take the toes out of my shoes so eventually Mum made me wear clogs. I didn't mind, it was after all true Yorkshire footwear. I remember once being dressed in a lovely little bolero with a wide skirt and with orders to take great care of them. I couldn't resist playing football and I caught my foot in the hem of the skirt and nearly tore it away. I didn't dare go back home for Mum to see so I went into the schoolhouse and together Mrs Lister and I sewed it back again.

I learned a lot in school which was to be useful to me in later life, particularly through reading and writing. I always enjoyed writing and receiving letters. I kept many that I think are going to refresh my memory as I write this book. Whereas most children left school when they were fourteen I stayed on until I was sixteen. There were reasons for this as Mum and I had plans for my future. I believe that those two extra years when Mr and Mrs Lister gave me occasional individual tuition were of the greatest value to me.

During the lunch break, or as we called it, the dinner hour, I'd go home for my meal. When I'd eaten it I'd go into the wash-house and turn the mangle while Mum fed it with the morning's washing. When school finished in the afternoon I'd go back to help Mum get Dad's tea, which was his meal of the day. After that was cleared up I'd have to knit so many rows of Dad's socks. This I found unrewarding work and they never seemed to get any longer. They did, of course, since I kept him provided with them for many years.

After knitting there was the needlework, the darning and mending, getting the children to bed and then getting there myself. On Saturdays as well as the ordinary jobs I had to clean and blacklead the kitchen range. The blacklead came in blocks like soap. It was kept in a jam-jar and every time I used it I'd have to pour cold water on it and work at it until it produced a sort of paste. This was brushed on to the stove and finally polished until it shone. When I'd finished I must have looked a terrible sight for I had porous skin which absorbed any of the blacklead that got on it, and plenty seemed to. The family all got a good laugh out of me on Saturdays which I thought was very unkind of them at

4

the time and more so now that I think of it again. Then the steel fender had to be emery-papered and polished.

I must say that by the time I had finished with it the stove looked a lovely sight. It deserved to be, because it was the most important piece of furniture, if I can call it that, in the house. It was the means whereby we lived. I shall never forget it; there was the oven on one side, the boiler on the other, and in between the grate and a wreckin, a sort of iron bar across the top. From this we would hang the kettle, a big black iron one which was almost permanently over the fire, or, when required, the frying-pan, one with a long vertical handle that hung over the flames. It could be adjusted by a chain which was fastened to the wreckin. In the evening our two cats would creep into the kitchen, jump up and sit each side of the grate, one on the oven and the other on the boiler. It's the kind of family scene one never forgets.

Another of my Saturday jobs was to clean Dad's boots for Sunday. In the afternoon whenever it was fine, we children would go out gathering wood for kindling. Studley Park was a good hunting-ground and there was a big copse near us, but we didn't dare go often since pheasants were reared there and the keepers didn't care to have anyone disturbing them. We almost used to welcome a storm or a high wind during the week because it made our task so much easier.

As I grew older Dad developed what was called in those days a weak heart, so it was the duty of the family to relieve him of whatever work we could. Then it was that I acquired another Saturday chore: lighting and stoking the church boilers as well as helping Mum with the cleaning and polishing there. Saturday was also bath-night which was just as well with me having done so much dirty work. In the winter I had to make do with a sort of wash-down. I'd stand naked in a large tin bowl of water in front of the kitchen fire, but in summer I used to luxuriate in the wash-house outside by heating the water in the copper and then filling the big dolly tub. Eventually the day arrived when Dad came back from Studley Royal with a lovely hip bath which they had discarded. We felt like millionaires from then on. I didn't know what it was like to lie in a bath until I went into service.

However, Sundays, while they were different, were not days of rest. I was awake more or less at the usual time, and went up to the church to stoke the boilers. If there was an eight o'clock communion service I'd ring the church bell and then act as server to the vicar. I went back home for breakfast and we all got ready for the morning service. Dad and I used to sing in the choir. I enjoyed that; occasionally I'd have to sing a solo which I liked even better. Sunday lunch, or Sunday dinner as we called it, was a sort of ritual. It was the meal of the week with the best of whatever was in the larder at the time and of course always a Yorkshire pudding followed by pies and tarts.

Nobody could accuse my Mum and Dad of being sectarian because as soon as lunch was over and cleared up, we children were sent to the Wesleyan chapel for Sunday School. I questioned Mum about the rights and wrongs of this one day. 'One place is as good as another,' she said, 'and I know where you are and that you're out of mischief.' I suppose it made a change. It also started our library, for as regular attenders we each of us got a book a year, an improving one like *John Halifax, Gentleman* which I found very hard going and didn't read until many years later.

The evening found us in church once again. You might think that we would have sickened of religion but I never did. Among the memories that I hold dearest are the services in Studley church. They were happy occasions with the farmers and villagers all cleaned and polished and dressed in their best clothes, singing at the tops of their voices. It was these weekly get-togethers that gave us a feeling of community and a sort of pride in belonging to our village. Studley church was very beautiful and it was ours. During my life in service I was helped by my religion and my childhood memories of it. Although we were expected to behave in a Christian manner it was seldom possible for us to go to church and be practising Christians as it would have interfered with our duties. I don't say this with rancour but as a fact.

Sunday was the only day our parlour came alive. No one was allowed in it during the week. It was the same in all the village homes. We had a piano, it was the symbol of respectability, which Mum had bought from her laundry money. We children had lessons at fourpence a week as we got older and although none of us learnt a lot we were able to strum a few notes to help as a background for our sing-songs. When the 1914 war came and the military camps were built nearby, Sunday nights at the Harrisons' were great occasions for the troops and for us. Mum used to sparkle as she sang 'Good-bye Dolly Gray', 'Two Little Girls in Blue', 'Keep the Home Fires Burning', and the other popular songs of the time, and even Dad would relax and be merry, partly as a result of the drink the soldiers had brought with them. It's odd, but to me the war was a happy time, the village and the countryside seemed to come alive with the marching feet, the guns and the uniforms. There were dances, Garrison concerts, more fun generally, and of course a few more babies around than there should have been!

But work had to go on and Mondays would see the laundry baskets arriving and the flags hoisted again in the kitchen. I think I should make it clear that Mum didn't just 'take in washing'; it was much more a full-time job, and a skilled one too. As I've said, she worked for the Marquess and Marchioness of Ripon, but she also did the laundry for Lady Baron of Sawley Hall, all their personal and some of their finer household linen. Even when the families went to London for the season it would still be sent to them by rail. Her employers were particular, and they could afford to be. In these days when it seems everyone is vying with each other to wash the whitest it may be of interest to know how my mother managed without any of the mechanical and other aids that are now available to everyone. Rainwater was collected in two huge wooden barrels from off the roof. It was carried by bucket to the copper, a brick-built boiler in a corner of the wash-house and heated by a coke fire from a grate underneath. When it was boiling hot the water was transferred to a long wooden tub where the clothes were carefully washed by hand in the best soap, which at that time was Knight's Castile. Things seldom needed scrubbing as they weren't particularly dirty, but if ever any hard rubbing was necessary it was done on a wooden scrubbing-board, the kind of thing that was used at the beginning of the pop music era as skiffle-boards.

When clean, the clothes were transferred into three different tubs for rinsing, aided by a dolly, a pole with three legs at the bottom which was turned by hand to move the clothes around in the water. If it was then necessary to boil them they were put into the copper and later rinsed yet again. Then they were put through the mangle and hung on two large angled clothes-lines in the garden where they were dried in the cleanest of country air. The more delicate things were, of course, washed entirely by hand.

The ironing was done on a table kept specially for the purpose under the kitchen window. There was an attachment that was fitted to the kitchen stove with two ledges which held the irons. This was kept red hot and Mum must have had eight to ten irons on it at any one time. There was one little round one with which she polished the gentlemen's collars and the starched dress shirt fronts till they shone, and to this day I have kept the gophering iron with which she would twist all the frillies on the petticoats and nightdresses to make them curl out. Once ironed everything was hung around our fire to air and finally carefully wrapped in tissue paper before being packed into the laundry baskets. One of the beautiful memories of my childhood comes from sniffing at these baskets before they were

8

closed. They were never scented with lavender bags, they didn't need to be because they had their own particular lovely clean smell, better even than that of new-mown hay.

When I tell people today of my father's earnings and the shillings my mother made from the washing and of how they managed to bring up a family of four children, who were fed, clothed and contented, they tend to dismiss it by saying, 'Of course things were different then and money worth so very much more.' Things *were* different. There was no National Insurance, so there was the constant fear of getting ill, of being out of work, of growing old without a family to look after you and of being buried in a pauper's grave. There was no electricity, no sewerage, no running water, no refrigeration; fruit and vegetables came and went with the seasons. I don't count radio, television, record players, cars and such-like because what you've never had you never miss, and there are some things you might well be better off without.

At that time thirty shillings a week, which was about our family income, I'll never know for sure, was only just enough for us provided everyone played their part in making do. We needed a good manager, good neighbourliness and co-operation all round. We fed well because we lived to a large extent off the land. Rabbits were our staple meat diet. Dad brought these home. He was always ready to do a bit of extra repair work in the gamekeepers' houses, and in return was allowed to set snares on the estate. A day I shall always remember was when Dad brought a couple of rabbits home and Mum turned to me and said, 'Right Ena, you're old enough to start skinning rabbits, you've watched me time enough, take them into the kitchen and see how you get on.'

Well, I got on all right until it came to the head, I couldn't seem to get the skin over it and I couldn't stand those eyes staring at me. I asked Mum if I could chop the head off but she wouldn't let me. 'Dad likes the brains and we don't believe in waste in this house,' but she did come and

9

help me. I soon learned, and I wish I had as many pounds now as rabbits I'd skinned by the time I was sixteen. I've eaten rabbit cooked in every kind of way, but even despite the variety Mum gave us we grew tired of it just as the apprentices in Scotland got sick of the sight and taste of salmon, but as I sit and think of my mother's rabbit pies now it starts my mouth watering. Although we didn't keep any chickens because Dad wanted the space for vegetables and fruit, which he was often able to barter for eggs, we were able to get old hens from the gamekeepers. Broody hens were much in demand in the spring to sit on the pheasants' eggs, and when they'd done their job and the chicks were hatched out Dad was able to buy them for a few pence each. Tough birds they were but Mum knew how to cook them and to get every bit of flavour out of them.

A great delicacy which again the gamekeepers helped to provide was fawn. The Marquess kept a deer herd and every so often it would be thinned out by shooting the old stags and some of the fallow deer. It was a great and welcome sight to see Dad arriving back home with a fawn slung over his shoulders. It meant that we should eat like fighting-cocks for days. Every bit was edible; the pluck or liver was particularly tasty, but I only know that from hearsay as it was always reserved for Dad.

We cured the fawns' pelts and the rabbit skins and sold them to a pedlar-man on his occasional visits to the village. Fish we bought from the weekly fish-cart, kippers being a great treat. Every so often Dad would have to open the sluices in Studley Park. He took a basket with him and came back with it full of eels. When I saw them my feelings were mixed. I liked the taste but hated the preparation. Having to skin them in salt played havoc with my hands and left them red and raw.

Now I have a secret to unfold. It's something I swore to Dad I would never tell but since it was over sixty years ago that I made the promise, and since there cannot now be any severe consequences I think he'll forgive me for breaking the confidence. Dad was a poacher. Not, I hasten to add, the kind that goes out in the dead of night with nets and snares, but nevertheless in the eyes of the law he was a poacher. He was a deadly shot with a catapult. He once boasted to me that he'd stopped a mad dog which was about to savage him by shooting it straight between the eyes. Whether that was true or not I don't know, but what I do know, because I've seen him do it often, is that he could hit a pheasant at a hundred feet.

I suppose in a way I was an accomplice after the fact because I acted as lookout and also used to help him make the lead pellets to use as ammunition. There was a field opposite our parlour which seemed to attract the pheasants. Come to think of it now it's possible that Dad used to put a bit of grain there as bait, anyway many a summer evening would find a bird pecking away in that field. If I saw it first I would alert Dad and together we'd go into the parlour and carefully open the window. He would take aim, there'd be a quick crack of elastic, and nine times out of ten down would fall the pheasant.

Now this was when it got difficult: the village policeman lived next door and since there were never any other crimes committed, poaching was his speciality. Dad of course knew his movements – everyone in a village knows everyone else's movements – so the execution was done when the policeman was on his beat. It was getting the body from the field into our house that was the difficulty. I at first volunteered to do it but Dad wouldn't hear of that. He didn't want my young character blackened. He'd wait until it was dark and then he'd collect it in a sack. He never got caught, though he must have been found out. As I've said, everyone in a village knows everyone else's movements and someone must have known Dad's because quite a few times when he went to collect the booty, it wasn't there. At first he thought he must have just stunned the bird, but he knew when he'd made a

certain kill and it sent him raging mad to think that someone was stealing his property, as he called it. I'd heard a
saying about honour amongst thieves and I wanted to repeat
it to Dad when this happened, but I didn't have the courage.
So it was, that from time to time our table was graced with a
pheasant. On his way to and from work Dad would also use
his catapult but only to shoot at jays or snipe. These were
considered as fair game by the authorities whereas pheasant,
partridge or grouse were sacrosanct.

Milk of a kind was always plentiful. I say of a kind because a farmer friend supplied the Studley Royal dairy at
Fountains with milk for their butter. After the cream had
been separated he brought the skimmed milk back as feed
for his cattle, but he always left a can at the end of our
cottage wall for us. We were also lucky with butter because
Dad had an 'arrangement' with the dairy and they gave him
a roll, about a pound and a half, whenever we needed it.
Another great treat that I remember was when the farmer
gave us 'beestings'. Beestings is the first milk a cow gives off
after it has calved. It was thick, rich and creamy and made
lovely curd tarts.

All our bread was baked at home. Flour was ordered by
the sack. Meat was bought from time to time but except for
Sundays this was for Dad only. In those days the man of the
house, the breadwinner, was considered all-important. He
had to be kept well fed, fit and healthy. It made sense. Without him at work we could all have starved.

Clothes were expensive. There were no cheap tailors or
dress-shops at that time. This might have been a problem
for us, but fortunately Mum was friendly with an independent lady who had a house in the village. I think they used
to meet when Mum was cleaning the church and this lady
was arranging the flowers there. I know Mum was able to
help her over a few things. She showed her gratitude by
giving Mum clothes, mainly for us children, but sometimes
there was a suit for Dad. They were secondhand of course

and they didn't fit straight away but Mum's needle soon remedied that. They must have been good quality things because they were inherited by both my sisters. My youngest sister Olive moans to this day about never having had any new clothes as a child. She's made up for it since, I'm glad to say.

Holidays were something we didn't know about. We never went away as a family. I don't think we missed anything. I had one day a year at the seaside and that was on our choir outing. I used to look forward to it, but it never came up to my expectations. I remember I was given sixpence to spend and out of that I bought a present for Mum and Dad. Mum went away for a couple of days each year to see her mother in Derbyshire and took one of the youngest children with her. Dad's recreation was umpiring for the village cricket club, and drinking a glass of ale. Since there was no pub in our village this meant a three-mile walk, which was all right going when he knew there was something at the end of it, but not the same and perhaps a little more hazardous coming back. In his later years Mum would keep a small barrel at home for him, or at least she said it was for him but I noticed she helped herself to a glass from time to time. My main recreation as I grew older was the cinema at Ripon. I'd cycle there and back and spend the fourpence I was now given for cleaning the church and doing the boilers; threepence it was to go in and a penny for sweets. There was one dance a year held in the village, the cricket club dance at the school. This was something Mum and Dad went to together; I was left at home to look after the children.

Our lives were really almost entirely centred on the house. A home which was run by careful planning and was kept going by small personal sacrifices and by us all working together as a team. Unkind people might say that we scrounged food and clothes and accepted charity, that Mum and Dad showed no pride. In one sense they'd be right, but in another my parents were the proudest I have known and for the right reasons. They could walk head high. They worked hard, they lived well, they looked after their own and helped others, they brought up a happy family, they gave us all the will to work hard and the knowledge of the satisfaction of a job well done. It wasn't the kind of teaching that was going to bring us a fortune, but it was a good grounding for the sort of jobs that were available to us at that time and it must have been rewarding to them both that they had their children's love and affection to the end.

My father's funeral was the outward sign of respect that there was for him. The entire village turned out to see him away. My mother lived longer and left Aldfield, otherwise I'm sure she would have been given a similar last tribute.

2 I Go into Service

The choice of a career for girls born into our circumstances presented no difficulty. Almost inevitably we were bound to go into service. I didn't mind what work I did, but there was one personal snag: ever since I could remember I had had the urge to travel. I know today that when you ask any children what they want to do, 'To travel', is almost always the reply. It's the fashionable thing to say. It wasn't when I was young, it would have been considered foolishness, so I didn't talk about it.

My mother was the first to know. We were very close and as I got older she used to confide in me and lean on me a bit. To my astonishment she didn't laugh when I told her, her 'We'll have to think about it,' was almost encouraging. She did think about it, because a few days later when we were alone together she said, 'Remember talking about your wanting to travel, my gal? It's not so difficult as it sounds. In service there are two servants who usually go everywhere with their masters or mistresses, valets and ladies' maids. If you're prepared to smarten yourself up a bit, I see no reason why you shouldn't be a lady's maid.'

So from then on that was my ambition. The 'smarten yourself up a bit' wasn't such a backhander as it sounded. By that Mum meant that I would have to learn French and dressmaking, and 'You'll have to stay on at school until you've learnt everything they can teach you,' she added. So the plan was made. It demanded no sacrifices from me, but it did from Mum and Dad. It meant that I should earn no money until I got my first job, that instead of contributing to the family coffers I should be a drain on them. I did suggest that I could go into service as a housemaid or kitchen-maid and then transfer, but Mum wouldn't hear of that. 'You'd be classed, you'd never get out of it. No, you've got to start as you mean to go on.'

It was arranged that I should have French lessons in Ripon, at sixpence each, and when I left school at sixteen I was apprenticed to Hetheringtons, a big dressmaking establishment in Ripon. The apprenticeship was for five years, but I only stayed for two. I'd got sharp eyes and an inquiring tongue and felt that I had learned by then all that I needed. I was also getting itchy feet and feeling guilty about not earning any money. So when I was eighteen I told Mum I was ready to apply for my first job. Again Mum's experience of service came in useful. 'You're not ready to be a fully-fledged lady's maid and it's no use thinking you are. I'll write off to an agency and see if there are any vacancies for "Young Ladies' Maids".'

She explained to me that young ladies' maids, or schoolroom maids, as they were sometimes called, were the junior equivalent of ladies' maids, who had to look after the daughter of the house. In my case it was to be the daughters because I applied for and got a job with Lady Ierne Tufton, and my charges were Miss Patricia aged eighteen and Miss Ann aged twelve. Understandably I was very excited at getting my first position, but strangely as I think about it now I wasn't in the least nervous. Nor was I frightened of London. I'd never been there but Mum had told me about it. She didn't warn me of the temptations and dangers there are there as some Mums did; she seemed to have trust in me or perhaps she thought that her earlier pronouncement, made in front of all of us, that if we girls got pregnant without being married it was no good us coming back home, she wouldn't open the door to us, was sufficient. I have often since wondered if she would have abided by what she said, but such was my fear that I never put it to the test. Mind you, at that time there wasn't much opportunity for thinking about such things, I had to set to making my outfit, print frocks and aprons for morning wear, and dark dresses for the afternoon and evening. Once again it was Mum who found the money for everything.

The train journey to London passed very quickly. I don't know whether Mum had said anything about not talking to strangers, but if so I ignored it. Everyone in my carriage soon knew where I was going and why, and I chatted to them all the way. I was met at King's Cross station by Jessie, the Tuftons' head housemaid. I had written to her and told her what I looked like and what I'd be wearing, so she recognized me and took me by taxi to the Tuftons' town house, 2 Chesterfield Gardens, Curzon Street, Mayfair. It was a large, six-storey house next door to the Earl of Craven. I particularly mention this because he later married the daughter of the Town Clerk of Invergordon. It caused quite a stir in society at the time. I was introduced to the other servants, shown my room and put to wait in the servants' hall until it was convenient for her ladyship to see me. I had time to reflect on things as I'd found them so far. The London I'd seen from the taxi was much what I had expected to find, the house if anything was smaller than I'd imagined, my bedroom, which I was to share with Miss Emms, was attractive and well furnished. I was not in the least daunted by my surroundings nor was I ever to be. Many people later expressed surprise at my easy acceptance of my new world but, as I told them, it takes a lot to impress a Yorkshire girl.

It was now that I didn't seem to be able to find my tongue. I don't know how long I sat there but it seemed like hours. When eventually I was taken upstairs and introduced to Lady Ierne I found her pleasant but stern. In turn I was introduced to Miss Patricia and Miss Ann and then handed over to Miss Emms, her ladyship's personal maid, to be shown the schoolroom and to have my duties explained to me. Miss Emms began by giving me a sort of background history of the family and then went on to describe their country estates, Appleby Castle in Westmorland and Hothfield Place in Kent. I learnt that there were two sons, the Honourable Harry who was in the army, the Hussars, and Peter, a schoolboy at Eton; he was the youngest of the family and I was later to become very friendly with him.

My timetable and duties sounded simple as Miss Emms said them, but were complicated in practice by temperament and the course of events. I was called at seven o'clock with tea by the under-housemaid, who also laid and lit my fire. This was a privilege and a distinction bestowed on me by the rules of the servants' hall. In my turn I had to clean the grate and lay and light the fire in the schoolroom, tidy, sweep and dust it and then go for my breakfast in the servants' hall, which would be given to me by the under-kitchen-maid. At eight o'clock I would call the two young ladies with their morning tea and gather up the clothes that they'd been wearing the night before. Doing this for Miss Ann was quite a task because she would fling them anywhere and everywhere. Miss Patricia was tidier. So indeed was Miss Ann after I'd been there a few months and was in a position to make myself felt. Then I would lay out their clothes for the day and prepare their baths, and finally when they were dressed make sure they were fully presentable.

While they were having breakfast I busied myself in their bedrooms and the schoolroom. I think I should explain here that the schoolroom didn't look like it sounds. There were no desks or a blackboard, it was an informal sitting-room with comfy chairs, bookshelves, games and a piano. The piano was considered to be Miss Patricia's property. She was a brilliant and gifted pianist and could have made a career out of music. It was her whole life and was so important to her because she had neuritis of the spine and was therefore unable to ride or play tennis or do the sort of things other girls of her class did at the time.

After breakfast my first job was to take Miss Ann to school. Generally the chauffeur would drive us in the car, or if it wasn't available I'd take her by taxi. When I got back I was, as it were, at Miss Patricia's beck and call. Whatever she wanted to do, I did. I'd go shopping with her or take her to the Aeolian Hall where she had her piano lessons and often used to practise in the studios. I would listen to her playing by the hour. It gave me a knowledge of and taste for classical music. When I say knowledge I wouldn't know the names of the pieces or the composers but when I hear them being played on the radio I can recall and enjoy them. It's the sort of nostalgia that other people get from hearing the popular tunes of the times. I would sometimes go to concerts with her too.

Shopping was easy from Chesterfield Gardens. It was within walking distance of Bond Street, Piccadilly and Oxford Street, though we only used Selfridge's or Marshall & Snelgrove in Oxford Street. The other shops weren't considered smart enough at that time. But buying was easy. The Tuftons had accounts everywhere so money never changed hands, except for little things. Sometimes we'd just go for a walk in the park. It was like Mary and her little lamb, me being the little lamb. Yet in fact I wasn't really supposed to be a lamb – more of a watchdog. I was there to protect her, not that I ever had to, but I suppose my presence was a deterrent. I was also there so that she wouldn't do anything rash or untoward. You might think that as my mistress she could have pleased herself what she did, but by the rules of society she couldn't; she mustn't demean herself in front of a servant. I'm not saying she would have, but my being there made it impossible. I suppose if she had broken the rules it would have been my duty to have told her mother, as I should have done, not directly of course – that was not my place – but if her ladyship had heard about it by gossip or hearsay she'd have said, 'Did Miss Patricia do so and so, while you were with her yesterday?' and I would have been bound to answer truthfully, not so much from conscience but because if I hadn't I'd have been dismissed on the spot with no reference, which would have meant that my next job would have been hard, if not impossible, to come by.

My relationship with Miss Patricia isn't easy for me to describe. We weren't friends, though if she was asked today she might well deny this. We weren't even acquaintances. We never exchanged confidences, never discussed people, nothing we said brought us closer; my advice might be asked about clothes or bits of shopping, but my opinions were never sought or given on her music or the people we met or on anything that was personal to either of us, nor did I expect it or miss it at that time. That was the accepted way of things. It was different with Miss Ann: she was younger and as she grew up was more open with me, that is until she went to finishing school in Switzerland. When she came back her attitude was the same as her sister's. We met again almost as strangers. Our relationship grew, but it was set in a different key; very much a minor one.

Whenever I wasn't with Miss Patricia I was kept busy at home. Clothes had to be repaired, cleaned and pressed. I didn't have to wash any of their things. All personal laundry was done at one of their country houses, Appleby Castle; it was sent and delivered weekly. It might be thought that pressing would have come easily to me having watched and sometimes helped Mum in her work, but she dealt only with lingerie. I had to learn how to iron the various materials their frocks and suits were made of and how to clean them if they became stained. Dry-cleaning was more of a last resort in those days; it was generally considered to be harmful.

As well as repairing clothes I made quite a lot of under-linen. Material would be sent from France and Miss Emms and I would make it up into pants, slips, petticoats and vests. Underwear was very different in those days, none of the flimsy bras and knickers you get now. Bust bodices, camisoles and petticoats were much more the vogue and corsets were worn from quite a young age – made and fitted personally of course.

Late in the afternoon I'd fetch Miss Ann home from school. She would then have to change and be made presentable to go down into the drawing-room to see her mother. Then Miss Patricia would have to be dressed for the evening and there would be more tidying up to be done. If Miss Patricia went out for the evening to the theatre, a concert, a ball or a reception, I was not called upon to go with her. Generally she would join a party and the hostess would be responsible for her. If not, a suitable escort or chaperone would be found for her by Lady Ierne.

Of course if she ever went away to visit I would accompany her and so it was that I learnt that very difficult art of packing. I say difficult, because by that I mean that while it's not hard to fill a case tidily, it is far from easy to pack it so that when you arrive at your destination you can take the things out in the same condition that you put them in – so that they are not creased, but ready to wear. I was taught some of this by Miss Emms, but there was a lot more that I had to learn by experience. Choosing what to take wasn't easy – mistresses before they leave are apt to be a bit hasty and short with you with their 'Oh, the usual things, you know what I like,' or 'I'll leave it to you, Rose,' but when you get to the other end and you haven't brought what they want it's a very different story, and you are to blame. I soon learnt to be relentless in my questions to them. Of course you could always send for what they wanted, but more often than not by the time it arrived it was too late or they found they didn't want it at all. Whenever we moved to Appleby Castle after the London season, almost the entire wardrobes would have to be packed and since we travelled by train it would be my responsibility to look after them. I'm proud to say that during my thirty-five years of service I never lost a piece. An interesting thing about those days was that ladies almost always travelled with their own pillow and some insisted on having their own bed linen, even if they were away for just one night.

A disadvantage about being a lady's maid was that I could never rely on having time off so I could rarely make any plans. This meant of course that an outside social life was out of the question. I couldn't have a steady boyfriend because he would never have put up with the haphazard hours. I didn't miss one. In a way I suppose I was a career girl. I wanted to learn my job, to get on. The thrill of discovering London was an excitement for me in my early years there. I enjoyed the theatre and the cinema, and the busyness of the West End with its shops and people was sufficient thrill for the raw country girl that I was. There was fun to be had in the house too for although we were all kept working we were a happy lot, and we'd break off at any time to make our own fun. The staff was almost all female, the war had seen to that. Practically every available man had been conscripted. There were a cook and two others in the kitchen, four parlourmaids, three housemaids, two ladies' maids – Miss Emms and myself – and a chauffeur; we didn't even have an odd job man. Nor was there a butler; his duties fell on the head parlourmaid, and Major Tufton's valeting was done by the second parlourmaid. The set-up would have seemed very strange to me a few years later, but then I accepted it because I knew no better. It was very much a time of women's lib below stairs.

When we went to Appleby Castle the staff was augmented. Then there were two chauffeurs, two odd men, four in the pantry (parlourmaids), four kitchen-maids and four housemaids. There were also the caretakers who looked after the place all the year round, and a number of gardeners. The terraced gardens that ran down to the river Eden were a beautiful feature of the place. Hothfield Place, although lovely, was seldom visited, but again there were permanent caretakers and gardeners. It was of course part of their estate and entailed, so therefore it had to be kept up. Since there were practically no men on the staff the discipline in the servants' hall was not so formal. 'Pug' was the name given to upper servants by the lower. I don't know how or when it originated, but according to Mum it was in use in my grandmother's time. The Pugs' Parlour was a sitting-room-cum-dining-room used by butlers or head parlourmaids, cooks, housekeepers, valets and ladies' maids. During my time in service meals were taken there by the senior staff at all times, but before the First War it was the custom that at luncheon they would have their first courses in the servants' hall with the butler presiding at the head of the table and the other servants seated in order of precedence, and then take their sweet course and coffee in the Pugs' Parlour. They were always waited on by the hall boy, odd man or under-parlourmaid.

I suppose the attitude towards our behaviour and conversation could be described as pernickity. I think that it was easier to accept the procedure when there were menservants and the butler was in charge. That was how the tradition had started. It wasn't the same somehow without them. Of course when I visited with Miss Patricia I went to houses where men had returned from the war. At first I found these servants' halls rather frightening. There was an awful silence during a meal but I soon found out that some sort of conversation would be taking place between the sexes by the playing of footsy-footsy under the table. The blushes and the occasional giggles gave this away.

But I don't want to give the impression that we were kept under. The staff at the Tuftons' was one of the happiest I ever knew or saw, and when we all went up to Appleby Castle we adopted a real festive spirit. In a way we looked on it as our holiday too. We got more time off and we'd spend it enticing the boys of the village away from the local girls. We went to all the dances for miles around. I suppose we were looked upon as sophisticated misses down from the big city. We were an attractive set, although I say it. I was the only one who didn't get married but I was partial to the boys and they seemed to be to me, and I was later engaged for nine years. All right, in those days long engagements were normal, but this got ridiculous. We hardly ever saw each other, so it was severed by mutual agreement. Even the cook there brought it off and that is saying something in her particular case. Gladys, the second parlourmaid, married the Mayor of Appleby's son, and mayors were considered something in those days. It was thought of as a big social coup in the servants' hall. Social coup it may have been for Gladys, it was one of another kind for the mayor's son. After their marriage he bought a large hotel in the area which together they managed and have continued to run most successfully. I reckon her time and training in service proved an invaluable help to him as it did to a lot of husbands in more ordinary homes. Nowadays most wives learn how to run a house by trial and error and in my opinion it is the errors that cause the rift in many a lute.

Marriage was the goal of nearly every woman servant. It wasn't easy for them. After the war men were scarce, the demand far outweighed the supply and a maid's limited and irregular time off was an added disadvantage. Then there was the having to be back by ten o'clock which made every date like Cinderella's ball, only you didn't lose your slipper, you could lose your job. There was no status in being in service, you were a nobody; marriage was the way out of it. Strangely there was not a lot of intermarriage between servants. I remember a footman who worked for Lord and Lady Astor marrying Grace the second housemaid. It wasn't very lucky for her, or for him either, because later he was shot and killed by a guardsman.

My ambition to travel was now being fulfilled but only in a small way and confined to Britain, places like Glen Tanar at Aboyne in Scotland, the home of Lord and Lady Glentanar; Glenakil, Tarbert, Loch Fyne to visit Lady Illona Campbell, the girls' aunt, Lady Mary Cambridge's house just after she was married near Ashby de la Zouch, in Leicestershire, and some of the Irish houses, though at the time there was a lot of violence there. I remember when we were staying with the Marchioness of Aberdeen in Shelbourne Place in Dublin, Harry Tufton's car was stolen from outside the house and thrown into the river Liffey. Another time when the Sinn Feiners were picketing the shops, I volunteered to go and fetch a joint of mutton from the butcher's. I managed to get in the back way and I walked out with it stuffed under my coat. I don't know what they would have done with me if they had caught me. I got a few queer looks, but it's my opinion that they thought I was a poor pregnant Irish girl. On my way home I heard a few shots fired and was told later that Sir Alan Bell had been taken out of his car and shot in the next street. I can't say that I cared for Ireland at that time.

I had one opportunity to travel abroad to Kenya with Miss Patricia. I was very excited at first when she told me about it. 'I'll give you the time of your life, but I'd better warn you that you'll meet a lot of spiders and insects.'

Well, that did it, that took the smile off my face. 'Then I'm not going,' I said, and that took the smile off hers because she could see that I meant it. The next day Lady Ierne sent for me and tried to persuade me, but I wouldn't budge. If there was one thing I couldn't abide it was creepy crawlies. 'They're as big as crabs I'm told, my lady, I should die of heart failure if I saw one.' She wasn't amused and things were uncomfortable between us for quite a few days. I did later go to Africa, but by then the D.D.T. sprays had been invented and I never travel anywhere without one.

After I'd been with the Tuftons for just over four years I decided I would like a change, a change of scene and of people and I hoped a bit more money. Twenty-four pounds a year wasn't a lot even in those days. I felt by now that I had learnt sufficient to qualify as a full lady's maid, and that I could leave the schoolroom behind me. It's never very easy giving in one's notice, employers are inclined to take it personally, as a slight to them. They don't consider that you have a life of your own to lead and that you have made plans for your future. It isn't easy for yourself either, loyalties, friendships and affections are hard things to surrender, but with me there was an overriding reason for leaving: my father was very ill and I felt my place was at home with him and my mother.

As I've tried to say, I had proved myself in those four years. Apart from learning the job I had earned and been given trust and responsibility, I had become reliable and I knew now that I could make it to the top. Although my Yorkshire accent stuck out like a sore thumb, as it was going to for the rest of my life, most of the other edges to my nature had worn smoother. I had learned a pattern of behaviour from the other servants and from the people I had served. I had got a good dress sense, I appreciated nice things, china, furniture, jewellery, and I'd developed a sense of humour which enabled me to laugh and get pleasure out of what I was doing where others might be moaning and groaning. This has enabled me then and since to live through the worst crises and on occasions to tolerate rough treatment without getting into a rage or tizzy. I learnt about the ways of society, and my place in it, what was and was not expected of me. I'd earned a good reference. In short I had discovered how to make the best of a good job.

It was as well that I decided to leave Lady Ierne when I did because I had been home only a short time when my father died, in his sleep. I know I was able to be some help and comfort to Mum and of course the money I had saved came in useful for paying the burial expenses. As I have said, it was a wonderful funeral. The whole village turned out and the church was overflowing. It was all fitting to the occasion and to the man. As a family we were sad but very proud. I stayed on at home for a year, and when I felt Mum was able to stand on her own feet, I went up to London, booked a room at the Hampstead Y.W.C.A. and called on Massey's of Baker Street, and Miss Sellars of Bond Street, two of the well-known domestic agencies of the time. Miss Sellars specialized in ladies' maids. She offered me a place in America, but I refused it because I felt that it was too soon to be so far away from my mother after my father's death. Two days later Massey's wrote to me and told me of a vacancy with Lady Cranborne at 25 Charles Street, Mayfair. I was interviewed and accepted. There was one snag to the job: I was told by her Ladyship that although she travelled abroad a lot, she would not be taking me with her. This did not suit me and I said so. I told her that I considered that travelling was an essential part of my employment. I thought that that would put an end to my going there, but it didn't. She smiled sort of thoughtfully and then said, 'Very well Rose, we'll see.' She didn't commit herself but I took it to mean that she had changed her mind and so accepted what I had asked for. I hadn't been there long when I met Bessie, Lady Moyra Cavendish's maid. Lady Moyra was Lady Cranborne's mother. 'She'll never take you abroad,' Bessie said.

'Let's wait and see, shall we?' I replied. I was right in my judgement; I travelled everywhere with her.

Although 25 Charles Street was only a small house, with two in the kitchen, two parlourmaids, two housemaids, myself, a nanny and a nursemaid, there was also the Manor House at Cranborne in Dorset, a beautiful country house. We were frequent visitors to the famous Hatfield House, the seat of the Marquess of Salisbury, since Lord Cranborne was his heir and indeed he and her ladyship eventually came into the title and the estates.

When I joined Lady Cranborne she was a lovely young lady in her early thirties. Although she had had two baby sons and had another one while I was with her, she'd a beautiful figure and carried her clothes to great advantage. Since the children were young I was able to get to know them well, indeed it was considered as part of my duties to relieve Nanny Woodman. She was one of the great figures of her world. The nursery at Charles Street was a delight and later the one at Hatfield was quite famous. She died in 1974 at Hothfield with the children and grandchildren looking after her.

Robert would have been ten and Michael about six when I went to the Cranbornes', and baby Richard was born a year later. I think I should explain that the children were called by their family name Cecil, a name that is famous in history. Being the sons of a Lord they put 'Honourable' before their names. It is one of the disadvantages of being born into the aristocracy, you have to keep changing your name whenever someone in the family dies. It makes it all very confusing for them and for anybody writing about them.

Michael was my favourite, I suppose because I spent more time with him. I hadn't been at the Cranbornes long before I had to take him to Switzerland for a holiday (so much for Bessie and her 'you won't travel.') I remember we shared a double sleeper on the train and Lady Cranborne insisted that he had the top bunk. I didn't sleep a wink all night for fear he would fall out. We had a lovely time together. Little boys are always so appreciative of what you do for them and he was a great companion. It was tragic that he should have died so unexpectedly while playing football at Eton when he was only sixteen. Richard, the youngest, was killed during the war.

Lady Cranborne was a loving and devoted mother. I say this because in my experience it was rare with the upper classes. Children I think were neglected – not where food, clothing or material things were concerned, but over the one thing that is perhaps more important than all of these – real love, love that shows. I'm sure that if you asked any mother of that class if she loved her children she would indignantly have said, 'Of course, how dare you ask such a question,' and she would have meant it, but love has to show when it's given. It's like a present, only more precious. Lady Cranborne had time for her children, which makes it so sad that two should have been taken from her when they were young.

My duties were similar to those at the Tuftons' except that I was only responsible to her ladyship. Our relationship was the same as I had had with Miss Patricia only more so. By that I mean that the division of class was more clearly defined. This in many ways had its advantages. I knew exactly where I stood, what was expected of me, what I could or could not say and do. I mention this now because this was the last position in which I had this kind of security. Lady Cranborne conformed to the accepted traditions of the time. By definition and by behaviour she was a lady. In my presence and in the presence of other servants, because otherwise I should have heard about it, she never deviated. She had set her standards and she never lowered them. I know this sounds hard to believe and dull to consider but in my opinion there was a lot to be said for it. For one thing it was easier to serve people whom you respected.

It was with Lady Cranborne that my ambition to travel was to be more fully realized. Almost every weekend we were away somewhere. In the summer it would be for social visits and in the winter for shooting parties – his lordship was considered a great shot and was much in demand. They both enjoyed the London season and Ascot was spent always with the Astors at Cliveden – exciting for me at first; little did I know that before long I should be living there and that it would be my home for almost all of the working life that lay before me.

We would move lock, stock and barrel to Cranborne Manor after the season. It was much the same pattern as at Appleby Castle, greater freedom, dancing with the farmers' sons and getting ourselves unpopular with the local village girls. I had a French companion for these dances, Mademoiselle Magnier, who taught the Cecil boys French, and who was also a great help with mine. She was very vivacious and attractive and she had the village boys falling over each other for her favours, but she took her job seriously. After she left us she was engaged by Princess Marina, the Duchess of Kent, to teach her children. I remember chatting about her to Princess Alexandra when she was sitting on my knee in the car coming from the station to Cliveden.

After we left Cranborne we generally went to the South of France as many of the aristocracy would be there at that time and we'd take over a villa for a few weeks, then it would be my turn to show the British flag at the local dances. Once we stayed at Eze with Lt.-Col. and Madame Jacques Balsan. She had been the Duchess of Marlborough in her previous marriage. It was a large house with a beautiful view of Monte Carlo and the Mediterranean, and there was a big house party. It was my first glimpse of French servants; they had a full staff including a butler and three footmen. I'd been told how much harder they worked and how they were more subservient than we were, but I didn't find it so. I was particularly astonished at the chauffeurs, who seemed able to use their employers' cars whenever they wanted to. Astonished but not worried – it suited me because I was able to go out with them sightseeing and enjoying myself.

From there we went to Rome to visit the British Ambassador and we stayed a few days at the Embassy. As I remember the butler and the lady's maid were both British but the rest of the servants were Italian. The servants' hall they tried to run on our lines, but it wouldn't have done over here: everyone seemed to be talking at once. The noise was unbearable; it must have driven the butler mad.

My knowledge of Italy and the Italians was strictly limited. One thing I'd heard in the servants' hall was that Italian men were hot-blooded. During our short stay I was to have proof of this. The first morning we were there as a footman handed me my lady's breakfast tray he pressed his hands over mine. 'Hello,' I thought, 'what's he up to?' Then I dismissed the incident. 'He was probably making sure I'd got hold of it properly,' I said to myself. I saw him once or twice during the day and each time he flashed a smile at me. I took it as a friendly gesture and gave him one back.

That night I was getting ready for bed and was standing in my voile knickers and vest when I saw a hand come round the edge of the door. I didn't stop to think. I was over in a flash and pressing the door against the obtruding hand with all my strength. I watched it go red and then purple and I could hear some nasty Italian words uttered from the other side; there is no mistaking curses whatever language they come in. They began getting louder and as I didn't want to wake the house I relaxed my pressure. The hand was quickly removed and there was a scuffling of feet down the corridor. I was taking no chances though so I dragged a heavy chest of drawers and pushed it against the door. After that I slept easily. The following morning I saw my sorrowful Romeo in the servants' hall. He looked at me with reproachful eyes and his arm in a sling. I didn't bother with the chest of drawers that night.

Before we went to Italy her ladyship spoke to me and told me not to mention the name Mussolini. I suppose he must have been coming to power around that time. I said, 'My lady, I've never heard of him till now and even if I had I couldn't pronounce his name.'

Again in Rome I came across the Astors. It was rather embarrassing. It was the morning we were due to leave the Embassy and I was in the Cranbornes' room packing when there was a knock at the door. I went to see who it was and there was Mr Bushell, Lord Astor's valet. 'What are you doing here?' I asked.

'Waiting for you to clear out,' he said rudely. 'My two are taking over this room, how much longer are you going to be?'

I tried signalling him to keep his voice down, but Lady Cranborne had heard. 'Who is it, Rose?' she asked. When I told her she put on an icy voice and said, 'Tell Lord Astor's servant to go away and that you will inform him when we are ready to leave.'

The trouble with Mr Bushell was that he was an excellent mimic and many's the country house where he has told that story in a hoity-toity voice to her ladyship's detriment.

From Rome we went to Lord Aberconway's house in Antibes (as fashionable then as it is today). We had a long spell at an hotel at St Jean de Luz. Miss Alix Cavendish, her ladyship's sister, was with us. She had contracted tuberculosis and it was thought the air would improve her health. I remember she brought her mother's maid, Miss Norman, with her. By now I was beginning to get familiar with other servants from the many great houses. This was to make my life easier and more pleasant in the future, also much more interesting since the more friendly one became the deeper was the gossip that was exchanged.

Visits to Paris became so common that it was not long before I knew it as well as I knew London. We always stayed at the Hôtel du Rhin in the Place Vendôme, a very nice comfortable little place opposite the Ritz. Most of Lady Cranborne's clothes came from Paris or were made from materials we bought there. I went to many fashion shows with her. Her favourites were those of Jeanne Lanvin and Madame Chanel. Although she would buy the occasional model I suppose I should be sorry to say that we cheated; we plagiarized. I had a very good memory for the cut and line of a frock and Lady Cranborne was clever at remembering the detail. Sometimes we'd even make quick pencil sketches, though we were careful never to get caught doing this. When we got back home we wouldn't make direct copies, we would take a feature of one dress and add it to a feature of another. Lady Cranborne's favourite material was Mousseline de Soie; unheard of today, it felt like chiffon but was just a little heavier. Her ladyship was easy to fit and to sew for because as I have said she was tall and slim and had excellent and generally simple taste. She was a great credit to me, and I mean what I say, for ladies' maids were very much judged by the way their employers were dressed; indeed it's always been my opinion that that is how I came to work for Lady Astor, though she never would have said so.

Much of Lady Cranborne's underlinen came from Paris, mostly made from triple ninon, beautifully appliqué'd by French seamstresses. The rest I made, copied from what she had bought. All the lace we bought there too, and gloves, and her shoes were from Pinet except for her heavy ones which were bespoke in London. For her tweeds and some suits she went to Lord Cranborne's tailor in Savile Row. It was a wonderful thing to be a young woman in society at that time. You could afford to dress, indeed you were expected to dress, elegantly, expensively and in the fashion, and remember fashions changed every year; today with most women it's only in their later years that they are able to buy good clothes, when their looks and their figures have deteriorated. I suppose that it why we see so much mutton dressed as lamb.

Now that I was a proper lady's maid I no longer wore print frocks. I was expected to dress simply, plainly, un-assumingly yet in fashion. I wore jerseys and skirts with a cardigan in the mornings and afternoons; after tea or if I was going out earlier I changed into a blue or brown dress. A string of pearls or beads was permissible, so was a wrist-watch, but other jewellery was frowned on. Make-up was not encouraged; indeed later I was rebuked for using lip-stick. When ladies and their maids were out together there could never be any mistaking which was which.

One habit that Lady Cranborne had that I didn't care for was that she would drive fast and often dangerously; indeed it was a common fault of the upper classes. They wouldn't be able to do it today, but they seemed to have a way with the police then. At the mention of their names constables would close their notebooks. Many's the narrow squeak I've had in a car with her ladyship. I remember once we were driving through the New Forest in her Lagonda; we'd reached Cadnam and she swung round taking up two-thirds of the road and hit an oncoming Rolls Royce on its side as it tried to avoid us. We rocked from one pair of wheels to the other but we stayed upright. When I recovered from the shock I looked back and there was the Rolls in the ditch. Her ladyship ignored the whole incident and went driving on as if nothing had happened.

'It's no good, my lady,' I said, plucking up my courage, 'you'll have to turn back. If you don't you'll get all the blame because the evidence is there on the road.'

She didn't reply, but a few moments later, after she'd thought about it a bit, she turned the car round and went back. It was as well she did because she'd hit Lord Wimborne's car and he had recognized her. There was a good deal of talk all round, although my opinion was never asked or given. Eventually they shook hands and that was the last we heard about it. No court case, no nothing. I remember that on our way home we broke an axle on Hammersmith Bridge and had to complete our journey by cab – by the way Lady Cranborne spoke you would have thought it was the makers of the car who were to blame, not the punishment she'd given to it.

And she did punish it; on another occasion when we were going to lunch with Lady Apsley, suddenly the car seemed to bounce all over the place. Eventually Lady Cranborne decided to stop and see what was wrong. It was obvious that one of the back tyres was torn to pieces. 'Oh well, Rose,' she said, 'we can't stop now or we'll be late for lunch.'

By the time we arrived there was nothing left of the tyre, the wheel rim was flattened and every part of my anatomy seemed to have changed places. Her ladyship didn't turn a hair, just got out as though nothing had happened. I imagine one of Lady Apsley's chauffeurs saw to the car because the wheel had been changed when we came out of the house.

I was with Lady Cranborne for five years. I might have stayed with her indefinitely: she was a pleasure to serve, my life was interesting, I was fulfilling my ambition to travel; unfortunately there was one stumbling-block, money. I was still only earning £24 a year and any request I made for an increase was flatly, almost rudely, refused. I don't know whether there was a conspiracy among the upper classes to keep servants' wages down, but everyone I knew in service at that time met with the same brick-wall attitude. The only way to get more was to change employers, and this couldn't be done too often otherwise you earned the reputation of being unreliable and having itchy feet.

Once again I had the emotions of loyalty and affection pulling at my heart-strings, with the added problem of my fondness for the children to contend with. But the strongest pull for me was always my mother and my family. Mum had struggled on gamely after Dad's death, but it was evident that she couldn't go on working for ever. I wanted to be in a position to buy her a little bungalow down in the south, nearer to myself and my sisters, and ten shillings a week wouldn't be enough for me to do this, so I hardened my heart and began to look around. It wasn't necessary for me to go to an agency. By now I was well enough known to the staffs of the big houses to be able to put the word round that I was thinking of making a change for something to be suggested to me through the grapevine. And there was the added advantage of knowing in that way everything about the job and the person I'd be working for. Employers used to set great store by references. They had to be immaculate, otherwise you stood no chance of the job. In my early days in service I thought that we ought to have the right to demand something of the same from our employers, before we decided whether to take the job on or not, but after a few years in work this wasn't necessary. We had a 'Who's Who' and a 'What's What' below stairs which contained more personal and colourful information about the gentry than ever the written version did. There was also a black list, and woe betide anyone who got on it. It could spell ruination for any hostess.

As it happened I didn't need recourse to the underground. Ascot week followed close on my decision to make a change and as always we spent it with the Astors at Cliveden. One evening I was standing outside Lady Cranborne's bedroom door; she had taken her bath and was making herself presentable before calling me in to dress her. I think that I should explain here that ladies never exposed their bodies to their maids. I never saw any of my ladies naked, except for Lady Astor, and then only when she was nearing the end of her life and needed me to help her do everything. This modesty may seem somewhat incomprehensible now; then it wasn't. Dignity at all times and in all places was very much the order of the day and while I think all my ladies could have preserved theirs even in the nude, some others had figures so grotesque that the memory of them when they were in the mood to command would have sent many maids into hysterics.

As I was saying, I was waiting outside Lady Cranborne's door when Lady Astor passed down the corridor talking to her maid, Mrs Vidler. She glanced at me and said, 'Good evening.' I'd visited Cliveden many times so my face was familiar to her. As she got farther down the corridor I heard her say, 'That's the maid for me.'

I'm sure she meant it as a compliment, but it ruffled my North Country feathers. 'Not if I've anything to do with it,' I said to myself. I suppose there were two reasons. I knew that over the past year Lady Astor had had difficulty keeping her maids and, as I've intimated, there was such a thing as a difficult employer as well as a difficult servant.

Also I thought it a slight on Mrs Vidler to say such a thing to her face. I was later to learn to turn a deaf ear to remarks like that and that pinpricks of that kind peppered your body when you served Lady Astor.

When I went down to the Pugs' Parlour I saw Mrs Vidler. I went up to her and said that I was sorry her ladyship had spoken the way she did. She laughed it aside. 'It's all in the day's work,' she said, then went on to say that she was leaving Lady Astor anyway as she had decided to go to America to seek her fortune.

'Would you like my job?' she asked.

Without really thinking I said, 'No.'

'Miss Wissie wants a maid, why don't you come to her?' Miss Wissie was Lady Astor's daughter, the Honourable Phyllis Astor, later Countess of Ancaster. She was then about eighteen. In a way I would be dropping in status back to a young lady's maid. Would it, I thought, be worth it?

'What's the money?' I asked.

'Sixty pounds a year.' That did it; status, like love, flew out of the window. 'Yes,' I said, 'I shall apply for it.'

I had reckoned without Lady Cranborne. I told her my intentions and asked for a reference. 'It's not convenient for you to leave, Rose,' was her reply. She had me over a barrel: I needed her reference. I'm not the kind that argues in a situation like that, nor do I resort to tears to try and win sympathy. I went away and thought for a bit. I was astonished when I saw her ladyship next that she brought the matter up. 'I've been thinking about what you said, Rose, I haven't changed my mind, I won't recommend you for Miss Wissie but I will for Lady Astor. I understand she wants a maid.' This was downright duplicity, I thought.

'Not me, my lady, I don't want to serve Lady Astor,' I said, 'and that's an end of the matter.' I wasn't to be daunted though. I'd got a reference from Lady Ierne. I didn't think it would be enough, but I wrote to Lady Astor's head secretary, Miss Kindersley, and put in my application. To my astonishment, two days later she replied and told me I had got the job. What's more I'd struck a blow for freedom, my freedom of choice at any rate. The next day I gave in my notice. Her Ladyship accepted it as though I had just passed a remark about the weather. When it came for me to leave she shook me by the hand, thanked me for all I'd done, and said she hoped I would get a nice position in the future. She didn't even ask if I had got a job to go to.

3 Meeting the Astors

I went to Cliveden on 14 August 1928, the day after Mr William Astor's twenty-first birthday, to take up my duties as Phyllis Astor's, Miss Wissie's, lady's maid. It was a red-letter day in my life because, as I've said, though I didn't know it at the time, I was to serve the family for the next thirty-five years. Therefore while this isn't intended to be a book about the Astors or Lady Astor, my life in service was inevitably focused on the family, and particularly on her, as indeed was everyone's around her no matter who they were supposed to be working for or what they were doing. She dominated the scene. 'Satisfy Lady Astor and everyone will be happy,' seemed to be the universal creed. I nearly said 'please' Lady Astor, but that was impossible: no matter what you did for her, she never let you see she was pleased. It was as though she thought it your bounden duty to serve her. Therefore my life, and the lives of the others whom I shall be writing about, will seem to revolve continually around her ladyship, and this may give the impression that my picture of domestic service is a special one and not a true reflection of the times. It's not the case. In general other servants lived as we did and other houses were run as ours were. It's only the personalities and the details that were different.

I was no stranger to Cliveden, as I've said, but it's one thing to visit a place and another to work in it. You see it through different eyes and of course distances become more important, that is the time it takes to get from one place to another. Attitudes towards the staff alter too. It is important to learn to understand their abilities, limitations and temperaments, and relationships have to be carefully developed. It was necessary at the start to learn something of the history of the family, and for this I turned to the man whom I suppose more than any other was to be the important and dominating figure in my life, Mr Edwin Lee, the butler. His christian name was the most unimportant thing about him; I can hardly ever remember it being used; he was known to everyone who visited us as Lee or Mr Lee. Even Royalty never had to be reminded of it. There were other great butlers at that time but Mr Lee I think would be acknowledged by almost all as the greatest. Mr Charles Dean, at one time under-butler to the Astors, later butler to Miss Alice Astor, Mrs Bouverie, Lady Nancy Astor at Eaton Square and the British Ambassador in Washington, although a great figure in his own right, still considers himself puny compared with Mr Lee. Behind his back, in the servants' hall, he was known as 'Skipper' or 'Skip'. To his face he was addressed as 'Sir' by male and female staff alike. I called him 'father'. How, when or why this happened I can't remember. I still marvel that I had the courage to be so familiar and that he allowed it. He never called me by my christian name and though we are still the greatest of friends today, he addresses me only as Miss Harrison.

Anyway, one evening soon after my arrival, he found time to tell me about the family. The first Astor he thought to be of any importance was John Jacob, who emigrated from Germany towards the end of the eighteenth century, first to England and then to America. He it was who founded the Astor fortunes, through dealing in furs and later buying land around New York harbour on which the present city stands. His estate was passed on for two generations, increasing in value all the time, until it came in the hands of William Waldorf, my Lord Astor's father. He was an eccentric and a bit of an intellectual. After his father died leaving him all his fortune, he decided to settle in England. This made him unpopular with Americans. Mr Lee thinks it was because he was making his money over there and spending it over here; a sort of absentee landlord. I could see the Americans' point of view because he really did spend. He bought Cliveden, two houses in London and a ruined castle at Hever which he had repaired. Then he built a mock Tudor village around it, where his guests stayed. He later also bought a title off Mr Lloyd George. A Viscountcy was given him for 'political and public services', but the size of the cheque was never mentioned. Apparently, although he was hoping that his eldest son Waldorf would marry into the English peerage, he didn't mind when he met my lady even though she was a divorcée and had a young son. He took to her at once; he must have done because when they were married he gave them Cliveden and several million pounds besides.

Mr Lee met his old lordship shortly after he went into service with Mr Waldorf. Despite his funny ways (he used to sleep with two revolvers by his bed, being in permanent fear that someone wanted to do him in), he seemed to Mr Lee a good-natured and generous sort of man, and not only to his family. He had a butler, a Mr Pooley, who over the thirteen years he was with him started taking to the drink. Eventually the old man could stand it no longer and he decided to sack him. 'Pooley,' he said, 'because of your bad habits when you're in the drink, I've got to ask you to leave, but because of your good habits when you're out of it and the time you've served me, here's something to take with you,' and he handed him a bank note.

When he left the room Mr Pooley looked at it and saw it was for a thousand pounds. As he said to his friends in the pub that night, over the drinks that he'd bought them, 'That's something worth getting drunk for.'

When he came to speaking of our 'Lordy', as he was familiarly called in the servants' hall, Mr Lee of course did not pass any opinion or judgement. I was left with the view that his character must be near-flawless, otherwise Mr Lee would not have stayed in his service. Don't misunderstand me, by that I don't mean that 'father' was pompous or

The Langhorne Family

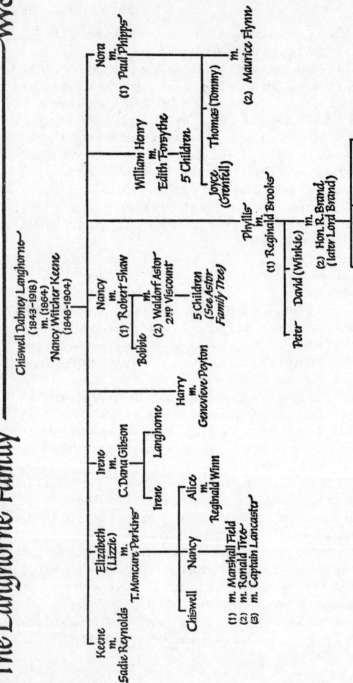

The Astor Family

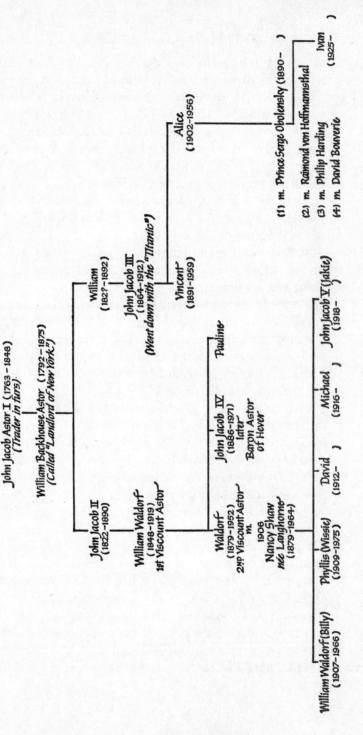

John Jacob Astor I (1763–1848)
(Trader in furs)

William Backhouse Astor (1792–1875)
(Called "Landlord of New York")

John Jacob II (1822–1890)

William (1827?–1892)

William Waldorf (1848–1919)
1st Viscount Astor

John Jacob III (1864–1912)
(Went down with the "Titanic")

Waldorf (1879–1952)
2nd Viscount Astor
m.
1906
Nancy Shaw
née Langhorne (1879–1964)

John Jacob IV (1886–1971)
later
Baron Astor
of Hever

Pauline

Vincent (1891–1959)

Alice (1902–1956)

William Waldorf (Billy) (1907–1966)

Phyllis (Wissie) (1909–1975)

David (1912–)

Michael (1916–)

John Jacob V (Jakie) (1918–)

Prince Serge Obolensky (1890–)

Ivan (1925–)

(1) m. Prince Serge Obolensky (1890–)
(2) m. Raimond von Hoffmannsthal
(3) m. Philip Harding
(4) m. David Bouverie

priggish, but he had his standards, those of his position, and he kept to them. It stood to reason that if his employer didn't measure up to them, he would prefer to work for someone who did. He would have been able even when I first knew him to have picked any job in the land. In the event I found Waldorf Astor what I can only describe as the epitome of an English gentleman. However extraordinary his father may have been, he had seen to it that his son was brought up as an Englishman of his rank, wealth and times should be. He went to Eton where he was Captain of Boats, while at New College, Oxford, he represented the University at polo, and got an Honours degree in history. He grew up with the British and foreign nobility, hunting with them and staying in their country houses or castles. His manners were easy and gentle; there was nothing assumed or false about him. He had his moral and religious standards but he didn't expect everyone to live in his way and showed wonderful understanding of human frailty in others. He loved and was proud of his beautiful wife and showed it in his every action all through his life. One knew that he couldn't have approved of many of the things she said or did, but he never showed it. If only she could have returned half the affection he gave to her he would have been a rich man in every way. I used to long for her to do it and I went as far as I could to tell her of my longing. It wasn't any good. She wasn't equipped to show love. He was a wonderful father; he tried to anticipate everything his children might want, though he didn't spoil them. Mr Michael, one of his sons, has written a book called *Tribal Feeling* about his family. Although most of it concerns her ladyship, it's my opinion that 'Lordy' was very much the head of the tribe.

Of Lady Astor's family, the Langhornes, there was not much Mr Lee could tell until he came to her father and mother. Chiswell Dabney Langhorne was born into a family that owned a tobacco estate in Virginia which was run with slave labour. The victory of the Northerners ruined him

and others like him. While fighting in the war he had met
and married Nancy Witcher Keene, another Virginian,
whose family was of Irish extraction. The first fifteen years
of their life together in the ruined Southern States was a
struggle. He had a variety of jobs, among them nightwatchman, piano salesman, tobacco and horse auctioneer. In-
security didn't prevent raising a large family, my lady being
the seventh of eleven. Her birth seemed to bring him luck.
A general whom he'd known during the Civil War employed him to handle his coloured labour constructing rail-
roads. He quickly advanced to become a contractor himself
and within a few years he had made a lot of money. He
moved from Danville, where her ladyship was born, to Richmond, the capital of Virginia. He lived there until she was
thirteen, and then with the philosophy that 'Only niggers
and Yankees work,' he bought a large estate and house called
Mirador near Charlottesville in the foothills of the Blue
Ridge Mountains, and retired.

My lady loved all the places of her youth and I was later
to visit them with her and share her affection. She left home
when she was seventeen and went to a finishing school in
New York. She later stayed with her eldest sister Irene,
who was by then Mrs Dana Gibson, wife of the celebrated
artist. It was she who inspired him to create the famous
Gibson Girl pictures. Through her, Nancy, my lady, met
a Bostonian of good family, Robert Gould Shaw, and eventually married him. According to Mr Lee he was a 'wild one'
and much given to the drink. So much so that after the birth
of her son my lady could stand it no longer, and left him.
It was Mr Lee's opinion too that it was Mr Shaw who gave
her her lifelong hatred of alcohol. During the next few
years and while divorce proceedings were taking place, she
visited Europe and England. She enjoyed a hunting season
here and it was on a journey for another visit in the autumn
of 1905 that she met his lordship, then Mr Waldorf, who was
on the same ship. They were married in 1906.

When he spoke to me about Lady Astor's character Mr Lee was guarded, choosing his words very carefully. He told me later that he hadn't wanted to say anything that might influence my opinion of her. He described her as a character, a great personality in her own right. 'She is not a lady as you would understand a lady, Miss Harrison,' I can remember him saying. By that he meant that she didn't conform to what society thought a lady's behaviour should be and to what had been my experience of ladies in service up till then. 'You won't find her easy,' was his final remark, but it was not a criticism. I understood him to mean that she was a challenge and that if one was able to meet it, it would be rewarding; or am I perhaps being wise after the event! Anyway I don't propose to sum her ladyship up, as I have Lord Astor, because it would be beyond me. What I felt about her can only come out as I write.

After this Mr Lee told me about the children, Mr Billy, twenty-one, Miss Wissie, eighteen, Mr David, sixteen, Mr Michael, twelve and Mr Jacob, nine – Jakie, as he was known to everyone. The ages I've put by them were their ages at the time I joined Lady Astor. 'You'll like them,' he said, 'and they'll like you.' One of the best things about being in service for any length of time is growing up with the children. He was right, for although I came so much later to the Astors than he did, this was something I shared with him. As I've said, her ladyship had another son by her first marriage, Bobbie Shaw. 'He's not an Astor,' Mr Lee said, meaning by this that he was different from the others. I found him different. He was the stormy petrel. It is my opinion that he felt he never quite belonged in their world and resented it. Some unkind things have been said and written about him, though never by the family. Some of the criticisms he has perhaps deserved, although, as I hope to show later in the book, no one demonstrated greater love or devotion to his mother than he did, particularly towards the end of her life.

That then was Mr Lee's outline, embellished by some remarks of mine, of the family that I was to serve. I say family for although I was employed to work for Miss Wissie, and shortly afterwards for Lady Astor, I had the feeling that I belonged to them all. Indeed, I did serve them all, because by keeping her ladyship happy, I made their lives a lot easier, and they used to tell me so.

It's difficult to understand about my job and my life without also knowing the places where I had to work, their size and the scale on which they were run. Cliveden, although the largest and the most famous, was only one of the Astor houses. The others were: 4 St James's Square, a great town house; Rest Harrow, Sandwich, Kent; 3 Elliot Terrace, Plymouth, what might be called their political house, which his lordship bought when he first stood for Parliament there; and Tarbert Lodge, on the Island of Jura in the Inner Hebrides, where the family went for deer-stalking and fishing holidays. I'm glad to say I only went there twice. That kind of isolated, open air life did not appeal to me.

I suppose we looked on Cliveden as the hub of the Astor estates although possibly more of my time in my early years was spent at 4 St James's Square. Cliveden may not be one of the most famous, but it is certainly one of the most magnificent country houses in England, and its setting on steep wooded heights looking down on the Thames from the north and on to an immense terrace and gardens from the south makes it one of the loveliest. It was only thirty miles from London which meant that it could be easily and regularly used every weekend as a home.

The house was composed of a centre block with east and west wings. On the ground floor of the centre block there was a huge front hall, the long drawing-room overlooking the river, the library with its panelling of rare Sabicu wood, the Louis XV dining-room, Lord Astor's study and Lady Astor's boudoir. Above were the main bedrooms with names like the Tapestry, the Rose, the Orange Flower, the Snow-

47

drop, the Lavender; also the day and night nurseries. In the east wing were guest rooms for about forty visitors. In the west wing were the offices and staff bedrooms. The basement contained the kitchens, the servants' hall, the Pugs' Parlour, the men's brushing-rooms where all the visitors' clothes were pressed and cleaned, the china room, the wine cellar, the butler's pantry where the silver was washed in teak sinks before being polished, and the silver safe. Along the passage were railway lines on which the food used to be wheeled from the kitchens to the service lift. This practice had stopped before I joined and the food was carried by the odd men on butlers' trays to the lifts and transferred to the large hot-plate in the serving room next to the dining-room. Considering the distance travelled it's amazing that meals were eventually served piping hot.

My room at Cliveden was large, well decorated and comfortably furnished with bed, two easy chairs, a couch and two big wardrobes. Unfortunately there was nowhere near at hand I could hang bits of washing, for although there was a laundry there were still some things I preferred to do myself. So I rigged a clothes-line across the room. It was like my childhood days, I always seemed to have underwear looking at me. All my lady's clothes were pressed and cleaned in my room so I was constantly dashing between floors with armfuls of things.

The inside staff employed to run the house were Mr Lee, the steward/butler, a valet, an under-butler and three footmen, two odd men, a hall-boy and a house carpenter; in the kitchens the chef, three kitchen-maids, a scullery maid and a daily; a housekeeper, two stillroom maids, four housemaids and two dailies; four in the laundry, two ladies' maids for Lady Astor and Miss Wissie, a telephonist and a night watchman. The outside staff was much larger, with estate maintenance men, gardeners, farm workers for the stud and home farms and chauffeurs. These men lived in cottages and rooms on and around the estate. Unmarried gardeners were housed in two bothies. A bothy provided dormitory-like sleeping quarters and a dining-room and sitting-room. Cooking and cleaning was done by the house-keepers, but the food was ordered and paid for by the men.

During the week the majority of inside servants would move to 4 St James's Square. In this way they were responsible for the running of two houses. It was a system that worked well and everyone was kept happy with the mixture of town and country life.

No. 4 St James's Square was a large and elegant town house of the eighteenth century. On the ground floor there were two large halls leading on to the Square, the morning room, the lower dining-room, Lord Astor's study, the controller's room and the menservants' quarters. Lord and Lady Astor's bedrooms and dressing-rooms were on the first floor and so was my lady's boudoir, also there were two drawing-rooms, the large dining-room and the ballroom. Above were staff and visitors' bedrooms and at the top of the house a squash court. In the basement were the kitchens which faced on to Regent Street, the Pugs' Parlour, the stillroom, the wine cellar, the butler's pantry and silver safe and countless other rooms, many of which were stored with furniture. There was a service lift to the top dining-room, but the food was carried to the lower one.

My room here, although attractively furnished and with a fitted carpet, was small considering the work I had to do in it. However there was a room nearby for the washing and drying, though since I was blessed with a fireguard I hung pieces on it to air and so once again was continually kept clothes-conscious.

Rest Harrow was built for the Astors in 1911. It was a seaside country house standing in large grounds near two golf courses, which Lady Astor used constantly when in residence. It was a comfortable house. There were two halls of which the inner could be used as a sitting-room; a drawing-room, a dining-room, schoolroom and kitchens on the ground floor and a patio leading to the gardens. Lord and Lady Astor's bedrooms were on the first floor, with three visitors' rooms. On the second were the day and night nurseries, more visitors' rooms and the servants' quarters In the gardens there was a miniature golf course, a squash court and kennels. The house had a resident housekeeper and housemaid.

Here my room was everything I could have wished. It had a lovely view out to sea, was light and airy and delightfully furnished.

No. 3 Elliot Terrace, Plymouth, overlooking the Sound, was one of eight terraced Victorian houses with a basement and five floors. The main rooms were therefore separated by staircases. The kitchens were in the basement, hall and dining-room on the ground floor, sitting-room and secretary's office on the first floor, Lord and Lady Astor's bedrooms on the second floor, visitors' rooms on the third floor and staff and spare rooms on the two top floors. There was a resident secretary in charge, a housekeeper, a cook and a kitchen-maid.

My room at the top of the house can very easily be imagined. It was typical of the Victorian period, a servant's attic. Fortunately it was better furnished than was usual and I found I was able to cope quite easily.

Tarbert Lodge was more like a farmhouse. It was comfortable, but comparatively spartan, not a place to be lived in, more one to come back to after a day's sport. It was run by the resident factor, a Mr MacIntyre, and his wife.

My immediate concern when I arrived at Cliveden was of course Miss Wissie. My friendship with Mrs Vidler, Lady Astor's maid, made settling into the house, and the job, much easier. She showed me around. Miss Wissie had her own suite, a bedroom, sitting-room and bathroom. She could, if she wanted, be independent of the rest of the house, do her own entertaining and have her meals sent up. She was a typical young lady of the times, good-looking with big dark brown eyes, a wonderful complexion, tall but slim. She took after her father and there was nothing of her mother in her. She was timid and shy and I think resented, at any rate in her younger days, her mother's theatrical and unpredictable behaviour. She had no dependence on her mother. I'd like to say that she'd cut loose from her mother's apron strings, but that wouldn't be very apt because I don't think Lady Astor ever wore an apron in her life, at any rate I never saw her in one. What I mean is she didn't look to her mother for help or advice. She got interference of course; none of the children could avoid that, nor indeed could any of the staff. I remember, soon after I joined her, that I went with Miss Wissie to her cousin Mrs Winn's home in Charles Street where she was to spend the night, to dress her for a ball her aunt, Lady Violet Astor, was giving for her at her house in Carlton House Terrace. Before we left Lady Astor called for me and told me that Miss Wissie had to wear a particular dress, white chiffon with a wreath of roses that I'd had to tack right round the back. Miss Wissie hated it and refused to wear it. Well, I thought, it can't really be that important, so I just made a few noises of protest and then let her have her own way. She wore a gold one and by the time I'd finished with her she was a sight for sore eyes. She was indeed the belle of the ball, everybody had said so, Mrs Winn told me the next day. When we got back to Cliveden Lady Astor sent for me and cross-examined me. 'I'm told Miss Wissie was the belle of the ball,' she said.

'I'm very pleased to hear that,' I replied. I knew what she was going to say next so I spiked her guns. 'I must tell you, my lady, that she wore the gold frock. I'm glad it worked.'

I sort of threw away the last line, knowing I was on dangerous ground. She must have been in a good mood for she let it go at that. She couldn't really have done anything else, you may think, with Miss Wissie being such a success; but as I was to learn later she most certainly could have. The great thing with Lady Astor though was to tell the

51

truth even before she asked for it; it took away the force of her attack.

Lady Astor was very generous to Miss Wissie over her clothes. She had a large and beautiful wardrobe for a young lady, but her mother supervised it. When she was in London we always had to go to her dressing-room together before Miss Wissie went out to a ball or theatre; and many's the time we've been sent back again to change. This didn't make my position easy with either of the ladies. However, after I'd been with Miss Wissie only a short time I was able to do her a service which I think endeared me to her. After I'd dressed her and we were going through her bits of jewellery to decorate whatever she was wearing, I'd say, 'There's nothing here that's worth while but I'm sure your mother has got something.' The first time I said it Miss Wissie said, 'You'll never get anything, Rose.' But I did. The hardest thing to borrow was her ladyship's pearls. Miss Wissie only had a small string, her 'nineteen and eleven-pennies' I used to call them. Well, one night after I'd discarded them I said, 'I'm going to try her ladyship once again,' and down I went.

'Here comes the sergeant-major,' Lady Astor cried when I went into her room. 'Well, what do you want this time?' She'd had her little joke so I thought, it's going to be now or never.

'It's your pearls, my lady.'

'I've told you half a dozen times, Rose, you can't have them,' she said.

'I know you have, my lady, but my name must be Bruce and, like him and his spider, I try, try again.'

It worked. She burst out laughing. 'You're not an ordinary spider, Rose, you're a tarantula,' she said, and threw her pearls at me.

Miss Wissie was both astonished and delighted. Nine times out of ten after that I was able to get them for her. With Lady Astor there was always the tenth time over anything. It was the same with her furs. I was soon borrowing those for Miss Wissie. After all, there's nothing distinctive about owning your mink, except of course its beauty and value. No one knew therefore that it was her mother's coat she was wearing.

Miss Wissie enjoyed dancing and the company of young men, though she was never one for gallivanting, not that she and I discussed this side of her life, but I should have heard about it from other sources if she had been. Her interests were few. She enjoyed riding and tennis but she didn't go in for the arts; at least not then. I was with her for part of the hunting season. We went together to a few country house parties in Leicestershire, Rutland and North-amptonshire, where the sport was most fashionable, and to the Duke of Buccleuch's place in Scotland, Drumlanrig Castle. I was of course responsible for looking after her riding habits and these weren't easy to cope with. Some evenings she'd come in soaking wet and spattered with mud, yet the next morning she would have to appear looking spotless. Fortunately she had an excellent tailor so the clothes never lost their shape. Both Miss Wissie and her mother rode side-saddle. It was interesting that when it became fashionable for young ladies to wear their hair short, and Miss Wissie had hers cut off, it was made into a bun, a piece of elastic was attached to each side of it and it was worn tucked under the back of her bowler. In that way she and other hunting ladies maintained the traditional style of wearing their hair.

I hadn't been with the Astors for more than a week or two when my urge to travel was really satisfied. In September 1928 I was asked to go to the States as ladies' maid to both Miss Wissie and Lady Astor. I was astonished and more than a little frightened; I hadn't yet become used to Miss Wissie's ways, let alone her tempestuous ladyship's. The reason that I was asked to go came about as a result of some double-dealing on Mrs Vidler's part. She wanted to leave Lady

Astor and she knew that if she handed in her notice in the normal way there would be trouble and her life would be made hell. So just before she should have been leaving with the two ladies she let me in on her ploy. It was this: they were expected to be away three weeks, and Mrs Vidler was going to plead that domestic troubles made it difficult for her to go. I would take her place, and directly we were out of the country she would give in her notice to the Astor office. She'd therefore be leaving immediately after we returned.

I didn't like being a party to it, but Mrs Vidler had my sympathy. It was never easy working out one's notice and with Lady Astor I could imagine the dreadful time she would have. Then of course there was my great desire to see America. I'd built up a sort of dream picture which can be a disappointing thing to have done, though as it happened the reality more than matched my imaginings. So I quickly agreed to fall in with the plot. Lady Astor wasn't particularly pleased when the news was broken to her; she didn't like other people's arrangements interfering with her own, particularly when she paid them, and she said so, but there wasn't anything she could do about it. Mrs Vidler did her packing, gave me one or two hints on how to treat Lady Astor, and suddenly there I was on Waterloo station with our tickets, twenty pieces of luggage and two ladies to protect and look after. If I had had time to think about it I should have felt like 'little girl lost', but thinking time was something Lady Astor didn't allow you when she was around: it was all talk and bustle.

We sailed from Southampton on the *Aquitania* on 22 September 1928, my first experience of a luxury liner, and I didn't enjoy it for the first two days; I was very seasick. Also I found that I had to share an inside cabin with three other maids. They had got themselves well installed by the time I arrived and I was left with a top bunk and hardly anywhere to put my things. When I tottered round to her ladyship after my first sleepless night I must have looked a pathetic sight because she took one glance at me and said, 'What on earth's the matter with you, Rose?'

When I'd explained she went into action. 'Miss Wissie's got two beds in her cabin. You must share it with her. Go and tell the purser.'

With the extra physical comfort I soon found my sea-feet and I was able to enjoy the rest of the voyage. I always travelled first-class on board ship after that. Some servants prefer to go tourist. I remember Mr Dean, who had been under-butler to the Astors before I arrived there and was later butler to her ladyship when Mr Billy came into the title, telling me how when he was butler to Prince and Princess Obolensky, he found he was always kept busy running errands for them when he went first-class. 'It was no holiday for me,' Mr Dean said, 'and it was made worse seeing the other servants having a good time in tourist. My opportunity came when I had to go and book to go to America. Six servants were travelling, me as butler/valet, a Russian chef, a footman, Mollie, Princess Alice's maid, a nanny and a nursery maid, and my lady was complaining at the price of the tickets. "It would save you money if your maid and I travelled tourist," I quickly said, and it was agreed that we should. Well, I had the time of my life for the first half of the voyage, with the run of the bars and the run of the girls.' (Mr Dean considered himself a bit of a Romeo.)

'Then one morning when we were splicing the mainbrace someone came in and said, "Your lady's outside looking for you." Well, I slipped out of the bar quickly, down the companionway and into the Prince's room and started busying myself. She came in a few minutes later and said, "I seem to have spent half this voyage looking for you, Dean."

' "I'm sorry about that my lady," I said, "I can't have been very far away though can I?"

' "I know where you've been. Even if I hadn't seen you it

would still be very obvious." And she made a little sniffing noise. "You're travelling first-class from now on." She handed me a ticket with my cabin number. "And here's another for Mollie" – her maid. No more high jinks for us on that voyage: we had to be at her beck and call from then onwards.'

When we arrived in New York Lady Astor and Miss Wissie left the ship to meet her ladyship's sister Mrs Dana Gibson. I stayed on deck with the luggage. If I was lost on Waterloo station, I felt like an orphan now. Eventually someone from the Astor office arrived and took the trunks, but I was still left with the twenty pieces of luggage. There were a number of coloured porters about so I asked one if he would see to the cases. He went to great lengths to explain that he was only allowed to carry two pieces, and beckoned to some others. Eventually I and my regiment of porters got down to the quayside to find Lady Astor looking for me. When she saw me she raised her hands in horror. 'Rose, and her ten little nigger boys,' she shrieked. I didn't know where to put myself, I felt so embarrassed for the porters. It was my first experience with coloured people and I expected them to take offence. They didn't: Lady Astor was the offended party. Apparently I'd been taken for a ride, as they say over there. One porter should have got a truck and taken all the cases; as it was I had to tip ten of them – or her ladyship did!

I found it hard to get accustomed to the treatment given to those with a different-coloured skin. The North was supposed to be more tolerant towards them and perhaps, speaking generally they were, but when we went to Lady Astor's home in the south in Virginia, they were much more a part of the family than servants were in England. They were almost loved, although rather as a pet dog might be loved, in a superior, tolerant, patronizing sort of way. When you met them they were expected to get excited, wag their tails and do their tricks, while you stroked and patted them. But despite this they still seemed to belong more. Outside the house, coloured people were looked down on, particularly by the poorer whites. It was the same as in England, everyone seemed to want someone they could feel superior to and this as much as anything else, I think, led to the decay of domestic service as an occupation here. Eventually servants were considered as the lowest of the low. Britain now has its own colour problem and shortly, it seems to me, by the way things are going, we shall soon be expected to despise the rich. Then my life will have gone full circle.

We spent the first night in New York at Mrs Dana Gibson's home on East 73rd Street. The size and the pace of the city seemed to get into me, which was just as well as I had so much to do and so little time to do it in, and since the next evening we had to catch a train to Virginia. Miss Wissie and Lady Astor shared what is called a drawing-room compartment on the train. We arrived at Charlottesville and later went to Mirador, Greenwood, the family home of the Langhornes. Although the family had married and moved away it was kept running by an Englishwoman, Miss White, nanny to Lady Astor's first son, Mr Bobbie Shaw, and later to her ladyship's sister Mrs Brand's two boys by her first marriage, Peter and Winkie Brooks. She was helped by a coloured butler and two cooks, Caley and Estelle, who were duly assembled on our arrival and given their pats on the back with beads and pearls for the cooks and cuff buttons and ties for Stewart, the butler. Although I may seem a bit critical, there's no doubt everyone enjoyed it and it was a happy occasion with fun, tears and laughter. It was at the time the expected and accepted thing.

Mirador was a large estate on which stood a roomy eighteenth-century house with a pillared porch, a marble hall and a curving Georgian staircase. It was set in the middle of the peach country in the foothills of the Blue Ridge Mountains. The scenery was very like the English countryside at its best, only on a larger scale with high mountains and massive valleys. I fell in love with the place directly I saw it and never had a change of heart. I was kept very busy during our few days there for apart from looking after the two ladies I had to keep arranging the flowers that arrived so continually that there was no room left in the house to put them; and answering the telephone that never stopped ringing. At first I left this to Stewart, but he kept forgetting names and getting messages wrong, so eventually Lady Astor insisted that I should answer it.

My main enjoyment on that visit was the food, the wonderful Southern cooking. Her ladyship felt the same way about it and we both put on a few pounds in weight. From Mirador we went to Richmond, staying with Mr and Mrs Sanders Hobson. Mrs Hobson was an old school friend of my lady's. Mr Hobson confided in me about Lady Astor: 'She was the wildest girl in Richmond,' he said. 'I ought to know, I was raised with her.' The Governor of Virginia gave a ball in honour of my two ladies. It was done in the grand manner that Americans are so good at, but also it had style. I think it was the occasion they both enjoyed most during their visit. Some of their enthusiasm even washed off on to me. From Richmond we went to Washington for two nights, which we spent at the Canadian Embassy. Then on to Boston, Massachusetts, and back to New York. Talk about a whistle-stop tour, it was all packing and unpacking for me. We'd only one night to spend with Mrs Gibson and I was looking forward to the rest that I hoped to have on board the *Aquitania* on our journey home. But I wasn't to get it. As our luggage was being wheeled out of the door Lady Astor waved imperiously at me. 'Take Miss Wissie's trunks and cases back, Rose. I've decided she will stay on here with you for the next three months. She'll be doing the American season.'

And we did. It was typical of her ladyship, as I was to find out, she'd change her mind as often as she'd change her clothes. But although I was shaken I wasn't sorry. It meant that I should have the opportunity of seeing more of America and I'd have only one lady to look after, who was much more predictable in her ways and in her moods.

Our permanent home during our stay was with Mrs Dana Gibson, though we travelled widely. Every weekend we'd be away. There was a continual round of dances and I would accompany Miss Wissie to every one. It meant many late nights for me, but her aunt was more considerate than her mother and I was always allowed to stay in bed until midday after a late return. This wasn't so much perhaps consideration on Mrs Gibson's part as the fact that in America maids expected much more time off than we did over here, so it was more the rule of the house. It happened everywhere we went, homes like Lady Granard's and at Vincent Astor's place near Rhineback, on the Hudson river. I came into contact with the staff of many houses. The thing that I found most extraordinary was that there was no overall mode of behaviour; every house seemed to be run differently, and there were so many nationalities in service there. Of course I was set in my ways when I went there but once I got used to the unexpected I enjoyed it. They were so immediately friendly and helpful, and I seemed to get a welcome everywhere I went. Although their hours were shorter and wages higher, they were expected to work hard. Their employers demanded their pound of flesh. One thing though that I could never get used to was that the butlers were called by their christian names. I used to imagine an employer calling Mr Lee, Ed, and shuddered at the thought – and the consequences.

We travelled back to Britain on 5 December 1928 on the *Leviathan*, a German ship we had taken as an indemnity after the war, it was fast and very comfortable. Apart from the enjoyment of my travels I'd got to know Miss Wissie well and I looked forward to many years of service with her.

On my return I was immediately summoned by Lady

Astor to give an account of our journeyings. Apparently Miss Wissie had spoken well of me, so I came in for no criticism. Then suddenly her face changed. 'You know Mrs Vidler has left me?'

'So I understand, my lady,' I said.

'Did you know she was going to?'

'Yes, my lady.'

'Then why didn't you tell me?'

'Because it was told me in confidence and in any case it was none of my business,' I replied.

'Very well, Rose, you may go.'

It was a curt dismissal and I could see she didn't like what I had said. I also knew she wasn't happy with the maid she had engaged temporarily and would be glad when she'd left. She would not have been if she'd known what was going to happen. She had arranged to employ the former maid of Beatrice the Infanta of Spain, and I think she felt that getting her was a bit of a coup. It wasn't. The maid lasted two weeks; she didn't even stay to collect any wages. She did what was called a moonlight flit; nobody saw her go, not even the nightwatchman. I suppose she couldn't stand the pace and decided just to put it all down to experience. Again I was cross-questioned, but this time I knew nothing. I must say at first I was a little bit amused by it, but the smile was quickly wiped off my face when I found that I'd got two ladies to look after and pack for, as we were going away for the weekend.

I bridged the gap until a Miss Byles joined. I'm afraid from the start it was clear that she wouldn't last long either. Whether her ladyship was going through a bad spell or what I don't know, but Miss Byles soon took on a haggard, worried and worn expression which never seemed to leave her. One day Mr Bushell, his lordship's valet, cornered me and said, 'A word in your ear, Rose, don't ask me how I know but her ladyship is going to take you away from Miss Wissie and get you to work for her.'

This aroused my Yorkshire obstinacy. 'Is she?' I said. 'We'll have to see about that.'

Then Mr Lee sent for me. 'Miss Harrison, I think you should know that her ladyship will be asking you to work for her shortly.'

'I don't think I'm up to it – I mean up to her standard,' I said.

His, 'She thinks otherwise,' was intended to close the conversation. However, when he saw the set expression on my face he said, 'Anyway, forewarned is forearmed.' I'm not sure but I think he had a word with her ladyship and told her that I wasn't going to be easily persuaded. She duly sent for me to her boudoir. 'Ah, Rose,' she began, 'I'm not happy with the way you're treating Miss Wissie.'

This took the wind right out of my sails. 'I'm sorry to hear that,' I heard myself saying.

'You do far too much for her,' she went on. 'She's not learning to stand on her own feet, she must be more independent and do things for herself.' I thought, You cunning old so and so. 'I'm getting her an inexperienced maid to replace you and I want you to come and work for me.'

'I'm perfectly happy where I am, my lady,' I said. But she'd got me cornered and I knew it.

'Of course you are, Rose, but it's Miss Wissie I have to consider.'

I knew she wasn't considering anyone but herself, but I couldn't tell her so. I wasn't going without a struggle. 'What happens if I say no?' I asked.

'Then I'm afraid you'll have to leave.'

'I'll go away and think about it.'

'Yes, you do that, Rose,' she said, all sweetness and honey.

She knew she'd got me, I'd really no option, I was happy there and since there was no point in cutting off my nose to spite my face, I later agreed. In a way I suppose I was flattered, but the feeling didn't last long, I hadn't time to think about myself. I was right about my limitations. It was

61

the concentration. I remember at school we were always being told to concentrate. Well, I think I managed it then. But with Lady Astor I found I was expected to do it for eighteen hours a day, seven days a week; and even when I had concentrated on doing something she would suddenly change her mind, and expect me to do the same – and at the same speed. Being lady's maid to her wasn't the job I'd learnt or been taught. As Mr Lee said, she wasn't a lady in the terms that my experience had led me to think of one. Nevertheless, even if she wasn't a lady, she was a great character and an international personality. So, there I was, I'd reached the top rung of the ladder for my kind of job. What I had to do was to stay there. It wasn't to prove easy and I swayed about a lot in the earlier years. Eventually I learned to be an acrobat.

4 My Lady and My Duties

When I began working for her ladyship I looked at her with professional eyes. She was short, five foot two, but slim. She had a good figure and carried herself well, though often she moved too fast for my liking. She was strong and had no time for illness or feminine weakness. She had adopted the faith of Christian Science at the beginning of the First World War. Before her conversion she had been a semi-invalid and spent a lot of time in bed, but while I was with her she was strong as a horse. Although she was small she made no attempt to increase her height by wearing high heels. Both her day and evening shoes had ordinary Cuban heels. Looking at her I was reminded of that Yorkshire saying, 'Good stuff in little room'.

Either she was very fond of games or she believed in keeping fit, probably a bit of both, for she was always taking exercise. She swam nearly every day in the summer in the river at Cliveden, or the sea at Sandwich; she played squash at St James's Square. She had got his lordship to build her a court for her own personal use. She played tennis and golf; there was a practice course at Cliveden. And she rode regularly until her later years. In the winter we always went abroad for sports; skiing and skating. It seemed there was nothing she couldn't do, and do well.

My duties were similar to those that I'd had before for the other ladies, only they were more so. I would go down to her ladyship at seven-thirty, collect her clothes from the night before from her dressing-room and take them to my room where I would have to press them later. At eight o'clock I would have my breakfast. I took hers up at eight-thirty and ran a cold bath for her; she took one both winter and summer. After her bath, it would then be nine o'clock;

she would read her Christian Science lesson. She wouldn't have this interrupted except for the most urgent of telephone calls, and I learned by trial and error what she considered urgent. After that everything was action. The political secretaries would be summoned and they would arrive at the double, feet coming first and their bodies following. The mail would be opened, the phone would start to ring or else she would demand a number. She always started her calls in a comical way: 'Hallo, is that you? Yes it's me.' Eventually the secretaries would be bundled off, almost pushed out of the door on the run, and her ladyship would demand her clothes for whatever exercise she happened to be taking that day. She seemed hardly gone for a moment and she'd be back, into a warm bath this time, which I'd prepared. She always slung her clothes into the bath after sport – squash things, golf blouses or tennis skirts. I suppose she wanted to make certain they were washed each time. I had seemingly endless sets of things ready in case there was any delay in the laundry. Then she would dress for whatever the occasion demanded that morning; for the House of Commons, for visiting, or shopping. After lunch she would change for the afternoon or, if she was relaxing, for golf, and she changed again for dinner. She generally got through five sets of clothes in a day. This required from me a deal of organizing, pressing, cleaning and repairing. Also there were perpetual messages to be run or delivered, shopping to be done either on my own or with her ladyship, and dressmaking or copying. I made many of her ladyship's things.

Lady Astor was always immaculate in appearance and she took a pride in being so. She treated her clothes well and was very tidy. When she changed she hung her discarded clothes on a hanger, put her hat on the hat-stand and trees in her shoes. She was particularly fastidious about her underwear. It was kept in sets in silk pouches which I had to make and decorate in his lordship's racing colours, blue and pink. Every evening I would leave one pouch on her stool and she would fold her underwear into it and tie the ribbon, and so it would be sent to be laundered. I'd heard of this being done before but I thought it was a habit only of elderly ladies. Her ladyship's underwear was hand-made in France, at some school for crippled girls, from a silk and wool mixture for winter, with knickers fitting above the knee, and of triple ninon for the summer, beautifully appliqué'd and sewn.

For the House of Commons she was impeccable in a tailored black suit, a double-breasted satin blouse lined with white silk with a collar and revers, and a three-cornered felt hat with a corded ribbon cockade: or a black all wool dress with white piqué collar and cuffs, and in the summer a thinner material black dress with either frilly jabots and cuffs or broderie Anglaise ones, which had to be spotless. I always had a number of sets of them by me and her ladyship never wore the same set twice before laundering.

I know her ladyship was often complimented on her appearance, but she never passed the compliments back to me. The nearest she got was when she said, 'Lady So-and-so would like to know how you keep my collars and cuffs so clean, Rose.'

I couldn't resist being a bit short with her. 'Tell her by washing them, my lady.'

She always wore black court shoes and black silk stockings, though when coloured stockings came into vogue she changed to steel grey. Her white suede gloves were from Paris, again only being worn once before being sent to the cleaners. Finally before she left the house she would fling a full length black cloak over her shoulders.

There was one thing which distinguished her, her button-hole. That was Frank Copcutt the gardener/decorator's contribution. He would send it up to the house if we were at Cliveden, or post it if we were at St James's Square, a fresh one every day. Her ladyship demanded white and it had to be scented. 'If a flower hasn't a scent, Frank, it isn't worth growing,' she'd say to him. He used to manage to meet her demands all the year round, concentrating on gardenias, tuberoses, stephanotis, lilies of the valley, and a lovely white orchid with a little gold centre which fortunately flowered in the winter; even this had a beautiful perfume. Though I'm sure her ladyship took her political responsibilities very seriously I think she also felt that being the first lady elected to Parliament she had to set a standard for those who followed. She only once slipped up and for the life of me I don't know why. It was one day shortly after I had joined her. 'I'm not wearing black today, Rose. Get out my red dress. It's time I looked different.' I tried arguing with her but got the now usual, 'Shut up, Rose,' for my pains. I don't exactly know what happened but apparently she was the laughing-stock of the Commons. She also put his lordship's back up. Whatever it was she was trying to prove, she didn't, and she never tried again.

Though I have gone into detail over her ladyship's clothes for the House of Commons it is because they always remained the same in style. This was not true of her others. She followed fashion, but she never attempted to lead it. She was never way-out. She was expensively but not extravagantly dressed. Simplicity was her keynote. It suited her personality best. It was as well she wasn't showing off all the time. Dressing her wasn't difficult; what was impossible was to attempt to keep up with her quicksilver mind. 'I didn't want this dress, Rose, I told you I wanted the purple,' was a common occurrence, and off I'd have to go to press it and bring it back for her only to find that she'd put on the one she had originally asked for. I'd try to say, 'Would I have put it out in the first place if you hadn't told me to?' only to get the reply, 'Shut up, Rose.' When at last she was dressed she'd stand in front of the mirror and go over herself in detail. If anything was wrong I was for it. 'She didn't let me forget a hairpin,' as the saying was amongst ladies' maids.

Perhaps because of the exercise she took she had a lovely complexion, which lasted her till the end of her days. She had few wrinkles, which I found astonishing since her face reflected her emotions and she practised these to the full in her constant contact with people. She used make-up very sparingly. It was through an unfortunate accident which happened shortly after I joined her that she was brought into contact with a make-up expert from whom later she was able to learn such a lot. She was playing golf one afternoon with a young friend of hers, David Metcalfe, and instructing him a bit as they went round. She stood too close behind him while he was driving, the club hit her on the cheek and she was very badly bruised. That night she was going to a State ball, which, on no account did she want to miss though not unnaturally she didn't want to go there looking as she did. The Bond Street firm of Elizabeth Arden was telephoned and it was arranged that one of their beauticians would come round to St James's Square to do her best to make her ladyship presentable. It was a very good best and Lady Astor was delighted. From then on for any occasion the same young lady would come and see to her ladyship's make-up. As a result Lady Astor learned some of her techniques and of course all preparations used by her were Elizabeth Arden's. She used scent sparingly, and always Chanel No. 5.

As I've said, she didn't mind how much she spent on clothes, so it came as a surprise to me once when some years later she asked me to go to Marks & Spencer's to choose a frock for her. 'Marks & Spencer's?' I echoed, astonished.

'Yes,' she said. 'I hear they have some very nice things there now. Anyway you go along and see.'

That was that, so I did. To my amazement I found a grey stockinette dress with delightful grey pearl buttons decorating it. It cost three pounds, nineteen and six. When I took it back I didn't sing its praises, I presented it to her and said, 'I don't know whether it's going to suit you, but if you don't like it or it doesn't fit, I can return it and get the money back.' That seemed to please her. I unwrapped it and she liked the look of it, then tried it on. It fitted her to perfection. When she heard how little it had cost, she seemed to like it even more. She almost wore it out, it was literally threadbare, something she never did with her other clothes. She'd come back and tell me that her friends had admired it and asked her where she had got it from.

'Did you tell them the truth, my lady?'

'No, of course not, Rose, they'd never have believed me anyway. I told them Jacqmar made it. [Jacqmar was a shop she used in Grosvenor Street] I expect they'll be round there tomorrow, trying to get one like it.'

The success of the Marks & Spencer's frock sparked off her ladyship's enthusiasm for the shop. I was never able quite to repeat our first success but I came near to it with some golfing skirts which also fitted perfectly and were much admired.

Hats were a big thing. I remember once when we'd been travelling in America and had returned to New York where we were spending the night before sailing, she announced her intention of going to look round Bergdorf Goodman, the big store on Fifth Avenue. 'Don't you come back with any more hats, my lady,' I said. 'The luggage is all packed and the hat boxes are full.' She waved me a perky good-bye and I knew then it would have been better to have said nothing, that my remark was now a challenge to her. True to form, back she came laden with parcels.

'I hope those are not hats you've got there,' I said.

'Rose, I just couldn't resist them,' she replied. She should have added, 'After what you said,' because that's what she meant.

'You'll have to carry them yourself,' I said, 'my hands will be full, as I told you.'

And she did carry them and when we got to Southampton I told her she must declare them at the customs. 'Oh no,

Rose, I'm not going to pay any duty on them. They've cost me enough already. If they ask for it I shall tell them they can keep the hats.'

But they did ask for it and she did pay it. Mind you, give her her due, she could wear hats and I think to some extent she influenced fashion. There was the case of Miss Welham who opened a hat shop in Knightsbridge. Lady Astor was one of her first customers. Not only did she go there regularly but all her friends did the same until Miss Welham had a very thriving business. She paid her debt to Lady Astor because when she died she left her £100; and how her ladyship appreciated it. It was to her in a way the widow's mite and as greatly to be treasured. Shoes and gloves were also a mania with her and whenever she went to Paris she'd come back laden with them. I'm glad to say she was very careful with gloves, I wasn't left with a box of odd ones as some ladies' maids were. I remember one saying to me, 'I must have thirty single-handers stored away and I am not allowed to get rid of them. My lady is certain she will be able to make a pair one day. At the rate she is going on I wouldn't be surprised. If there was a society for one-armed gentlewomen perhaps she would let me give them to it.' I could guess how she felt.

Lady Astor wasn't too good with umbrellas, particularly in later life. She would meet a friend in the street, start chatting and hang her brolly on an iron railing if there was one nearby so that she could use her hands for gestures. When the conversation was over she'd often walk off and leave it there. Many's the journey of hers I've had to retrace looking for one.

Another accessory that was in constant use when I first joined her was fans. She had a beautiful collection from many countries. The feathers that looked so gorgeous with their tortoiseshell handles needed great care to keep them fresh and clean. It seemed a shame when they went out of fashion. I think her ladyship missed them because she used them to great theatrical effect when she was talking to visitors and friends. Eventually, I'm glad to say, she gave them to Miss Joyce Grenfell, the actress, who is a niece and a friend as well. Yet another accessory of that time which also followed fans into retirement was lace. Lady Astor had a most beautiful collection which I was able to learn from. It was eventually all boxed up and put away though I did keep some to use on her black velvet dresses, coffee-coloured collars and turned-back cuffs, rather as they were worn in King Charles's time. Lace had to be cleaned most carefully and ours was always sent to a specialist cleaner.

Of all the things committed to my charge the jewellery caused me the most concern. When I first joined her ladyship I was given a list of all that she owned and I had to sign for it. It ran to about five pages of foolscap; I've got it to this day and nothing will make me part with it. It now shows where every piece went to and to whom it went. It has proved very useful even since her ladyship's death and it will always serve to give me a clean bill of health. It really is extraordinary when you think that I, a servant earning £75 a year, should be given the care of jewels whose value ran into hundreds of thousands of pounds. I alone knew the combination number of the safe. I expect there was a copy of it kept in the office but her ladyship could never remember it, which was fortunate for me since she couldn't take anything without my knowing about it, and although she wouldn't thank me for saying so she had a very poor memory over certain things. The very valuable pieces were of course kept in the bank in St James's Square; this was a condition imposed by the insurance people, but I was sent to collect anything as it was required, and again had to sign for it. What would have happened if I had lost anything I don't know, it's something I don't like to think about, but it would have been a long time before they could have got its worth back out of my wages; I should have had to have lived to be as old as Methuselah!

Perhaps the most valuable of all her ladyship's jewellery was the Sancy diamond. Its history fascinated me as much as the diamond itself. It was bought in Constantinople in 1570 by the Seigneur de Sancy, French Ambassador to Turkey, an almond-shaped beauty faceted Indian fashion on both sides. When Sancy became French Ambassador in Britain, King Henry IV of Navarre asked to borrow it. Sancy agreed and sent a messenger with it. He never arrived. His body was found, but not the diamond. Sancy, believing in the boy's loyalty, explored further, and it was discovered that he had swallowed the jewel. It was later sold to James I of England, then to Cardinal Mazarin and then to Louis XIV. After the French Revolution it went to Russia and finally William Waldorf Astor bought it for her ladyship. When I used to handle it I thought of all the places it had been, particularly the messenger's stomach. Talk about Jonah and the whale! It caused a bit of excitement while it was with the Astors, and me a few anxious moments. When war was declared in 1939 his lordship decided that everything of value should be moved from London to Maidenhead. Mr Lee came to me and said, 'I've just had a message from Lord Astor, saying, would you take the Sancy diamond to Cliveden when you next go.'

'It's in the bank,' I said.

'No it isn't, his lordship's cleared the bank and he says you must have it.'

Well, I was nearly out of my mind with fright, yet I knew I was right. After all I wasn't likely to forget whether I'd got a few hundred thousand pounds' worth of diamond in my possession, was I? I phoned Miss Jones, Lord Astor's secretary. 'Oh, he's just spoken to me about it, Rose,' she said. 'He put it in his pocket and forgot that it was there.'

'Put it in his pocket and then said that I'd got it,' I shouted down the phone. 'Wait till I see him, I'll give him a piece of my mind!'

'You can do it now, Rose,' came the reply in his lordship's voice. He'd taken the phone from Miss Jones. 'It was very naughty of me.'

'Naughty, my lord?' I said, 'it was criminal. You nearly murdered me, I was just about to have heart failure.' I must say that for the next few days whenever he saw me he put his head in his hands and turned away.

I wasn't the only one to have suffered through that diamond, Mr Lee informed me. 'It happened,' he said, 'some years before you joined, Miss Harrison; there was a ball at St James's Square and Lady Astor had lent the diamond to her sister, Mrs Nora Phipps, to wear on a gold chain. In the early hours of the morning her ladyship came up to me and whispered, "Mr Lee, the Sancy diamond is missing."

' "Missing, my lady, do you mean Mrs Phipps has lost it?"

' "Yes," she said. "Who do you think has taken it?"

' "If you mean do I know who the thief is, my lady, it's a question I can't answer, but aren't you jumping to conclusions?" She was.

' "What about your men?" she said, knowing I'd hired some additional staff for the evening.

' "Do you think they're honest?"

'I looked hard at her. "Be reasonable," I said, "What would the likes of us do with the Sancy diamond? The moment we tried to get rid of it we'd be arrested."

' "What about the band?" she said.

' "The band has nothing to do with me, my lady, it was booked by your secretary." It was Ambrose and his orchestra who were so popular at that time that they were engaged for all the big society balls; hardly likely to have wanted to combine rhythm and crime. "If it's a question of theft, my lady, it would more likely be one of your guests, they would be in a better position to dispose of the diamond. If you believe it to have been stolen I suggest you ring Scotland Yard."

'She went to his lordship but he wouldn't hear about calling in the police. It was just as well. I informed all the staff that it was missing and the next morning at seven one of the under-housemaids came to my room with the Sancy diamond in her hand. "Mr Lee," she said, "is this the thing there's all the fuss about?" She'd found it under a carpet. It had probably been swept under by the ladies' long dresses. And that, Miss Harrison,' said Mr Lee, 'was the mystery of the Sancy diamond.'

Mr Lee always spun his stories delightfully, and I must say I liked the housemaid's reference to the famous diamond as a 'thing'. It seemed to put it in its place. Once Mr Lee got into his stride he was a hard man to stop. He went on to tell me about the time her ladyship's pearls were missing. 'It was in 1919, Miss Harrison, just about the time society was getting into gear again after the First World War, and when her ladyship had won her seat in the Commons, for Plymouth. There'd been a party at the house in Elliot Terrace and the morning following Lady Astor sent for me and said, "Lee, my pearls have been stolen."

' "I'm sorry to hear that my lady," I said. "When and by whom?"

' "It must have been last night," she said, "and I don't know who took them."

' "Then you mean they're missing, my lady."

' "I've searched everywhere and so has Miss Samson." Miss Samson was her lady's maid though she'd only been with her a short time. "They must have been stolen. Ring the police."

' "Very well, my lady." I tried to convey that she was being a little hasty, but I had to do as she said. The sergeant came round and true to form he started off with, "What's her maid like?" It was always the staff that came under suspicion. I tried to explain that it was unlikely that she could have taken them because she'd have no means of getting rid of them, but he still wasn't convinced.

' "She's the one most likely to have done it, I'll question her first." He interviewed her in the library. Poor Miss Samson, she came out blazing with fury and with tears running down her cheeks, just in time to hear her ladyship say, "We've found them." Apparently her secretary, Miss Jenkins, had turned out the waste-paper basket in her room, and discovered that the pearls had dropped in there. When I next saw Miss Samson I thought it only right to express my sympathy for what had happened, and she told me her story. Apparently, that bullying sergeant had written out a statement for her to sign admitting that she'd stolen the pearls. When she wouldn't he insisted on searching her.' Then Mr Lee's voice dropped to a horrified whisper: 'Do you know, Miss Harrison, she told me that he had even put his hand inside her breeches.' I must say I found it hard to keep a straight face, not at what the sergeant had done to Miss Samson, but because Mr Lee found it impossible to refer to her undergarment by its familiar name of 'knickers'.

We did have a real burglary at Cliveden while I was there. It was during the summer; a painter had left a ladder at one of the bedroom windows and the thief managed to get into my lady's room and take some small pieces of jewellery which were lying around. I think he must have been disturbed because there were a number of valuables left behind and none of her drawers had been opened. The police and the insurance people came and investigated but they weren't able to find whoever had done it. A few days later his lordship called me in to see him. 'We think it would be a good thing if we changed the safe, Rose. Instead of a combination we shall have an ordinary type of lock, and there will be two small keys, one for Lady Astor and one for you. They'll be a gold colour and we'll buy you a gold bracelet and you can carry it on that.'

I had to think very fast. 'That won't do for me at all, my lord,' I said.

'Why, what do you mean, Rose?' He wasn't used to

having his decisions challenged and it was the first time I'd done it.

I said, 'I'm the only person who knows the combination of the safe at present, but only you and her ladyship know that I'm the only one. If I'm seen carrying a key on my wrist everybody will realize what it's for, and if a wrong 'un finds out I may end up with my wrist cut off. Oh no, my lord, that won't do for me at all.' He laughed a bit but I could see that what I'd said had gone home.

'All right, Rose, we'll leave things as they are for the time being.' He had to allow himself a loophole as regards time, but nothing further was ever mentioned about it after that. Now I don't want you to think that I was a coward and that I was really afraid about my wrist, but I knew that if her ladyship had access to the safe I would never be able to keep track of where her jewellery was, and my life would have been made a misery. But I couldn't very well tell his lordship that, could I?

Apart from the Sancy diamond and the pearls, the other special pieces of jewellery were the tiaras. Her ladyship had five. The most beautiful and valuable was the Astor heirloom, the second was a bandeau of diamonds and pearls, the third aquamarines and diamonds, the fourth she bought herself – it was of spiky diamonds – and the fifth was an imitation of the first. It was used by her for the less important occasions and she also often lent it to her friends. All her most precious jewellery was expensive to wear because from the moment it left the bank until its return there was a special insurance premium in operation. Not that she ever stopped to think about that. She loved wearing it and she often used too much for my taste. She'd turn round to me and say, 'How do I look, Rose?' and I'd reply, 'Haven't you forgotten the kitchen stove, my lady?' earning myself the customary, 'Shut up, Rose!'

Then she had a big sapphire and diamond chain which she'd separate and wear as bracelets, one on each wrist, and two large diamond earrings, as large as cobnuts they were. One of these she lost one night at some 'do' at the Café Royal. There was the usual hullabaloo about thieves. I was round there first thing in the morning and collected it straight away. A cleaner had found it and handed it in; just another example of how honest staff were at that time. One of her favourite pieces was a sapphire and diamond tee that she had won as a prize at golf when she was partnering the Prince of Wales, later Edward VIII. She wore it as a scarf pin when she went out golfing. It was lost and found, lost and found, trampled on, repaired and finally replaced. Rood's, the jewellers, must have made a lot of money from that piece alone.

I wonder how widely the kind of relationship jewellers had with their clients is known. It wasn't just making a sale and that's that. It was as if you had your jewellery on loan from them. They cared for it in every way, cleaning, repairing and resetting. Pieces were photographed and detailed and if lost, replaced, so that you couldn't tell the difference. Jewellers were all courtesy and kindness towards ladies' maids and were prepared to teach you how to clean things and keep them looking their best. I take my own small bits to Cartier's or Rood's from time to time and I'm always greeted as one of the family, even though I can now be of no value whatsoever to them. It's just one of those things that makes a lifetime spent in service worthwhile.

I remember once how useful Cartier's were. It was one of her ladyship's stormy days when nothing went right or was right. She was getting at me and finding fault with everything. She picked up a bracelet and said, 'Look at this, Rose, it's absolutely filthy, don't you ever clean my jewellery?'

I gave her a bright smile and said, 'Filthy, my lady? Then what a good thing you noticed it. You see it came back from being cleaned at Cartier's this morning. I'll pack it up and return it to them, and perhaps you'll enclose a note saying how badly they've done it.'

There was no 'Shut up, Rose,' this time, it would have been 'Shut up, my lady,' only I didn't have to say it.

The restringing of the pearls was a regular event and it developed into a ritual. Miss Grace from Hopkin Jones, the Warwick Street jewellers, did them. We would ring up and make an appointment, I would get the pearls from the bank, and together we'd climb to my bedroom and on a table there she would restring them with me supposed to be watching her like a hawk, to make sure she didn't replace any; she couldn't have stolen them without doing this because when they were finished I had to count them – they were strung 42, 46, 49 and 54. I still carry the numbers about in my head. Well, I knew it was all a charade really, so did Miss Grace, and so I expect did Queen Mary's maid, because Miss Grace used to restring her Majesty's necklaces. Still it had to be gone through. It was at the jeweller's insistence. You see it covered them against any later accusation, and their good name was their stock-in-trade. I don't think I have ever seen a more beautiful clasp than those pearls had; it was an emerald snap with six diamonds on either side – whoppers they were.

Although we had occasional dramas with the expensive jewellery, these pieces more or less looked after themselves because their appearances were not everyday affairs. It was the smaller pieces that caused me the most concern. These her ladyship treated casually, lending them here and there, and sometimes even giving them away, without telling anybody. I needed eyes in the back of my head to keep tabs on them. Her furs sometimes caused me similar worries. When I first went there these were not officially made over to my charge. By that I mean I wasn't given a list and made to sign for them. Nevertheless in fact I was held responsible and after an altercation with the office over one that went missing it was decided that they would from then on as it were be my property. This suited me. It was no good being half responsible, all or nothing was what I wanted, and I got it. A list of furs will I think show the scale of things in those days. Lady Astor had a long sable cape (for the opening of Parliament and state occasions), a mink, a nutria, a black broadtail and a Persian lamb; she had a short mink jacket and a short mink cape, short and long sable stoles, a chinchilla cape, a sable tie (made from three skins she brought back from a visit to Russia), a black velvet evening coat lined with white ermine and some of her hats were decorated with expensive furs.

Bradley's of Bayswater were responsible for cleaning, repairing and remodelling. I don't think I shall give offence if I say that they were the leading house for furs at that time, though Bayswater seemed a bit provincial for such a company. The altercation to which I referred earlier was over the Russian sable tie. I had sent some of her ladyship's furs, including that one, to Bradley's for cleaning, and when I unpacked them on their return I found it was missing. Bradley's swore it had been sent. After her ladyship cross-examined me it seemed apparent that she believed what Bradley's had said. As I said to her in no uncertain terms, that meant that I must have stolen it, as I was the only person to have handled the furs on their return.

'No, I believe you, Rose, I know it's out of the question that you would do such a thing.'

'But you still think Bradley's sent it; that doesn't make sense to me,' I said. 'The only right thing for you to do, my lady, is to call in Scotland Yard and I won't rest until you have.'

She did this and an inspector questioned me very thoroughly, which I didn't mind. By a stroke of good fortune I'd kept the tissue paper that the furs were wrapped in, and I was able to demonstrate, by repacking, those that had been returned and how they had arrived. Now today, people who like me are economical, because they have to be, keep tissue paper for re-use. It was a firm rule of her ladyship's that it must never be used twice, and that went for my things as well, so it was strange that I'd kept it. Anyway the inspector then went to Bradley's. Two days later he called at St James's Square and I was asked to go and see him. He was with Lady Astor and he said, 'I have to tell you, Miss Harrison, that the mystery has been solved. There was never any question of you being under suspicion, neither are Bradley's staff to blame. There was a third party involved, but we are not taking proceedings against them, and the matter will now be dropped.' It all sounds a bit strange as I write it, but it was clear as daylight to me. One of her ladyship's acquaintances must have persuaded Bradley's to part with it, the police had found out who it was but it had been decided not to pursue the matter. In society at that time dog did not eat dog. The only mystery to me was that we never saw the tie again.

Valuable coats are always a great worry. Unlike jewellery, which as it were never leaves the person when it's worn, coats have to be continually put in the charge of other people who don't necessarily give them the protection or the care they need. Then again they can be easily forgotten, particularly when the warmer weather comes along. I must say that generally speaking Lady Astor took care of hers and very rarely did I have any real worries over them. I think too that at that time people were more honest. I also know the police were more effective, probably because there were more of them. The constable on the beat was a great comfort, a good friend and a link with the local police station. It was easy to ask for help, it was always forthcoming and given in a friendly way. It was the same on the railways, and you can imagine I used them a lot not only on our lengthier travels but shuttling backwards and forwards between Cliveden and London every week, with a multitude of trunks and cases.

I was to learn over the years how to pack for every conceivable period of time, climate and occasion and to be ready at a moment's notice to do so. Whenever I travelled by train I would tip the guard and porter well. They got to know me and would look after me. They gave me a lot of useful advice about taking care of luggage and I think largely because of the trust and friendship that was built up between us I am able to say that I never lost as much as a piece of ribbon. People complain about the railways. I don't. I've found that if you treat the people who run them properly and try to realize their difficulties and the things that can happen that are beyond their control, you can travel in comfort and with an easy mind.

I've mentioned that I tipped well: it was with her ladyship's money and advice. I always had a reasonable float given me by the office and accounted for by me at the end of each month. It was sort of petty cash, but it had to be quite a sizeable amount as her ladyship was continually running out of money and having to rely on me.

That then is the bare bones description of the duties of Lady Astor's personal maid. The spirit and the flesh follow later.

5 Coming to Terms with My Job

What sort of person was I as a result of my experience over the last nine years? I hadn't changed, or I didn't think I had. I believe character forms during your childhood and you never grow away from it, indeed that you never really grow up. So I was young in heart. I've not mentioned my love life which nowadays is called sex life, but I prefer the earlier way of putting it. Perhaps I've given the impression that in service there wasn't a lot of time for that sort of thing. Let me put it this way: we didn't give it the amount of thought that it seems young people do now; there were so many other things to think about. Still, I didn't neglect the romantic side by any means, and I got a lot of fun from it, but while it's something I enjoy recalling it's a personal thing and in any case would make very dull reading.

Professionally I was, I thought and indeed still think, highly competent by the standards of the day. If you enjoy your work as I did, I don't think you can help but become good at it. I'd developed the skills I'd begun with and learnt many others. I'd travelled a lot for my age and become a Marco Polo for my class. I'd met people and enjoyed them and I was able to get on well with my colleagues below stairs and my employers above, or so I thought until I began working for Lady Astor. From the start she knocked the stuffing right out of me. I had imagined things would be quite easy; after all I'd managed to get by when I'd looked after both her and Miss Wissie on our trip to America, but that I found didn't seem to count. It was in a way as if I was with a complete stranger. Difficult though the job was I know I could have done it left to myself, but I wasn't. The moment I began one thing she wanted another. She was quite unpredictable and always unappreciative. She was sadistic and sarcastic. If I reminded her of something, she'd say, 'I never need telling anything twice, thank you, Rose.' She mimicked me, not out of fun but to hurt. She'd change her mind purposely over her clothes, accuse me of not getting things right, and then call me a liar if I protested to her. She shouted and rampaged like a fishwife, though without using the bad language.

It all seems strange as I tell it now, and I don't think anybody knew at the time quite how bad it was. I just wasn't used to ladies behaving in that way towards servants. Gradually it wore me down. I began to think I was to blame, that I'd lost my grip on the job. I did forget things. My work went to pieces and so her criticism became justified. I had too much pride to go to anyone and ask for help. When I told Mr Lee about it some long time later he said, 'Why didn't you come to me, Miss Harrison, that's what I'm here for. It wouldn't have been easy, but I would have sorted things out with her ladyship.' He would have, too, but at the time I saw it as my battle, something I had to fight for myself and I'm glad I did for both my sake and her ladyship's.

The change in our relationship was not something that happened subtly over the years. It couldn't have been. I should have either collapsed or given in my notice if things had only altered gradually. I can pinpoint the day, indeed the time almost to the hour, when I got the resolve and the strength to come to grips with the situation. I'd had a very bad morning of it, with her ladyship at her most demanding. After lunch, feeling both physically and mentally tired, I went to my room. I began thinking about my work and the way my life was going. Then my thoughts switched to my childhood, my early ambition, the efforts Mum and Dad had made for me. I was back in our village, in the school, in our cottage, in our church, singing in the choir, and thinking about the beauty of life then. I don't think I was consciously praying, but suddenly something seemed to touch my spirit, I had a feeling of inner happiness and release. It was as though I was in a trance. I allowed myself to drift.

I don't know how long it went on but gradually the dreamy feeling fell away and my body took over again. I didn't hurry it, the sensation was so relaxing and enjoyable. When I came to myself it was as though I'd gained a new strength. I didn't feel tired, the things that had worried me almost to death now seemed insignificant. It had all been my own fault. I'd allowed her ladyship to walk over me and make mincemeat out of me. I now knew that my work had been right; where I'd been wrong was in not defending it and myself when we were both under attack. I saw her in a different light, not as a mean spiteful person any more, but as someone who in her own way was putting me to the test. She wanted a maid in her own image and she thought she could get one by destroying me and then building me up again as she wanted me to be. She hadn't succeeded and from now on she wasn't even going to get the chance. Two could play at her game, and henceforth two did. What had begun as a battle gradually mellowed into a kind of game between us. It went on for thirty-five years; neither of us won, neither of us lost.

For a day or two I went about my work with a light heart and any nasty remarks fell off me like water off a duck's back. Then one morning in London Miss Dorothy, from Bertha Hammond's of 16 Old Bond Street, came to do her ladyship's hair. Perhaps it is interesting to recall here that on my lady's recommendation Mr George Bernard Shaw had his hair and beard trimmed and washed at Bertha Hammond's. As I went in to remove the breakfast tray Lady Astor said, very testily, 'Rose, give Miss Dorothy a cup of coffee.' I poured her one from the Thermos jug on the tray, put the cup on the dressing-table and left. About five minutes later my bell rang and I went to her ladyship again. Angrily she pointed to Miss Dorothy's cup and said, 'Take that thing away, you should have done it hours ago.

How do you expect Miss Dorothy to work with dirty cups lying about?'

I stopped in my tracks and looked long and hard at her ladyship through the mirror. From my expression there was no mistaking how I felt. I then looked at Miss Dorothy, who was obviously thoroughly uncomfortable, and left.

Two more minutes and my bell rang again. 'Rose, why have you given me a thick dressing-gown to wear in the middle of the summer? Get me a thin one.'

'I can't get you what you haven't got, can I?'

'Very well, Rose, buy the material and make me one.'

'No I won't, my lady. You've got the money go and buy one yourself.' I gave another look at her in the mirror, and another glance at Miss Dorothy who looked as if she was frightened to death, and left.

Three or four minutes later the bell went again; so did I. 'Rose,' she said, 'don't you ever dare speak to me as you have this morning. I don't know what's come over you.'

'My lady,' I said, 'from now on I intend to speak as I'm spoken to. Common people say please and thank you, ordinary people do not reprimand servants in front of others, and ladies are supposed to be an example to all, and that is that.'

I left the room feeling triumphant. I'd stood up to her, I'd protected myself, she could sack me if she liked, but if she did she was in the wrong, not me. Half an hour later my bell rang again. 'This, my gal,' I said to myself, 'is it.' I wasn't the least bit afraid.

'Rose,' she said, as I entered the room, 'I apologize for my behaviour this morning.'

I'd won. Now I was torn between two stools: should I say, 'And so do I, my lady,' so making things easier for her? I didn't. I thought no, if I do it will mean things are all square. So I just said, 'Thank you my lady,' and went.

Now all this sounds very trivial, but if you want to know how it was possible for two people to live closely for thirty-

My mother, who died in 1953
aged 85

My father, who died in 1922
aged 54

With my younger sisters Ann
and Olive and brother Frank :
taken in the 'good old days'
when a poor family were all
bound for domestic service

In memory of
many pleasant
suppers at the
Harrisons. J C Dowd Lt.
23/11/17

Our home at Aldfield, near Ripon. It was built of stone in 1676 and the walls are a foot thick. The church behind is ten years older. Our garden was full of old world flowers and many people used to ask my mother if they could paint the cottage. We were never lucky enough to get one of the paintings

I had this picture taken for my parents soon after I entered service

During the First World War Mother and Father used to entertain soldiers from Catterick Camp for tea. Two lady drivers were billeted on her; one drove Lt. O'Dowd and later married him. Lt. O'Dowd drew this for the family autograph book. The kitchen is exactly as it was in 1917

One of my first employers: Lady Cranborne dressed for a pageant

Phyllis Astor

When I joined the Astor family in 1928 I was 'young lady's maid' to the daughter, Phyllis, known as Miss Wissie

Just to show what good-looking children Lady Astor had; David, her second son, a very handsome young fellow

Lady Astor wearing the Astor tiara with the Sancy diamond in front; her dress is pale blue satin with coffee-coloured guipure lace. These are the Astor pearls: the rows contained 42, 46, 49 and 54 pearls; I shall never forget the numbers

The dining-room at 4 St James's Square. Lady Astor's portrait is the famous one by Sargent. The mixed flowers were arranged by Frank Copcutt, the decorator, who later became head gardener. He was allowed to use only low containers and fern was forbidden

How the Cliveden menservants were dressed: brown livery, yellow striped waistcoats, brown coats with brass buttons. Here are the valet, the butler, two footmen, the coachman and the groom of the chambers

Edwin Lee, a great butler of his time, Lady Astor called him 'Lord Lee of Cliveden'. To have been trained by him was a reference in itself. Now retired, he loves to recall the days when he was king of his castle. Here he is with Arthur Bushell, Lord Astor's valet

Gordon Grimmett, the footman, at Rest Harrow

Dinner & Reception Feb 25th 1922

The Duchess of Devonshire   Lord Astor
Lord Revelstoke   Countess of Wemyss
Lady Ridley   Rt Hon Austin Chamberlain
Lord Lee of Fareham   Lady Lee of Fareham
Mrs Lyttelton   Lord Desborough
Mr C.P. Scott   Mrs Austin Chamberlain
Mr Snowden   The Duke of Devonshire
Mr Winston Churchill   Mrs Lloyd George
Lady Moyra Cavendish   Mr Garvin
Hon Evan Charteris   Mrs Spender Clay
Mrs Winston Churchill   Earl Winterton
Col Clay   Mr Garvin
Mrs Thomas   Lord R Cavendish
Sir E. Grigg   Mrs Brand
Mrs Winteringham   Hon. J. H. Thomas
Marquis of Londonderry   Lady Desborough
Lady Kerry   Mr John Sargent
Lord Derby   Lady Londonderry
Lady Frances Balfour   Hon. A. J. Balfour
P.M. Mr Lloyd George   Lady Astor

Dinner. 40.   Reception Approx. 850

A page from Mr Lee's 'black book', his own record of guests at Cliveden.
A reception or dance for several hundred was not at all unusual

Cliveden, Buckinghamshire

Lord and Lady Astor at the
time I first went to them. On
the terrace at Cliveden

odd years it is important. For me it was a turning-point and
so it was going to be for her ladyship though she didn't
know it then. She couldn't change her nature any more than
I could. I had created a situation between us and named
the rules. It was to be a battle of wills and wits and therefore
I had to keep mine about me. It wasn't long before I saw
how right I was. We'd been at it hammer and tongs and
finally I said, 'You're unkind, my lady. I don't think you
realize how hurtful you can be to people.'

'Oh yes I do, Rose, whenever I'm hurtful I mean it, and
I enjoy it.' She was like a tigress as she said it.

I said, 'Right my lady. Now we know where we stand.'

She laughed then, but still I knew she'd meant what she'd
said, when she said it. As another argument reached its
climax, she cried, 'Rose, it's my ambition to break your
spirit.'

'I know it is, my lady. There's two of you trying to do it.
You and the devil. And neither of you will succeed.'

She didn't care for that one, being coupled with the devil,
with her strong preoccupation with religion. I'd got to learn
quite a bit about Christian Science while I was with her
and I'd throw it back at her. 'How can you think that way
my lady? Your book says, "A person who thinks good and
does good is good." You must learn to practise what you
preach.' That put her back on her heels. So did my reply
to her when she was being critical. 'You know Rose, if you
were the perfect maid you would arrange my collar for me
before allowing me to go down to dinner.'

Quick as a flash came the Christian Science phrase, 'It's
because I'm imperfect that I am here to try and perfect
myself. Remember, my lady, there's only one perfect
person.'

She often tried to get at me through my speech. 'You
and your Yorkshire accent,' she'd say, 'why don't you try
and speak properly?'

'Do you really want me to go around aping the kind of

people you entertain my lady, speaking with a plum in my mouth? Never, I'm Yorkshire and proud of it. Me I am and me I mean to stay.'

Then another time she was finding fault and started making comparisons. 'The difference between us, Rose, is that I was born to command and have learnt through experience how to deal with people.'

'The difference between us, my lady,' I said, 'is that you have money. Money is power, and people respect money and power so they respect you for having it.' It wasn't really true, there were so many other things about her that people respected, but beggars can't be choosers when it comes to words. She'd use my rank to belittle me. 'You're as bad as a housemaid, Rose,' she said to me once.

'You ought to know better than to speak to me like that,' I replied, 'my sister Ann is a housemaid, a good one, and she's a good person. I expect there are a lot of them who are better people than me. You've no right to talk of housemaids as though they are the lowest of the low, you only belittle yourself.'

Oh, I let her have it that time, and she took it. Give her her due, after she'd got over the initial shock of my talking back at her, she learnt to accept it and to expect it. It wasn't long before I began to suspect that she enjoyed it and therefore goaded me purposely. Anyway she never seemed to bear any malice. Another time when she was talking disparagingly about servants I said, 'I'm surprised that you think of maids that way, my lady. Wasn't it only yesterday that you were saying in the House of Commons that more girls ought to go into domestic service? If any possible recruit were to hear you now I should think they'd have second thoughts.' I got a quick, 'Shut up, Rose,' for that one, but now, when she said that, I looked on it as one up for me.

There were times when she suspected that I wasn't very busy and she couldn't bear to think that she wasn't getting her money's-worth out of her servants. An occasion I remember was when we were down at Sandwich, and she asked me how I was enjoying the holiday. 'Very much, my lady,' I said. This must have started her thinking that I wasn't doing enough because half an hour later she rang for me and told me to produce the sewing work that I'd done for her that week. Well, that was tantamount to me being there on trial. It was an insult and I took it as such. As it happened I'd been very busy making sachets for her underclothes and edging scarves from material that had been sent from Paris. I took it all down, plonked it in front of her and stormed out of the room.

Again my bell rang. Her ladyship said, 'Rose, I like your work, but I don't like your attitude when I ask to see it.'

'My lady,' I said, 'you treat me as if I was new and un-trained. You show no trust in me at all. I can read you like a book. Just because I said I was enjoying the holiday you thought I wasn't doing my work, so you decided to check up on me. I don't like it my lady and it won't do.'

'I'm sorry, Rose,' she said.

'So am I, my lady,' I replied.

There's no doubt that some of the blame for our set-to's lay with me. It was a clash of temperament. Perhaps we both fed on it. Sometimes it used to worry me. I'd end up by saying, 'You know, my lady, it's dreadful the way we go on at each other; you make me ashamed of my own sex.' Once, I remember, things got so heated that she really lost control and landed out at me with her foot. I made to catch it but just missed. 'You wouldn't have floored me, would you, Rose?' she said, when she pulled herself together.

'I certainly would, my lady,' I replied, 'just as you would have kicked me if I hadn't moved away in time.' Then of course we both burst out laughing.

As the years passed our relationship mellowed and the rows became more like verbal skirmishes. Apparently, though I didn't learn this until later, they were a topic of amusement and conversation not only among the servants, but with the family as well. Eventually I was told that Lord Astor would go to his dressing-room when we were having an altercation, to listen in and have a good laugh. When I heard this I was astounded that he allowed a maid to talk to her ladyship as I did. Mr Bushell, his valet, said that he probably thought it better that she should take it out on me and so spare himself. I don't know. I suppose it could be true. One thing I do know is that I discovered the key to understanding and working for Lady Astor: she didn't like people who kow-towed to her and she didn't like 'yes' men.

So far I haven't been very complimentary about her ladyship. While I am at it I think I may as well complete this one side of the picture. That there is another you can be sure, otherwise I could never have stayed with her. She was such a mass of contradictions that it's impossible to generalize about her. She could be mean, mean over money and sometimes mean in spirit. It was about six years after I had been with her that I thought I deserved a rise in salary. Seventy-five pounds a year wasn't a lot of money even then. I approached her ladyship. I could see she didn't like me for doing it, but she said she would see what she could do. She spoke to the secretary. The next month my wages were raised by five pounds a year. I was disappointed and disgusted. I said nothing. Some time passed and one day her ladyship said, 'Oh, I've been meaning to ask you, Rose, have you got your rise in salary?'

'Yes thank you, my lady,' I answered, 'I've got my extra threepence a day.' She flushed a bit, but no more was said. I'd learnt my lesson. I never asked for another rise, and I never got one. At that time goodness was supposed to be its own reward.

Her ladyship could be mean too over small purchases that I made for her. 'Fancy buying that! Couldn't you have made do?' That sort of thing, and once when I took some cakes to eat myself after they had been taken from the drawing-room, she went for Mr Lee as if he'd lost the crown jewels.

He didn't give me away, but when I heard about it I told her that I was the culprit. 'Oh, if he'd told me that I wouldn't have minded, I thought it was one of the other servants,' she said.

'And why shouldn't they have the occasional crumb from the rich man's table?' I demanded.

'Shut up, Rose.'

Black or white, that was Lady Astor. That there was so much white was the wonder. She was spoilt from birth, for despite what her mother is supposed to have said, 'I've had eleven children, all unwanted,' the Langhornes were made to feel very much wanted, with everything that money could buy and the other things that money couldn't, like love and happiness. She enjoyed the outdoor life and the débutante scene in New York. All right, her first marriage was not a success, but to what extent did she try and make it one? She ran back home a number of times, beginning with the second night of their honeymoon. She blamed the drink, but a lot of men drink, particularly if their wives are a bit unstable. After she was separated, and later divorced, from Mr Shaw, she toured round Europe so she could forget the unpleasantness. Then she had the wonderful good fortune to meet and marry his lordship, a great gentleman, a kind husband, and one of the wealthiest men in the world. From what I've heard of their early years together he lavished everything upon her, love as well as his worldly goods. She was pampered in every way. I reckon that treatment would have destroyed most women, but that her ladyship survived it and became the great person that she did shows a phenomenal strength of character that her worst enemy couldn't help but admire. From what I knew it was her love and feeling for others that saved her from becoming a spoilt darling. Cleverer people than I have talked about her as a supporter of causes. I believe that behind every cause was a person, someone she could identify herself with. She never talked politics to me, she only talked people, and I would later see the plight of these people turned into causes. She is famous for those she entertained. There's no doubt she enjoyed meeting them. Entertaining with her was like an industry. Many people are said to have used her for their own ends, but she used many of them to make the lot of the poorer and more insignificant easier.

During the First War the Astors built a military hospital for Canadian soldiers. It was a model of its kind and was all paid for by his lordship. By the end of the war it could hold over six hundred patients. One of these, a Mr Guy, stayed on to work for the Astors in the estate office. He never stopped singing her ladyship's praises. 'I reckoned I was a goner, Miss Harrison,' he told me, 'nothing they did for me seemed to help. Then one morning along came her ladyship, only she was plain Mrs Astor then. "What are you so down in the mouth for?" she asked. "You look as though you think you're going to die."

' "Well, it had crossed my mind, madam," I said.

' "Nonsense, that's not the kind of spirit that's going to get you better. I'll tell you what," she said, "if you pull yourself together and get well quickly I'll give you a gold watch." Well, from that moment on, everything seemed to go all right, despite the fact that I had to have four more operations. Every time her ladyship came to the hospital she came to see me and sort of dangled that gold watch in front of me. When I was on my feet again sure enough she gave me one, and here it is.'

I'm sure that gold watch was taken out more often to illustrate his tale than it was ever to look at the time. There were to be many other people that her ladyship assisted, as I was able to see for myself during the next war. Her generosity was not confined to the sick or disabled: she also often helped with the education of the children of the workers on the estate. Mr Lee tells a story which apparently was one her ladyship was very fond of using when she had a party in the lower dining-room at St James's Square. She sat at the end of the table; opposite on the wall were two pictures, one of the first John Jacob Astor and the other the Sargent portrait of herself. During dinner she would point at them and say, 'That's the man who made the millions and that's the woman who's spending them.'

People found her what is called an easy touch. I've seen her give five pounds to a street beggar. This used to irritate me because they'd lie in wait for her, and it infuriated Mr Lee because he would be constantly answering the door to them. He was always meticulous in his treatment of them though, asking if they had an appointment to see her ladyship before dismissing them. It was a rule of his that was passed on to all the footmen. 'Never judge a sausage by its skin,' he'd say. 'There's many a duke dresses like a dustman, and many a dustman who tries to dress like a duke.'

If I was irritated by beggars in the street it was nothing compared with my feelings when her friends asked her for money. 'You'll never get it back, my lady,' I used to tell her, watching her sign cheques for hundreds of pounds, 'and it'll only make them worse.'

'Shut up, Rose,' she'd say, but sometimes she took my advice. At any rate, my telling her made her think twice. There was nothing I could do about the Grand Duchess of Russia – Xenia her name was. She'd been given a grace and favour house at Hampton Court by the royal family. Her ladyship would do anything for her; she gave her suits, dresses, underwear, got her anything she asked for and she gave her cheques. I'd say to her ladyship, 'She's got more money than you have, my lady,' but she wouldn't listen. When this Xenia died she left three hundred thousand pounds, and not a penny to Lady Astor. Then there was another of her friends to whom my lady was always giving money, presents and clothes; she died worth eighty thousand. How they could ask I don't know. There was more pride amongst the poor than among some of the aristocracy.

Yet as I have said, her ladyship had her mean streak.

There was a trick that she would play on me: 'Would you like a chocolate, Rose?' she'd say.

'Thank you my lady, I would.'

Then she'd take one out of the box, bite into it, hand it to me and say, 'You can have this one, it's a kind I don't like.' I'd take it and throw it into the waste-paper basket. 'You'll want that one day,' she'd say.

'Not after you've bitten it, I won't, my lady.' She did it to me a number of times. I suppose she was waiting for the day I'd change my mind. I never did.

Then there was another lady, whose name escapes me, who used to bring her mending to Cliveden and sit doing it in the drawing-room. 'Rose, it worries me, Lady so-and-so doing all this mending, she must need money very badly.'

'I don't agree, my lady, it's probably by mending and patching that she keeps her money, and if you take my advice, you'll keep yours. I'm certain I've more darns in my vest than she has.' I knew this particular lady's maid and she'd told me what her mistress was like, a nasty, cuning woman.

There was one occasion when I slipped up badly. Lady Astor had given a black coat she'd had trimmed with mink to a very deserving case. She asked me to pack it. I thought quite naturally that she would want me to remove the fur and keep it, so I unpicked it and took it to show her ladyship. 'You can now go and sew that on again, Rose,' she said. 'When I give something away I give the whole thing, not just a part of it.' I went upstairs with my tail very much between my legs. She was generous with her clothes to me and gave me many of her things. Not all ladies were like her. It didn't suit them to think that their maids were well dressed when they went out. I never wore anything I was given by her when I was with her, it didn't seem right to me, not that I think she would have minded.

Over the years she became very fond of my mother, whom she always made a point of meeting if she could whenever

Mum visited me. She was continually offering me clothes to take to her, absurd things like evening dresses and cloaks. When I refused them she'd say, 'Why, Rose? I'm sure your mother would like them.'

'My lady, to begin with she's twice the size of you, and even if she wasn't they'd look absurd on her.'

'I just don't understand you, Rose, if your mother doesn't want them why don't you just take them and sell them like other maids do?'

'And what would you think of me, my lady, if I was like them?'

'Shut up, Rose,' she'd say, and get on with something else. She'd think of the staff when we were on our travels. One Christmas when we were away she asked me what I thought the indoor servants would like for presents. I was always ready with a quick answer on such occasions. 'Why don't you send them a Virginia ham each, my lady?' This touched her American loyalty.

'What a good idea, Rose, go to the estate office and order them.' I did. They suggested a tinned one each, which may have been her intention, but I pooh-poohed that idea.

'No, I'm sure she means them to have a proper one,' I said. Was I popular when I returned home!

I shall always remember one Christmas some two years after I had joined when the presents for the women staff misfired. My lady, thinking perhaps that everyone had her own passion for hats, told Miss Irvine, her personal secretary, to buy one each for the maids; I'm glad to say I wasn't included. It was of course an impossible task, but Miss Irvine made the worst of it. She bought identical hats in a variety of colours and sizes, all costing the same two and elevenpence, as was apparent since the price tags were left on.

On Christmas morning the servants' hall was a riot, anger at first, but after a while the maids began to see the funny side and demonstrated it. Some hats were pulled over eyes and ears, others perched on the backs of heads. The footmen joined in the fun and Arthur Bushell minced round the room giving a remarkable imitation of her ladyship. Then someone started a football game with them and finally they all ended up in a splendid blaze in the fireplace.

Another time her ladyship said, 'I think I'll take the maids some lace collars and cuffs back as a present, Rose.'

'Whatever would they want them for?' I asked, 'nylons would be much more to their liking.' It was a time when they were in short supply over here. Again it worked and I was sent to buy them three pairs each.

My greatest scoop though came very much later. Christmas had come round again and with it the usual question. I was ready. 'My lady, you told me that you've left the maids a piece of jewellery each in your will. Why don't you give it to them now, when they can give you their thanks and also enjoy wearing it?'

She clapped her hands with delight. 'What a splendid idea, Rose, I'll do it.' She did, and was able to see the surprise and pleasure she had given them written all over their faces. I got my piece too!

Her ladyship was very stubborn; it was in her nature. If she didn't want to do a thing it was the devil's own job to persuade her to do it. I didn't try, it wasn't my place, but the boys and his lordship did, and nearly always failed. She couldn't listen to reason. She was a creature of instinct and it sometimes failed her. She didn't know the meaning of the word tact; I suppose she thought she could afford not to, but none of us can do that. Apart from the times she wanted to hurt she often did it without intending to. This caused pain for others, and herself. There were only three people she allowed to dominate her: Queen Mary, and her sisters Irene Gibson and Phyllis, Mrs Brand.

If outward and visible signs are anything to go by I think she loved Mrs Brand more than anyone else outside her immediate family. I was with her ladyship at Eydon Hall when she died. It was one of those unnecessary deaths. Mrs Brand had been out hunting, got soaking wet, caught a cold and instead of looking after herself allowed it to develop into pneumonia. When Lady Astor heard the news she was almost out of her mind with grief. Mr Blyth, Mrs Brand's butler, came rushing to me and said, 'Go to Lady Astor, she needs you.' When I arrived at her rooms she was screaming, crying and praying. I took her in my arms and comforted her as best I could in my gruff Yorkshire way. Somehow it worked, her sobbing quietened down and whether it was that she had for the moment lost her inhibitions and could allow herself to give rein to other emotions I don't know but she turned to me and she kissed me. It was then that I knew she had affection as others had. It was just that she thought it a weakness to show it, which of course was nonsense; all feelings need an airing now and then.

It's funny though how people who control their own emotions seem to like and need a show of affection from others. This was the case with her ladyship. On her birthdays when I first went into her room I'd greet her, give her a kiss and say, 'I'm afraid I haven't got a present, my lady, that's all I have to offer.'

'And that's all I want from you, Rose,' she'd say, as if I'd given her the earth.

I think I should make it plain that affection was the only emotion I can think of that her ladyship did not display. Others could have done with toning down quite considerably; they got too much exercising for my taste. Like the good actress that she was she could cry to order, and like a baby she frequently did so, so as to get what she wanted.

Women, according to men, are unpunctual creatures. With Lady Astor unpunctuality was a disease and it made my life that bit more difficult having to work against time. When at last she was ready for whatever occasion it was, I then had to cluck round her like an old hen to get her away and meet a volley of 'shut up, Roses' for my pains.

Then his lordship would say to me, 'Please see Lady Astor is on time tonight,' as though it was my responsibility. Eventually, on important occasions, I would put all the clocks and watches on a few minutes; I couldn't do it too often or she would have tumbled to it. By the time I went to work for her she had learnt that trains usually left on time, but that was all. The only two other occasions when her ladyship was punctual were for Royalty or when she went to claim her seat at the House of Commons, a corner seat above the aisle. I think she'd have waited up all night if necessary to make sure she kept the same one.

With Cliveden being so near to Windsor Castle it was easy to anticipate the time Royalty would arrive and have everyone in position to greet them. Mr Lee had an arrangement whereby the Castle would phone him directly the visitors had left, and he knew almost to a second the time it took for them to get to us. Foreign Royalty too generally came from the Castle. There was one embarrassing occasion that Mr Lee recalls when King Gustav of Sweden was expected. On the signal from the Castle he posted two footmen on the door and went to tell Lady Astor. She was nowhere to be found. Search parties were sent out and Mr Lee arrived back at the door at the same time as his Majesty. He had no option but to say he couldn't find her ladyship. 'Never mind, Lee, how are you?' said King Gustav, as he was taken through to the drawing-room, and together they engaged in conversation. Suddenly Mr Lee spotted her, playing golf in front of the house. He pointed her out to his Majesty, who roared with laughter and, ordering Mr Lee to stay in the house, made his way out to surprise her. 'I'll put her off her stroke,' he chuckled, as he left the room. Mr Lee, who was on terms with many of the royalty, found the Swedish King one of the most easy and charming that he knew.

As time went by, and as her ladyship and I grew accustomed to each other, we became closer, though anyone listening outside the door to one of our ding-dongs wouldn't have thought so. Unlike my previous ladies, or any others that I knew of through other maids, she confided in me on personal matters. I've never, nor would ever, betray her confidences. There is a kind of Hippocratic oath like doctors have, with servants. Mr Lee saw that it was observed. 'Peeping Toms have no place here,' he'd say, if he heard even the whisper of an indiscretion. Anything more than that meant instant dismissal.

Gossip of a certain kind wasn't discouraged, and I think most of us enjoyed it. I know I did, but it was as well to know where to draw the line. Life isn't any the worse for living to certain rules. At any rate I know we had a very happy staff at the Astors'. I noticed the difference as I visited around with her ladyship. I suppose I'm making these remarks because I'm leading up to her attitude towards sex. Obviously a personal maid knows certain things about this side of her lady's life. I shall talk about it now not as it concerned her relationship with his lordship, but from her comment and behaviour in general. She was hotblooded by nature. She had five children. Yet she was fastidious and so was her husband. They disliked even the most witty or sophisticated reference to anything of a sexual nature and coarseness was not tolerated. Any guest who wandered over the border of what they considered acceptable would never be asked to come again. This was common knowledge among their class and few ever were indiscreet. In a way I suppose her ladyship was like Queen Victoria in her attitude to sex. To them both it was an intensely personal thing. A remark of Lady Astor's that was often quoted was, 'I can't even tolerate seeing two birds mating without wanting to separate them,' and this was often used to try and show that she was frigid. I don't see it that way. She was an inveterate match-maker, not with her own children, but with other people's. She liked good-looking, virile young men, but the parading of sex embarrassed her, so did vulgarity.

She could often be wild. Some people say it was the Irish in her. I don't think so. The Irish haven't got the monopoly of wildness. It's my opinion that it came from her Southern American upbringing and was an inheritance from her father. It was something that came out in so much of her life – in Parliament, at her parties, in sport – and it was so unpredictable. It used to worry his lordship no end. One of the worst moments was when T. E. Lawrence, Lawrence of Arabia, came to visit us. He was one of her ladyship's closest friends. He'd driven over on a motor-cycle. He and her ladyship must have been talking about it because suddenly both of them got up, rushed outside, jumped on his bike, her riding on the pillion, and drove off at top speed in a cloud of dust down the drive.

They were only away for a few minutes, but it seemed an eternity, and his lordship was beside himself with worry and embarrassment. They came back, if anything faster than when they'd gone away, and stopped in a skid on the drive. 'We did a hundred miles an hour,' she screamed, but she didn't get the enthusiasm back that she expected. I know I was thanking God for him having answered my prayers. His lordship just stalked away furious. Unfortunately that kind of reception didn't stop her. There was always a next time and we knew there would be.

That incident of her ladyship's ride on Lawrence's motorbike was brought back to me with some force. Shortly afterwards it fell to Mr Lee to take a message to her ladyship telling her of his death as a result of a fall from his bike. She was entertaining at the time and she hadn't even heard that he'd been injured. As Mr Lee says, it was a terrible shock to her. He had to assist her to her room. As usual on these occasions, I had to take over. Another's grief is almost as bad as one's own, and in any case it was as though the whole house had suffered a loss. We all of us liked him, all, that is, except Arthur Bushell, his lordship's valet. For some reason he couldn't tolerate him. I don't know why.

It was at Lawrence's funeral that Mr Winston Churchill and her ladyship for once got close together. As Mr Churchill was leaving afterwards she ran to him and caught hold of his hand, and they stood in silent understanding with tears running from their eyes.

Her ladyship always treasured Mr Lawrence's memory even after Richard Aldington besmirched him in his book. I didn't read it, but I'm told it was the truth. Even so her ladyship refused to believe anything bad of him. He was her friend and she was nothing if not loyal.

All my employers seem to have been fast, sometimes dangerous, drivers and Lady Astor was no exception. Even as a passenger she was dangerous. If we were late, which was often, she'd sit in the back shouting at Mr Hopkins, her chauffeur, to spur him on. It was as if she'd put her shirt on one of his lordship's horses. It had its consequences. Many's the time she and I have ended up on the floor of the Rolls. In retrospect it was funny. There she'd be sitting, smartly dressed in her black suit and three-cornered hat and with her white buttonhole, then the brakes would scream and the next moment she'd be lying on the floor, skirt above her knees, hat askew and hair falling down and eyes blazing with fury like a wild cat. Poor Mr Hopkins would have to explain, while I got her back into some sort of shape again. He couldn't very well tell her she was at fault.

My worst, or best, driving experience with her, depending on which way you look at it, was one morning when we were going to the House of Commons, and she was driving. The roads were icy and we'd had one or two nasty moments before we got to London. You wouldn't have thought so though, the way she drove down Constitution Hill. Suddenly, when we were in the Mall, I noticed the Guards Band coming towards us followed by people on both sides of the road. Her ladyship saw them too and put on the brakes. The wheels locked and we went sliding down towards the band. Their music sort of petered out and without waiting for any orders the musicians broke ranks, and I don't blame them. We went sliding on through where they should have been, then her ladyship got control of the car again and drove off as fast as she could screaming with laughter as we went. I was soon joining in; after all we were still alive and she'd got to face the consequences, I hadn't. There weren't any. I imagine someone must have taken her number and reported her, but she got away with it, she always did. Another habit of hers was going across traffic lights when they were red. She was continually being stopped for it, but either she charmed the policemen or they knew what was good for them; for she was never prosecuted.

One quality that I loved in my lady above all others was her gaiety and her sense of fun. I once said to her, 'If you ever find me dead on the floor you'll know I died from laughing thinking about something you've said.' When she was in her happy moods she would make a figure of fun of anybody or anything. Sometimes it was malicious, but it was always amusing. She was a wonderful mimic of the pompous British, Americans from the South and coloured people. She was sometimes accused of showing off, but it was always by people who hadn't got her gifts and so were probably envious of them. Anyway, what would she gain by showing off to me? There would be times I'd be treated to a half-hour monologue, and I'd be bursting my stitches all the time. She was particularly fond of taking off Margot, Lady Asquith, wife of the one-time Prime Minister. She even had a special set of false teeth for the performance and some evenings when she thought she'd be called upon to entertain, I'd have to make sure they were in her handbag. It was her ability to see fun and make fun that made her so popular with young children.

An event of the year was her ladyship's children's party.

It was held at St James's Square in the ballroom, with the food in the top dining-room. The ballroom would be covered with imitation grass and it was laid out like a garden fête with stalls or toys, sweets, balloons, lucky dips and games. The children were given a bag of money as they came in, chocolate money wrapped up in tin foil or gold foil according to what coins were represented, and they went around the stalls 'buying' whatever they wanted. There were conjurors and Punch and Judy shows. All the society children would be there with their mums.

I particularly remember one just before the war when there were three queens present, Queen Mary, Queen Marie of Yugoslavia and Queen Elizabeth, with of course the Princesses Elizabeth and Margaret. Queen Mary was always called upon to judge the fancy dress competition. I used sometimes to wonder really who the party was for, for the children or their mothers. It certainly wasn't for the nannies who brought their charges along. They handed them over at the door and then went below stairs. The servants' hall would be seething with them, much to the disgust of the permanent staff. Nannies weren't generally popular with servants. Nanny Gibbons, the Astors' nurse, was an exception; she knew how to behave towards them, but most of the others were considered to be a stuck-up lot.

Lady Astor always invited my mother to come and she'd send the Rolls to Walton-on-Thames to fetch her. This used to embarrass Mum. 'Whatever will the neighbours think?' she'd say, so I arranged with the chauffeur to stop at the top of the road and walk down to her bungalow to fetch her. When she arrived she'd sit in the cloakroom and watch as the visitors came in. She loved it. The time when all the queens were there Lady Astor must have mentioned my mother to Queen Mary, because when she was leaving she turned to her ladyship and said, 'Where is Miss Harrison's mother? I'd like to meet her.' Mum was duly produced, made what passed as a curtsy and had quite a long chat with her Majesty. It really made her day.

Royalty noticed servants. They may have been the lowest of the low to the man in the street but they were given the importance they deserved by the more distinguished. That sounds snobbish I know, but after all who is it that sets the standards? Lady Astor was wonderful to my mother, who in turn of course worshipped her. She'd never hear a word against her. This I occasionally found irritating because if I went to visit Mum after some particularly hard tussle with her ladyship and was giving vent to my feelings she'd always take her ladyship's side. 'Anyone would think she was your daughter,' I used to say.

Lady Astor was continually giving gifts to her. I remember the first time, it was just before Christmas. 'I'd like to get your mother a present, Rose,' she said, 'What do you think she would like?' It was in the early days and I was a bit on the defensive.

'It's kind of you, my lady, but we children can take care of the things she needs,' I answered somewhat churlishly.

'Shut up, Rose, if I want to buy your mother a present I shall. It's my money and I shall spend it as I like. Now go away and think, I'll give you ten minutes.'

I didn't know what sort of thing to suggest so I went for advice to Mr Lee. He said, 'Why don't you ask for a turkey?' I thought this was an excellent idea. A turkey had never found its way into our house before and I knew Mum would love one.

Sure enough, ten minutes later her ladyship rang for me, and again put the question. I told her what I'd decided on, but added, 'Just a small one, my lady, because a large one wouldn't fit into her oven.'

'Go out and get her one then, Rose, and buy all the things that go with it.'

I wasn't having that. 'No, my lady, it's your present, not mine, and you don't know that I'm not the sort of person

who knows no limit when it comes to spending your money.'
So she told Miss Irvine, her secretary, to go to Fortnum and
Mason. It wasn't just a Christmas turkey Mum got, it was a
Christmas everything, for she sent her one of their hampers.

Lady Astor took an interest in all the members of my
family, indeed for a time my sister Olive was cook to Miss
Wissie, at her house in London. She was an exception to the
rule; many mistresses didn't think that servants had parents,
let alone brothers and sisters. Of course her attitude affected
my work. To have someone putting pleasure in my mother's
way, who got so little out of life at the time, gave me the
incentive to try twice as hard. But I don't want anyone to
think that that was the reason for her ladyship's kindness.
She gave without any thought of return.

I haven't spoken about my own social life, that is my life
outside work; the reason is that I didn't really have any.
With her ladyship leading such a full life, eighteen hours
a day, seven days a week, it just wasn't on. You may say that
time off was due to me and that by the terms of my employment I could have demanded it. You'd be right and I
would have got it. But what would have been the consequence? Someone else, unused to my lady, would have taken
over, she would almost certainly have got into a tizzy, I
would have come back to things in chaos and my lady in a
tantrum. It wouldn't have worked. It would be sheer arro-
gance to suggest on my part that I was indispensable. Indeed when I was ill I was replaced temporarily, but it would
never have been worth the candle to have had weekly dis-
ruptions. I snatched time when I could to get out, when I
thought I knew that her ladyship's appointments would
keep her away long enough, but I was sometimes wrong.
Predicting her movements was never really possible and
she'd always straightaway ring for me on her return with the
inevitable, 'Where have you been, Rose?' if I was there,
and 'WHERE'S ROSE?' if I wasn't.

My sleep was something that was precious to me and I

guarded jealously the hours between nine in the evening and six in the morning. It was seldom I was in bed later than ten o'clock. Without regular rest my job would have been impossible as it was necessary for me to have a clear mind and a fit body. This was something I'm glad to say that Lady Astor understood and respected.

Although there was little opportunity of pursuing a social life outside I think the Astors were aware of this and did their best to compensate. There was a club at Cliveden which was presided over by his lordship. The sporting side was very strong. We had our own football and cricket teams, with regular fixtures, our own boat on the River Thames, and the staff could use the tennis courts and the golf course when the family weren't in residence. Alternate weeks there would be a whist drive or a dance.

There were two big days each year: the summer party, a sort of fête with a flower show and knitting and needlework displays, sports and all the fun of the fair for the children of the estate, with a big dance in the evening. Despite the Astors' dislike for strong drink there was beer for the men and wine for the women. The other big day was the Christmas party, and this was the one I enjoyed most. The house was decorated in traditional style and there was a huge Christmas tree in the front hall on and around which were presents for all the staff. They weren't the 'useful' gifts that some employers gave, like black stockings, aprons or lengths of material to be made up into uniforms, but personal things. Everyone seemed to be studied individually.

The family would all be gathered together and a few of their more intimate friends would be invited. In the evening there was a fancy dress dance, and this was the occasion I particularly looked forward to. Perhaps there's something of the actress in me. I loved dressing up and showing off. Choosing what to go as was also part of the fun. My success in my first Christmas there may have fired my enthusiasm. It wasn't actually my first Christmas with the Astors, that

I'd spent in America with Miss Wissie. I decided to dress up as 'Eliza comes to stay'. I wore a black and white gingham skirt over a red checked one, a high-necked white blouse with a bright yellow tie, a pair of black gloves with holes in, and I borrowed Miss Wissie's riding coat. On my head was a tiny straw hat with a tall, straight pheasant's feather and on my feet, lace-up boots. I carried a big handbag, a broken-down umbrella, a small tin trunk that the previous hall-boy had left behind, with a suspender hanging out at one end and a piece of lace at the other, all bound up with cord, and to complete the picture I persuaded her ladyship to give me a celluloid cage with a bird in that she had in her boudoir. Before the parade I had a glass of port which enabled me to walk round to the manner born. When Lord and Lady Astor saw me they exploded. I'd never seen them laugh so much, so I suppose it was a foregone conclusion that I should win the first prize.

Arthur Bushell, his lordship's valet, also enjoyed the occasion. He went as Nellie Wallace and delighted the staff with his antics. I think he must have had more than one port because as he passed her ladyship he lifted up his skirt, and showed her his green knickers with a union jack on the behind. 'How do you like my greens, my lady?' he inquired. She was not amused.

'Arthur,' she said, 'you're disgusting,' and she meant it. However Arthur was irrepressible. He was always going just that bit too far for her ladyship's taste. I think he did it purposely, she knew it and was always ready for him.

That costume of mine was a continuing success. Many of the big houses around Cliveden gave servants' dances and some members of our staff were generally invited. It was easier for me to get away as they always took place after dinner. I got quite a few laughs out of it too. One night I decided to go to a dance at the Wharncliffe Rooms. I came up our area steps into St James's Square and stood waiting for a taxi. I attracted the attention of many of the passers-by and I could hear some whispering about the terrible state of affairs there was for servants. One man and woman stopped in their tracks as they were passing me; they mumbled together and the man fumbled in his pocket and with a gruff, 'Here you are, my dear,' thrust half-a-crown in my hand.

I was at a loss for words but true to my costume I dropped a curtsy at him as he went on his way. Just at that moment Mr Hopkins drew up in the Rolls. I went over to him and he offered to drive me to the dance. I didn't like to look to see if the generous couple had noticed, but if they did they must have got the shock of their lives. So did the photographer when I reached the Wharncliffe Rooms, for I suppose seeing a Rolls drive up and Mr Hopkins helping me out he thought I must be somebody, and kept his camera snapping at me. Then as I was going in he rushed up and asked me my name – 'Rose Harrison, Lady Astor's maid,' I told him. I wished I'd had a camera for his face was a perfect picture. There was nothing he could do though. I hadn't asked to have my photo taken.

One of the social events of the year in London for us was Lady Malcolm's Servants' Ball, which was held at the Albert Hall. It was a charity affair, with employers buying tickets for their staff at prices we could never have afforded. My 'Eliza comes to stay' took first prize there too, which Lady Astor considered a feather in her cap. Today it would seem incongruous to contemplate holding a servants' ball. I don't suppose anybody would go. To begin with there are so very few servants around and those that there are don't acknowledge the word, and would think the whole idea lowering. We didn't.

So, although today our social life might seem a bit dull and mundane I recall it with nostalgia. We had a deal of fun heightened possibly by the hard work that surrounded it. My life was made more enjoyable by the travelling I did and even at home it was never boring; my lady's unpredictability saw to that. Then, despite the size of the staff, I think most of us had the feeling of belonging. I've already mentioned Michael Astor's book *Tribal Feeling*. I suppose when he wrote it he was considering the family, but the feeling went wider than that. It brushed off on all of us, on some of course more than others. I must have got covered in it. After all, and I direct this remark to Mr Michael, 'You left home when you were eight to go to your preparatory school. After that it was a place where you spent your holidays. I was there continuously for thirty-five years so I feel as much, if not more, a member of the tribe, even though I may have been a more savage one.'

6 Entertaining in the Grand Manner

Entertaining both at St James's Square and Cliveden was done in style and in the grand manner. Lunch and dinner parties and receptions were so frequent they became a commonplace. Not that that meant there was any less work, but it was like a drill: everyone knew what was expected of him and more or less did it automatically; so it became easier by constant repetition. My part was to get my lady presentable and ready on time. After that I went to my room and did the necessary pressing and cleaning and getting ready for the following day, though this was often interrupted when she wanted me to take her something or to run messages. But there was always an inquest in the servants' hall afterwards so I had a very good idea of what went on in each department.

There were two types of party: 'My town style and my country style,' as Lady Astor would call them. The 'town style' at St James's Square was more formal, with a majority of political guests. The 'country style' at Cliveden, while none the less correctly presented, had a feeling more of family and friends. She invited a mixed bag of people and since many were staying in the house there was a greater ease, more of the person and less of the face. This was also reflected in the dinner services used, the food served and, strange though it may seem, in the flower decoration. Her ladyship was very proud of the distinction between her two types of entertaining and was immediately critical if she felt that one had encroached on the other.

Mr Lee kept a guest list of many of the dinner parties in his little black book. Whether he got bored or blasé after I joined the staff I don't know, but he stopped doing it and just recorded the event. He lent me his book and it was fascinating to read the names of those invited in the years from 1911 onwards; it was like dipping into history. The list was impressive both socially and politically. These were people who were used to the best and were prepared to be highly critical since they, themselves, were accustomed to entertaining on a similar scale. It was not only the dinner either, for immediately after dinner there was often a reception of up to a thousand people. This was generally held in the ballroom, depending on its size, as of course were the dances when they were given.

It was a feat of organization to mount occasions of this kind. Each department had its own task, though often these as it were interlocked. Mr Lee as butler was in charge of the whole production and it was for him to see that everything finally came together. The first thing his men had to do was select the silver from the safe at Cliveden. This safe was a sight to behold. It was the size of an average room and as you walked round it it was like looking at a treasure trove. His lordship had inherited and bought gold and silver ornaments, silver cups, candelabra, candlesticks, plates and cutlery, and had added to them the trophies his horses had won. All service was done from silver plates and salvers. Although everything in the safe was kept polished it was always refurbished before use. Mr Lee had set his standards when he was a footman and under-butler, and was famed for the condition of his silver. He saw to it that his demands were met. It was an unpleasant task. It began with red rougeing; this gave the silver a dark appearance which looked so much better, particularly under light. This rouge was put into saucers, mixed into a paste and then rubbed on with the fingers and rubbed in hard. The silver was then highly polished with cloths and leathers. Polishing silver this way played havoc with the footmen's hands, but Mr Lee insisted that there were no short cuts; and he was not above showing a new footman himself how he should do it.

The Astor Households, 1928

Controller — 4 St. James's Square
(Miss A.M.Kindersley)
1 Accountant *(C.H.Swinburn)*
2 Assistant Accountants

Nursery — CLIVEDEN
Nanny *(Miss Gibbons)*
2 Nursemaids
1 Governess *(French or German)*

Astor Estate Office
(H.J.Forster Smith)
2 Clerks

Estate Maintenance
Foreman *(Bert Emmett)*
6 Painters
2 Carpenters
2 General Workers
1 Bricklayer
Plumber & Mate
3 Electricians
1 Clockwinder *(part time)*

Gardens
Head Gardener
(W. Camm)

Forestry
3 Foresters

Gamekeeper
(Ben Cooper)
1 Assistant
Gamekeeper

Stables:
Hunting
& Riding

Head Groom
(W. Brooks)
3 Men

Outside Foreman
8 Gardeners
1 Bothy Housekeeper

Greenhouse Foreman
6 Gardeners
1 Decorator
1 Bothy Housekeeper

Men Servants
Valet *(Arthur Bushell)*
Under Butler
3 Footmen
1 Hall-Boy
2 Odd-Men
1 House Carpenter

Kitchens
Chef *(Monsieur Gilbert)*
3 Kitchen-Maids
1 Scullery Maid
1 Dairy Maid

Housekeeper
(Mrs.Moore)

Stillroom
Head *(D.Dolby)*
1 Maid

Head Housemaid
(Lottie Moore)
3 Under-Housemaids
2 Daily Maids

SANDWICH — Rest Harrow
Housekeeper-in-Charge
(Mary Day)

Gardener/Handyman
(F.Kington)

1 Housemaid

JURA — SCOTLAND
Factors
(Mr. & Mrs. Macintyre)
Boatman/Fisherman
3 Ghillies

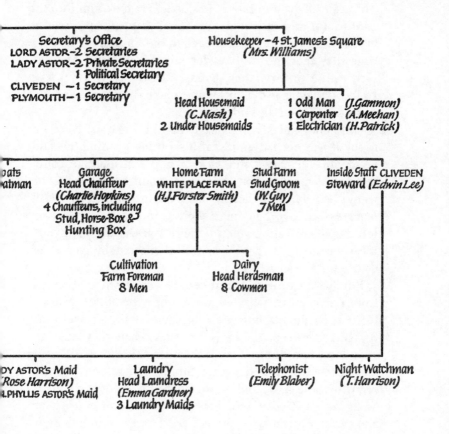

Secretary's Office
LORD ASTOR – 2 Secretaries
LADY ASTOR – 2 Private Secretaries
           1 Political Secretary
CLIVEDEN – 1 Secretary
PLYMOUTH – 1 Secretary

Housekeeper – 4 St. James's Square
(Mrs. Williams)

Head Housemaid
(C. Nash)
2 Under Housemaids

1 Odd Man   *(J. Gammon)*
1 Carpenter *(A. Meehan)*
1 Electrician *(H. Patrick)*

oats
atman

Garage
Head Chauffeur
(Charlie Hopkins)
4 Chauffeurs, including
Stud, Horse-Box &
Hunting Box

Home Farm
WHITE PLACE FARM
(H. J. Forster Smith)

Stud Farm
Stud Groom
(W. Guy)
7 Men

Inside Staff CLIVEDEN
Steward *(Edwin Lee)*

Cultivation
Farm Foreman
8 Men

Dairy
Head Herdsman
8 Cowmen

DY ASTOR'S Maid
(Rose Harrison)
a. PHYLLIS ASTOR'S Maid

Laundry
Head Laundress
(Emma Gardner)
3 Laundry Maids

Telephonist
(Emily Blaber)

Night Watchman
(T. Harrison)

PLYMOUTH – 3 Elliot Terrace
Secretary-in-Charge
Housekeeper *(Florrie Manning)*

Cook
1 Kitchen Maid

Chauffeur

Many of the visitors remarked on our beautiful silver and once the Argentine Ambassador, a Mr Carcano, asked Mr Lee to show him how it was done. He took him into his pantry and demonstrated, and then wrapped up a packet of the rouge for him to take back to the Embassy. The next time they met the Ambassador said, 'It's no use Lee, my men refuse to dirty their hands with the stuff. I suppose you won't come as my butler and make them?' He knew it was a vain hope as he said it.

Only once did Mr Lee nearly leave the Astors. Needless to say it was her ladyship's fault with her goading, her unreasonable demands and lack of appreciation. He could stand it no more and one evening announced to her that he would be leaving at the end of the month. Quick as a flash her ladyship saw the danger she was in. 'In that case, Lee, tell me where you're going because I'm coming with you.' That finished it; they both fell about laughing, and of course Mr Lee stayed.

But back to the silver; it was driven down to London from Cliveden in what we nicknamed the 'Black Maria'. Gordon Grimmett, one of the footmen, used to travel with it. He remembers the early twenties when they used an open lorry and slung a canvas sheet over the boxes. 'It must have been worth well over a hundred thousand pounds, even in those days, and we never had a thought about it being stolen. Today we'd probably have an armoured car and three outriders to protect it. There's a moral in it somewhere, Yorkie,' he said. Mr Lee was proud to boast that he had never lost any silver, though recently he admitted to me that that was not strictly true. 'As far as the family were concerned I didn't. There was once though when a silver dish went missing. We hunted high and low for it, but with no luck. So the next day I went to the silversmiths with a similar plate and had it copied. I paid for it personally. Of course I knew I didn't have to, but it kept my record straight with the Astors.'

The seating plan for the guests was prepared by her lady-ship with the help of Miss Kindersley, the controller. This was more difficult than one would think: there were so many things to be considered. First was precedence. Royalty was easy, so really were the Dukes. It was when you came to the Lords, Marquesses, Generals, Bishops and such-like that the trouble started. Rarely were mistakes made. *Burke's Peerage, Debrett* and *Who's Who*, the books of reference, saw to that. But we did occasionally get mixed up with Indians, and with their caste system they were the quickest to take offence. Mention of Indians reminds me of the time when Mr Gandhi came to dinner. His meal took a lot of sorting out. During it her ladyship offered him some American pecan nuts. 'Oh, Lady Astor,' he retorted, 'be British and buy British.'

As well as the business of precedence there was the question of who should sit next to or opposite whom! Political or social adversaries or personal 'bêtes noirs', and incompatibles, had to be separated. Of course in the choosing of guests this had been considered, but it was occasionally impossible to leave opposites out. Sometimes there would be two or more tables, which made things easier, but as Miss Kindersley confided to me, Lady Astor then tried to hog the most important or interesting guests for her table. Eventually Mr Lee would get the plan and have name cards printed so there could be no mistakes. Sometimes on his advice places would be changed. He was, as it were, overseer at these parties and knew more than anyone who got on well with whom.

There was one particular thing about parties that always seemed to get her ladyship and Mr Lee hot under the collar: that was the size of the chairs and the seating accommodation. Her ladyship would insist on getting as many people round a table as possible and this gave little room for manoeuvre either for the guests or the footmen. Mr Winston Churchill always complained. One particular night he refused to eat anything, but he must have been watching throughout the meal because at the end he said, 'Thirty dishes served and no damn room to eat one.' Sir Montagu Norman, Governor of the Bank of England, also used to grumble, but it didn't worry her ladyship when she was told about it. 'They can both afford to lose a little weight,' she said to Mr Lee, but he was testy about it and took their criticism personally.

The butler and footmen were of course liveried servants. The everyday livery was brown with yellow and white striped waistcoats, and a red and yellow piping down the side of the trousers. The dress livery was brown jackets, striped waistcoats, breeches, white stockings and black pumps with gold buckles, and of course white gloves; no serving was done with bare hands except by Mr Lee, who only served the wines and liqueurs. I must say that when I first saw the footmen in their get-up, although they looked very smart I couldn't stifle a laugh; to me they looked like a swarm of wasps. Mr Lee as butler was more distinguished than the others. He wore a navy blue tail coat, black breeches, black stockings and the same black pumps. The men were provided with two sets of livery and these were changed regularly, usually every two years. Less formal wear for them was morning suits, and in the evening, dress suits, black tie and tails.

Gordon Grimmett tells the story of how he joined the Astors, as second footman, in the early twenties and of his experience with the tailors. 'I'd been to Campbell & Hearn, the footmen's agency in North Audley Street, and was given a card and instructed to go and be interviewed by Mr Lee, butler to Viscount and Viscountess Astor at 4 St James's Square. I went down the area steps of this imposing building wondering what was in store for me. I pressed the back-door bell and was greeted by a young lad. "What's your business?" he inquired. I handed him the card and he said, "Hmm, Grimmett, not, I take it, the Australian cricketer?"

and he smirked. "I'm Eric, the schoolroom boy, follow me and I'll take you to see the skipper."

'I met Mr Lee in his sitting-room. "What's your Christian name?" he said.

' "Gordon, sir," I answered.

' "Very well, Gordon, where have you worked over the past years?"

' "With the Marquess of Bath, the Honourable Claud Portman and Mr C. H. Sanford."

'I thought this an imposing list, but by Mr Lee's expression I could see he was not impressed.

' "Done any valeting?" I said I had. After a few more brusque questions he rose and said, "Right, Gordon, we'll go and see her ladyship." By the way he said it I was convinced I was not going to get the job. He took me to what I learned later was Lady Astor's boudoir, told me to wait outside while he informed her ladyship of my presence and left me for what seemed a long time, with my heart now nearly in my boots. Finally the door opened. He beckoned me in and said, "This is Gordon, my lady, applying for the post of second footman." I looked at Lady Astor, a beautiful trim figure of a lady with a smile like a spring day (I was to learn later how quickly it could turn to winter).

' "A very good afternoon to you, Gordon," she said. "He looks a big strong boy, Lee. Where is your home, Gordon, and have you a mother and father?"

' "I have a mother and father and my home is in Ascot in Berkshire, your ladyship," I replied.

' "Well now, isn't that nice. We have a country house at Cliveden, near Taplow in Buckinghamshire. You will be able to go home to your parents regularly." Then she sped towards the door.

' "How soon can you join us? We want you in one week's time. Good-bye, I must fly to the House of Commons." And out she went.

" 'You can consider yourself engaged," said Mr. Lee, I

thought a trifle unnecessarily. He told me my wage would be £32 a year, with two shillings and sixpence a week beer and laundry money, not for my general washing, just for the starching of white shirts and collars. I discovered that any beer I wanted would have to be bought outside, but that was not encouraged. It had to be mentioned in the terms though because it was the tradition of that time. I was then instructed to proceed to visit Robert Lillico, their tailors in Maddox Street, to be measured for suits and livery.

' "Are we allowed to choose our own patterns, sir, for the morning suit or do you insist on 'pepper and salt'?" This was a footman's term for a grey and white pinhead suiting which many families instructed their tailors to supply their menservants with, which looks, as it was intended, a servants' suit.

' "Within reason you may select any pattern you wish," was Mr Lee's noncommittal reply.

'I went to Maddox Street and was duly measured by Mr Lillico. When he'd finished he drew me aside by the arm and whispered, "Dear boy, you are entitled to a long pair of woollen pants to go under your livery trousers, we give them with each suit. If however like many other footmen you don't choose to wear them, go downstairs and my brother will give you something in their place."

' "Downstairs" I found was the cutting-room. Seated at the table was brother Bob surrounded by three other men who like myself, were being fitted for livery. All had glasses in their hands. "Ah," he greeted me, "another no-nonsense pants man, I presume. Come and sit down and join us." He then took a glass and filled it with whisky from a cask at the end of the table. "Here you are, Astor, this is your reward." He replenished his glass and wished me luck in my new job.

'I eventually staggered out into the air a little worse for drink, but not so far gone as not to wonder what my clothes would be like when I got them, for brother Bob was the cutter and how he could work after paying the footmen for their pants and drinking the health of each one was beyond my comprehension. In the event my clothes fitted perfectly and I was later to join Bob in many similar celebrations, but I never ceased to wonder at his capacity.'

For any big dinner and reception Mr Lee would have to engage additional footmen. He had his own list of trained men who were willing to do extra work. They were mostly retired servants from the Colonial Office or the India Office. He was constantly being praised for their smartness and bearing. The business of serving and clearing dishes was done like a drill. It was something that Mr Dean learnt while he was with us, and practised later when he was at the British Embassy in Washington. He recalls an occasion there when Lady Dean, the Ambassador's wife, decided that they must give a served dinner party for Princess Alexandra during her visit there. As Mr Dean said to me, 'The trouble about having royalty in the States, Rose, is the number of people who expect to be invited to meet them, which is why generally they go in for buffet suppers and cocktail parties. But Lady Dean felt that Her Royal Highness must be tired of these affairs and wanted to do it in the old style. "How many could we seat in the ballroom?" she asked.

' "It's no good guessing," I said, "we'll have to try it and see." We did a mock layout and decided that we could cope with a hundred and ten guests.

' "How many footmen will you need?" she asked.

' "That depends, my lady, on the menu."

' "On the menu?" This surprised her.

' "Yes, you see if you have a simple menu we can manage with one man a table, but if we are serving sauces and side dishes, we shall need two."

'She went to the chef and it was decided that it would be a complicated menu. So I needed twenty-two to serve and since with a large party of that kind I would only be able to supervise I engaged another four to serve the wines. I was able to have a short rehearsal with them, as Mr Lee did. I told them to look to me for their cues to serve and to clear, and apart from one man who jittered with nerves and had to be quietly removed, the whole thing went off like clockwork. The following day Lady Dean asked me to go and see her and, unlike Lady Astor, who could never bring herself to do such a thing, congratulated me on the evening. "How did you manage to control all those footmen?" she asked.

' "That, my lady," I said, "was as a result of my training under 'Lord Lee of Cliveden', Lady Astor's butler." Her ladyship always got some of Lee's credit, I suppose she deserved it.'

Although Dean is not an uncommon name it was in a way extraordinary that our Mr Dean should have been butler to Sir Patrick Dean. It was also occasionally embarrassing, particularly when he was answering the phone. Mr George Brown, when he was Foreign Secretary, found it all a bit bewildering, as Mr Dean told me. 'His Excellency and Lady Dean with their two sons had been to meet Mr George Brown at the airport. When they arrived back at the door I opened it and said, "Welcome to the Embassy," to sort of make the Foreign Secretary feel at home. Some Labour ministers I knew looked on us as a stuffy lot and seemed a bit ill at ease in our presence. Sir Patrick then introduced me: "This is Dean, our butler." I was wrong to have worried about Mr George Brown not feeling at home. "Another bloody Dean! That makes five. What sort of place is this, Barchester bloody Towers?" Everyone laughed of course, and I took to him right away. He seemed to be able to get on with anyone and his visit was a great success.'

Although our footmen were liveried they did not 'powder'. 'Powdered' service more or less went out after the First World War, though Mr Lee remembers it well. 'It was only done for the more formal parties. It was not resented by the men even though it made the top of your head feel as if it was in plaster. When we had dressed we put a towel over our shirts, damped our heads and then sprinkled our hair with the flour we'd been given from the kitchen. It pulled a bit at the roots as it dried but there's no doubt it looked very smart indeed,' he said, almost wistfully. Nor did we have 'matching' footmen. These were what they sound; men of the same height and build. They had them at Buckingham Palace and probably still do; and at ducal establishments.

Again, when I was talking about them to Mr Lee, he went into a reminiscent mood. 'You know, Miss Harrison, I was only turned down once for a job when I went to be interviewed, and that was for Lord Derby's place. They wanted to match one of their footmen and I was an inch and a half too short.'

'Too short!' I was amazed, for Mr Lee stood six foot one and a half in his stockinged feet.

'Yes, his lordship liked them tall, it gave tone.' Mr Lee liked ours tall too, none were under six foot, but they didn't 'match'.

I haven't yet mentioned the food and the kitchens. I think of the kitchens even now with trepidation. On big party days, or even the day before, they were places I kept out of, and if they were sensible so did everyone else. They were hives of activity but you were likely to get stung if you interfered with the staff in any way. Some days beforehand her ladyship would have worked out the menu with the chef. We had two chefs while I was there, though Monsieur Gilbert was the one I knew best. Mr Lee of course had known many. 'Papillion was the finest of them all,' he confided to me, 'a truly great chef.' Papillion was with the Astors before the First World War. He died in 1914.

As with footmen, the number of extra chefs who had to be called in depended on the size and kind of dishes on the menu. At times we engaged four, one for each main course, but generally it was two. As I've said, I kept away from the kitchens, but after I'd been there a number of years and Gilbert had got to know me, my sister Olive, who was working as a kitchen-maid, was allowed by him to watch occasionally when a dinner party was on. She had been used to good service, but our parties were an eye-opener to her. She particularly loved to watch the sugar chef at work. He'd decorate the sweets with spun sugar, and was an artist first and a chef after. Apart from decorating the sweets he made decorative sugar baskets for the petits fours in various designs: beehives, letterboxes, birds' nests. Once I took a rose basket he'd made home to Mum, she kept it until it became a dirty brown colour and disintegrated in the sun. She said she just couldn't bear to throw it away.

It was dangerous work this chef had to do, because the sugar had to be kept near boiling-point all the time, but by the way he worked at it you'd have thought that he was playing with plasticine. What most people, and this included Lady Astor, don't realize is that with a dinner party the kitchen is working to almost split-second timing. One minute a dish is ready to serve and the next it's past its best, as anyone who has cooked a soufflé will know, and it's the same with many other dishes. It's heartbreaking for a chef when he sees hours of his work spoilt, and four heartbroken chefs in one kitchen is the stuff nightmares are made of.

It was another job of Mr Lee's to co-ordinate with the kitchen, get the guests in and see that courses were served, eaten and cleared on time. Getting the food from the kitchen to the dining-room hot, decorated and ready to serve was the job of the odd men. Every house had at least one, some two or even three. As their name implies they did anything and everything that wasn't one of the duties of others of the staff, and often some of theirs too if things got hectic.

Some of them were not as other men are, by that I mean they were often lacking in brain power and had little ambition (once an odd man, always an odd man). They were strong – they had to be with the fetching and carrying they had to do. Their interests were mostly limited to beer and baccy. I never knew one who was married, but they were willing workers and good friends. Mr Lee reckoned he could spot an odd man at a hundred yards. 'It's the way they walk, Miss Harrison, their legs are buckled, toes turned in and they always look as though they're carrying something heavy.' Well, odd men did carry heavy things and very heavy trays for dinner parties. Sailor, one of ours was called. Mr Lee and he got on very well, they were like man and dog. Sailor I think worshipped him, though he'd never have admitted it, but at a word of praise his face beamed; a reprimand was like a whipping. He was excellent at carrying from the kitchen, I never knew him to drop anything. In fact I only once remember that kind of accident: a footman dropped a plate of savouries. Fortunately it was outside the dining-room, in the serving room. Mr Lee heard it go and he and the footman were able to retrieve most of the contents. I was a bit sorry for the offender later when Mr Lee was reprimanding him. 'The plate was scalding hot, sir,' he said.

'Of course it was, and rightly so, lad, but you're hired to hold it and hold it you will in future, even if it burns you to the bone, do you understand? Fingers heal, food doesn't.'

Yet Mr Lee could be unexpectedly kind. At a dinner there was once nearly a disaster which could have turned into a social scandal. A public figure of some standing was talking to Lady Astor as a footman was serving him. 'I need a skivvy for my kitchen, can any of your servants recommend one, do you think?'

Give her ladyship her due, she tried to temper his speech. 'What kind of servant do you want?'

'Oh, any little slut will do.' The footman stepped back and went white as a sheet. 'I had some sort of sixth sense that things weren't what they should be with him,' Mr Lee told me. 'I moved over as quickly as I could and caught his arm just as he was about to pour the hot sauce over the guest's head. There was no doubt about it, he told me that was what he was going to do when I got him outside.'

Mr Lee didn't so much as reprimand him when he'd heard his story. He didn't say a word; he went to the sideboard, poured a glass of port, handed it to the footman, patted him on the back and said, 'Come back in when you feel you can.' Mr Lee saw Lady Astor the following day and complained of her guest's conversation. 'He had no right to speak like that about servants, even behind their backs, my lady, and in our hearing, it's unforgivable.' He didn't mention the footman's reaction to what had been said.

'You're quite right, Lee, and that man will never visit us again.' She asked for the footman to be sent to see her, and she apologized to him. It would seem that my earlier remark to her about her reference to housemaids had struck home.

Mr Lee's men were kept busy at parties. For dinner he and two footmen received the guests in the hall and removed their cloaks and coats. There was a large cloakroom which was manned by attendants if there was to be a reception later. Arthur Bushell would often be there and of course it was fertile ground for his humorous imitations. He could always be relied on to raise a laugh in the servants' hall the following day. His mimicry had to be seen to be enjoyed, but his demonstration of Queen Mary twirling around on her feet like a model on a revolving plinth while her coat was taken off can be easily imagined. According to Arthur, King George V grunted in and out of his.

Before dinner drinks would be served in the smaller dining-room, again by the footmen, and after the meal and during the reception the pace would really get hot. Tremendous activity both inside and outside the house. The police were informed beforehand; Mr Lee would tell them how many were expected and from that would be decided the number of police required. He tells a story of how on his first big party as butler, he stopped all the traffic in the area through his inexperience. The Astors were giving a dinner for Lord Balfour with a reception for a thousand. Mr Lee went to Vine Street police station and asked for three constables to report to him for traffic control. It was the time of mixed carriages, both motor and horse. The constables duly came and were given their instructions. Within minutes of the guests beginning to arrive there was a complete shambles: the whole Square was jammed with cars and horses, with chauffeurs and coachmen – never friendly at the best of times – exchanging curses. It appeared that the confusion was the fault of the police; one would not take orders from another, so they each acted on their own initiative.

Poor Mr Lee, it took him the best part of an hour to get order out of chaos. As he said, when he described the incident, 'It was a lesson to me. If you have to delegate command there should always be a person in command to delegate it to. From then onward I had an Inspector to supervise, and a sergeant and two constables to direct operations. We never had any trouble again.'

Another essential employee was the linkman. As the guests left he was the man who called up the carriages to the front of the house, with as little delay as possible because once people have decided to go they don't want to be kept stamping their heels in the hall, neither are they any longer wanted by the staff, cluttering up the place. Linkmen carried lanterns or torches to signal with, but other essential qualities to go alongside were a strong voice and a piercing whistle, the kind errand boys could produce in my young day by putting two fingers in their mouths and blowing. It was a talent I always envied, but was never able to copy. There was one danger with linkmen: they had a lot of time waiting about with nothing to do except get cold. It seemed they thought that the best way to keep cold out was to put drink in, and the consequences could be more disastrous than twenty bolshie policemen.

The announcing of guests was a necessary part of the general production. The engagement of an announcer was another of Mr Lee's responsibilities. He always tried to use the same man, a Mr Batley, who combined a distinguished figure with a clear and attractive voice. He could make even a plain Mr and Mrs sound important. Announcing can be quite a strain; nobody likes to hear their name fluffed or mispronounced and it requires a degree of concentration. It's also hard on the voice if there are large numbers, so Mr Lee would often take a turn after the first three or four hundred guests. He was no mean performer. I think he liked the feeling that there was nothing that he asked people to do that he wasn't able to do, and do well, himself. During the reception the footmen would be busy serving drinks and food, snacks and petit fours, with occasional warm dishes, so the kitchen was still kept busy. I used to marvel at the appetites of some people who after a large dinner would continue to stuff themselves for the rest of the evening. Bigger eaters people were then than they are today.

Many of the receptions were 'dry', that is to say, no alcoholic drinks were served, or expected. Many's the hip flask though that was surreptitiously produced and by all reports the gentlemen's cloakroom was used more for the consumption of whisky than it was for its real purpose. Both his lordship and my lady were teetotal. Mr Lee respected this, but also in a way regrets it. He was not able, he thinks, to become a real connoisseur of wine, like many of his colleagues. This may have been to his ultimate advantage because although the others may have been connoisseurs, some later became drunks, and many's the good butler who has had to be retired as a result. In any case it's my opinion that Mr Lee is being over-modest. Because of his lack of personal interest Lord Astor left the buying and care of wines completely in his butler's hands. Hawker's of Plymouth were our suppliers. Mr Hawker was Chairman of the Conservative Association there, so his lordship didn't have much option.

As butler at dinner parties Mr Lee was responsible for the preparing and the serving of wine. He always tasted it when each bottle was opened so that he would be ready if there were any complaints. 'It was a real drop of good,' he'd say to me afterwards, and since many of our guests were surprised at the choice and quality of the wines it confirmed my view that he knew more than he would admit to. I've seen him demonstrating the decanting of port and claret to the footmen; both were put through a muslin. He'd talk about 'bending' the bottle of port. He was particular about the right temperature. He'd put the claret on the hotplate at a moderate heat. 'It needs just a very slight warmth, nothing like as hot as some people seem to think. You'll get to be able to sense exactly when it's right.'

Mr Lee was particularly proud of his claret. One day her ladyship decided that it would be a good compromise if she served claret cup at her reception. She summoned Mr Lee and told him. 'Very well, my lady, I shall have to order some from Hawker's.'

'Haven't we got any in the cellar?'

'Yes, but we cannot possibly use that, it's the very best vintage.'

Her ladyship was not impressed. 'You'll order no more till that's used up. I'm sure my guests will appreciate having very best vintage claret cup.'

Mr Lee was shocked and stunned. 'We eventually used thirty-six dozen bottles. Bloody sacrilege!' He must have felt it deeply; it was one of the very few occasions he ever swore.

White wine he felt was at its best when it was slightly chilled, though champagne he liked ice-cold. He didn't believe in fridges for it, he was more accustomed to ice. If we were having a reception where drink was to be served he ordered two hundredweight of ice which was broken up and put into a bath; there was a bathroom on the floor near the drawing-room which could easily hold two hundred bottles; these were replaced regularly during the evening. When there was just a dinner party he'd use a wine tub in the serving room which could hold up to three dozen bottles. He told me he learnt early how to draw the cork from champagne without losing any and without maiming anybody. 'I gently unscrew the cork, cover it with a napkin and by tilting the bottle to one side I find the cork comes away easily and quietly. There are some idiots who think that you're supposed to hear the "pop" of the cork. We had such a one at Freddie Wynn's, Lord Newborough's place in Mount Street. I was in livery at the time. The butler pointed this bottle at the ceiling. It went off with the deuce of a bang and the cork rebounded on to his lordship's head.

"That sounds like a good bottle my lord," he said.

' "Sounds like a good bottle, you fool, it nearly blew my bloody brains out. Good wine don't sound good, it tastes good." '

There was another butler he'd heard about who had lost an eye on account of champagne. 'He couldn't understand why the cork wouldn't come out, so he peered down to see. It's like looking down a gun barrel to find out if it's loaded, you need only do it once.'

Mr Lee took the port and liqueurs round. The port he only carried once, leaving it at the head of the table to be passed round to the left, when the glasses required replenishing. 'It's as well to limit the choice of liqueurs,' he said, 'otherwise if you leave it to personal preference, you can be bobbing backwards and forwards all the time. I only served brandy, crème de menthe and kümmel.'

The Astors' reputation as teetotallers was universally known. Once, in 1923, when King George V and Queen Mary were guests of honour, the King's equerry took Mr Lee on one side when they arrived at the house and handed him two decanters, one of port and the other of sherry.

Apparently the monarch wasn't prepared to give up his little drop at the whim of his host and hostess.

Mr Lee didn't say anything at the time, but as the equerry was leaving he handed him back the full decanters, with a 'Hardly necessary, I think you'll agree, sir.' Mr Lee rather enjoyed having royalty to lunch or dinner, not just for reasons of status, but because all guests had to be in the drawing-room a quarter of an hour before their Majesties were due to arrive, otherwise they were turned away. 'Royalty are the only assurance of punctuality in this house, Miss Harrison,' he'd say.

A similar thing happened the first time the Prince of Wales came to dinner. By now Mr Lee was very much in command. Major Metcalfe, his Highness's equerry, rang him: 'I'm going to send a bottle of brandy round for the Prince, Lee,' he said. 'I want you to see it's available for him at any time.'

'That would be no compliment to your hosts, sir,' he replied. 'I'm sure his Highness will appreciate the brandy we will be serving.' In fact Major Metcalfe was only obeying instructions, as Mr Lee found out when he went round with liqueurs after the meal. In answer to his inquiry the Prince said, 'I'll have a little of your excellent brandy, Lee,' and he said it with a twinkle.

When the last guests had gone Mr Lee paid all the servants he had hired. He had a hundred-pound float as petty cash, and he accounted for it weekly to the office. He could at any time get up to fifty pounds from them without reference and, like mine, never at any time was his account questioned. The Astors gave and expected perfect trust. Finally he would go to the footmen's pantry, where they would be giving the silver a preliminary clean. Many evenings he would take a bottle of wine with him. 'I reckoned they deserved a little something extra for their pains.' Some people occasionally took a little extra without being asked. One night, as Mr Lee was offering these last drinks around, he noticed that Sailor, the odd man, was missing. He made inquiries. 'The last time I saw him,' said the under-butler, 'was when he was helping me uncork the champagne in the bathroom.'

'You blithering idiot, I told you never to let Sailor anywhere near the drink. Now we're in trouble. Find him.'

As it turned out there was no trouble, apart from the Astors being a few bottles of champagne short! Eventually Sailor was discovered in the secretary's room stretched out on her bed, drunk to the world. He was carried shoulders and feet by two of the men and slung into his own room. 'All's well that ends well,' Arthur Bushell said, when they'd reassembled.

'It's all right saying that, but supposing the secretary had been staying overnight?' answered Mr Lee.

'That was too much for me, Rose,' Arthur said. 'I had to clear out fast, I've got a very vivid imagination.'

'Everyone worked hard on those nights, Miss Harrison,' Mr Lee said to me recently, 'but we got a deal of enjoyment out of it. The people I was sorry for were the scullery maids. Poor little devils, washing up and scrubbing away at the dozens of pots, pans, saucepans and plates, up to their arms in suds and grease, their hands red raw with the soda which was the only form of detergent in those days. I've seen them crying with exhaustion and pain; the degradation too I shouldn't wonder. Well, let's hope they got their reward in heaven.'

There's one person's work I haven't yet mentioned. Like the others it was an all the year round job, but it was more intensified when there were parties: that is the decorator's. He it was who, perhaps more than anyone else, set the scene. The decorator was the gardener who was responsible for the flowers inside the houses; when I say flowers this covers everything that grew. Sometimes we had shrubs as large as small trees. The decorator I knew best was Frank Copcutt, who later became head gardener. Frank joined the Astors when he was young, but he was experienced because he'd been in good houses ever since he began as a boy. He came to us from the Rothschilds. At first he thought he was slumming it. He was disappointed with the greenhouses and the shrubs. 'With the Rothschilds I only had to express a wish for something and it was provided.' I don't think it was the fault of the Astors, although her ladyship was always mean over bulbs; it was the devil's own job to get her to buy any, but when she saw them in other people's houses she'd cry out for them. He blamed the general shortness on Mr Camm, who was head gardener when he joined. He died in service shortly after Frank arrived and when Mr Glasheen took over he went on a spending spree and things got better.

Frank was very much a greenhouse man and he worked wonders at Cliveden. It wasn't long before he caught her ladyship's eye and so was appointed as decorator when the vacancy occurred. 'While in a way I was flattered at getting the job, frankly, Rose, I was scared stiff. It was something I'd never done before. I knew Lady Astor particularly liked mixed cut flowers. The arranging of these is an art in itself, and of course I knew she could and would be difficult. When I first went to St James's Square Mr Glasheen came with me to show me the ropes. Eventually Lady Astor got me on my own and said, "Look George" (I wanted to tell her my name was Frank and that George had been her last decorator, but I couldn't, so George I remained for well over a year). "Look, George, there's one thing I want you to understand." She seemed very stern so I thought, "This is your first dose, my boy," and trembled inwardly.

'She went on, "Your predecessor was with me for six years. I expect you to stay much longer than he did." Well, that didn't seem too bad a start. Then she said: "Another thing you'll find, you will arrange the flowers for the tables and elsewhere, and you'll probably be pleased with what you have done. Then I shall come in and say, 'I don't like them, take them all out and start again.' And you'll do it without any argument."

'Well, that was getting it straight from the horse's mouth. "Right, my lady," I thought. "I know where I stand, even though I shall feel a bit uncomfortable in the position." I told her I didn't know anything about the arrangement of cut mixed flowers. "You'll soon learn," she said, as she walked out of the room. This cut flower business had really got me worried, but you know, Rose, Nature has a way of sorting things out for you. It had for me anyway, for the next Sunday I was walking to Cookham to church and as I went down the hill I looked over to a little footpath at the side and into the meadow which it crossed. There amongst the grass was the most glorious display of wild flowers. On my way back I stopped and studied them. There were some spikes, some medium, some small, and the colours seemed to melt into each other. "That's it Frank," I said to myself. "Keep that picture in your mind and you can't go wrong. You model on that field." And I did.

'When I'd done the bowls the next day her ladyship came in and said, "I thought you told me you'd never arranged mixed flowers before."

' "No more I have, my lady."

' "George," she said. "You're a liar." That was the compliment I got. It was the only kind she knew how to give, but it was enough, it gave me confidence from then on.'

I asked Frank if he had told her where his inspiration had come from. He hadn't, which was a pity because I know it was something that would have delighted her. Frank was a great one for putting Nature first. There was another time when Lord Astor wanted to plant azaleas and rhododendrons in a place that looked bare. 'Come down here in four weeks' time, my lord, and say the same thing,' Frank said. His lordship did, and saw the most wonderful carpet of bluebells. 'Thank you, Frank, it would have been sacrilege to have interfered with that.'

'You see, Rose, as Shakespeare says in that sonnet about your namesake, "Every fair from fair sometime declines." So a garden has to be planned, not just for today but for the whole year round.

'The first thing to be thought about when decorating for a party was the general area: the hall, the staircase and the ballroom. These were large areas and could be set off with shrubs, forsythia, almonds, cherries, laburnum and wistaria, things of that kind. Standard fuchsias and standard geraniums were also useful and colourful. Planted around these would be primroses, polyanthus, forget-me-nots, the smaller border plants. These would all be forced in the greenhouse. If I could get her ladyship marigolds at Christmas-time she was more pleased than if they'd been orchids. Medium-sized flowers we put in "coffins", containers which are miniatures of the real thing. They were packed in with clay and overlaid with moss, and provided what we called ground cover. Her ladyship was particularly fond of geraniums, she was later President of the Geranium Society; this may have been very nice for her but it wasn't for me – geraniums are the most difficult things to take from one place to another, their petals fall away at the slightest touch. Many's the beautiful plant that has left Cliveden only to be brought in, quite bare, at St James's Square.

'Once the main area had been dressed came the difficult and dangerous decoration, that of the tables. I say dangerous because it was here that her ladyship could and did interfere. Before I travelled up, and indeed some time before the party, it was my business to find out what dinner service was to be used, because my flowers and plants would have to blend in with it, not always easy particularly in winter when there was no recourse to outside blooms. Another of her ladyship's foibles was her dislike of fern. I was seldom allowed to use it anywhere, which was a great limitation to have put on me, particularly for table work.

Another hardship was that Lady Astor wouldn't have anything of any size on the table; it interfered with her talking to and looking at her guests. She had to put up with it though when we used the gilt or silver. Then things had to be taller because of the size of the containers. It was very easy for me when they used silver, you can do anything with silver. Gilt too is reasonably easy, but some of the china, as I say, was a real challenge. The oval tables at St James's Square were hard to cope with. I'd have to climb on to them to get the centre decoration arranged, and there'd be the footmen around shouting advice, sometimes abuse.

'I wasn't the only one to climb on those tables. I remember Mr Lee meeting me in the hall the day after a party. "Hello, Frank," he said. "Just the man I want to see. You and your flowers nearly wrecked my dinner party last night."

' "I'm sorry to hear that, sir," I said, "what did I do wrong?"

' "Nothing in my eyes, but her ladyship saw you as a criminal when she looked at the table decorations. Why didn't you check them with her?"

' "She wasn't back from the House of Commons when I left."

' "No more she was, she came back late and there was royalty to dinner. Well, she came into my dining-room, took one look at your flowers, screamed, kicked her shoes off and climbed on to the table, knocking my glass and silver all over the place and spilling water on the table-cloth. Then she started pulling your centre-piece to bits, saying nasty things about you as she was doing it."

' "What did you do?"

' "The only thing possible under the circumstances. As I've told you, she was already late so I said to her, 'This won't do, my lady, you're ruining Frank's work and my work. If this is the way you want to run your dinner party you must run it yourself. I want no more of it.' And I left the room. As I knew she would, she came running after me. She looked pathetic in her stockinged feet. 'Don't worry, Lee, I'm going to change now.' She dashed back in the dining-room, picked up her shoes and raced upstairs with them in her hand." I must say she didn't look so pathetic when she saw me later in the day. I got similar treatment from her as I'd had from Mr Lee, starting with, "You nearly wrecked my dinner party." Oh well, it was all in a day's work,' Frank ended philosophically.

'Other plants that we grew that were her ladyship's pride and joy were the poinsettias,' continued Frank. 'They weren't like the small ones you see today: ours grew to six foot and made a wonderful indoor show at Christmas. Orange trees were another delight, though they couldn't be relied on to be in fruit when you wanted them. Still a little subterfuge could work wonders. I remember having a beautiful pair at the foot of the staircase for a wedding reception at St James's Square. Everyone was commenting on them, they were in blossom and fruit. His lordship came up to me and said, "Wonderful orange trees you've got there, Frank, a pity we can't have them in the house at Cliveden."

' "Why not, my lord?" I asked.

' "Well, the fruit's bound to drop when they're travelling," he said.

' "I don't think so, my lord, we'll take it off before we move it, and put it back on again at the other end." And I showed him how it had all been attached by wire.

'As you know, Rose,' Frank said to me, 'her ladyship was not much given to paying compliments.' I was able to assure him on that point. 'But she did occasionally pass on what other people said. There was a party for the Prince of Wales, and her ladyship told me she wanted something different for him this time, as he was a frequent guest at the house. "What do you suggest, Frank?" Well, I told her that I didn't think we made enough of the water garden.

There are many beautiful varieties of water-lilies that would make lovely floating decorations. "But don't they close at night?" They do of course, but I said I thought if I put them into the boiler-room until just before dinner, then opened them by hand, that they'd stay open throughout the meal. She agreed we should try, but we had to have alternative arrangements standing by. We didn't need them. Everything worked perfectly and though I say it as shouldn't, they were a lovely sight. I had them in bowls with a big white centre lily *Gladstoniana* and two red ones, *Escarboucle*, on either side.

'Some two or three days later her ladyship saw me at Cliveden and said, "Frank, I thought you'd like to know, two of my guests came up to me after the dinner and said that while they'd enjoyed meeting the Prince of Wales, they'd enjoyed seeing my plants and flowers more – and particularly those beautiful lilies." She didn't add that she had liked them too, but that was the way life went. For all her ladyship's moods and tantrums I grew very fond of her. There's nothing like flowers for bringing people close. I was always a shy sort of chap, I'd had the stuffing knocked out of me as a child, and she seemed to sense this. It didn't stop her going at me hell for leather when she was in a mood, or me giving as good as I got, but at other times she seemed to understand and almost to mother me.'

The picking, packing and arranging of fruit also came under Frank for big parties. On ordinary days the arranging for luncheon and smaller dinner parties would be left to the housekeeper or another of the servants, and if Frank was around while they were doing it I'd hear him grinding his teeth and muttering under his breath, 'They just don't know how to treat it. The pains we go to over the years to create and preserve the wonderful bloom, and they wipe it away in a few seconds with their clumsy fingers.' And the fruit at Cliveden was wonderful, everyone said so. The grapes, peaches, nectarines and the most glorious 'black' strawberries. I've never seen anything like them before or since. There was always fresh fruit no matter what time of the year it was, and of course a lot was given away. The same kind of scrounging that goes on the world over. 'What beautiful strawberries. How do you grow them? Wouldn't my father/mother/sister/brother just adore these. Oh, you will? How awfully kind of you.' The Colonel's lady and Judy O'Grady are sisters under the skin.

It was the same with plants and flowers, her ladyship was always generous with these. As a rule the gardeners accepted it philosophically, but, for the fortnight before Ascot week, they were like Scrooges. Which brings me to Cliveden and the entertaining that was done there, in her ladyship's 'country style'. It was the perfect house for weekend parties: the hall and reception rooms were compact, and the beautiful terrace was ideal for outside entertaining.

Cliveden was easy of access, and the river and the gardens and the nearby golf and tennis courts provided everything a visitor might wish to enjoy. And believe me they were enjoyed. The resources of the house were strained to their limit, and I include the servants when I talk about resources and limits. We'd move to Cliveden lock, stock and barrel on Friday, and I've already described the packing and unpacking that that entailed. Guests would generally start arriving on Friday evening. They were many and various. We could accommodate up to forty though I'm glad to say we only rarely had that many. While St James's Square had been largely political and high society, Cliveden was more for friends, relations, visiting Americans and personalities of every kind, though of course the 'Cliveden Set' on which I shall later pass the domestics' opinion, didn't get called that without some reason as there were generally a few politicians there as well. The atmosphere there was gayer, friendlier and more relaxed and the pace a little slower, though it could hot up at times. Her ladyship en-

joyed the company of literary people and sometimes actors.
She rarely entertained musicians. I suppose she thought
writers had more to say and of course Cliveden was one long
buzz of conversation while she was there. I don't think she
appreciated good music but she loved the songs of the
American South and was a fair performer on the mouth-
organ. I remember her once going to the opera at Covent
Garden; she didn't see all of it; she was late of course and
had to cool her heels in the foyer until the first act was over.

Bernard Shaw was her greatest literary friend, an ill-
assorted couple I'd have thought. I believe they were
brought together by the Labourite Margaret McMillan,
whose nursery schools her ladyship fought for in the House
of Commons. Their friendship was later cemented by a
visit to Russia together and they remained close until Mr
Shaw's death, which even though he was ninety-four came
as a shock to my lady, and which she took badly. I was
surprised at this because in his later years I thought he found
her ladyship too overpowering and too oppressive for him
and had made this plain to her.

The Irish writer Sean O'Casey and his wife were also
regular visitors. Of the political and other talk that went
on I'm afraid I can say little; I wasn't there. I'd get snippits
from her ladyship during the day, but I'd plenty of other
things to think about. There would be some chat in the
servants' hall, but, as I say, Mr Lee didn't encourage gossip
of this kind, and again they mostly spoke of things that
concerned them. Even in our private chats 'Father' didn't
comment much. He used to say, 'It's difficult if you start
getting interested in what's being said when you're among
the guests because if you do your concentration goes. Also,
as I've told my fellows, it's easy to spot a servant who is
following a conversation. His expression changes, particularly his eyes, and it's out of place to do it. Another thing
that is most difficult is when some guest, who doesn't know
any better, tries to draw you into a conversation. Very hard.

I just answer noncommittally and withdraw. It's entirely another matter when they talk to you alone. Many's the interesting conversation I've had with people then.'

The footmen would always be particularly busy at weekends. Not everyone would bring his own valet and of course some of the guests didn't even have one, so the footmen would have to look after one gentleman each or sometimes more. It was the same with the housemaids and the ladies, though some preferred to look after themselves. This way the footmen got to know quite a deal about their charges because despite what is said to the contrary, men tend to talk and confide more in their servants than do women.

At Cliveden guests tended to be up later than in London, probably because they were staying. Many liked to play cards, bridge or poker into the early hours of morning, so there would have to be the groom of the chambers and a footman on duty. It was the groom of the chamber's duty to look after the cards. These would be regularly changed; a pack would be used for two nights and then discarded. In big houses they were ordered by the gross.

Compared with some servants we had it easy after dinner. Some establishments would give supper on top of dinner parties. When Charles Dean went as butler to Miss Alice Astor, when she was married to Prince Obolensky, these were regular occurrences. All right, generally they were cold buffets, but this meant cooking and decorating whole salmon, turkeys, hams and game pies, as well as providing a range of sweet dishes, chilling and decanting wine and then looking after the guests; often until dawn broke. My sister Olive worked for Alice Astor for a few weeks in the kitchen, but even after so short a time she felt the strain of the late hours, and had to leave.

Prince Obolensky was a near-penniless Russian exile, so Alice Astor's millions came in useful. Like her ladyship, he believed in spending and his friends and brother exiles encouraged him. Mr Dean remembers an evening when the Prince and his cronies were drinking after dinner and recalling the death of Rasputin, the monk whose influence and dominating personality caused havoc amongst the Russian Royal Family. They told the story of how the Prince and his friends had decided that it was time he was put out of the way for good. They invited him round for tea and, knowing his weakness for cream cakes, poisoned some, the coloured ones. Suspecting a trap, it was some time before he could be persuaded to eat, and to their dismay he selected two white cakes. Over-confidence and greed however eventually got the better of him and he ate a third and duly expired – or so they thought. They dragged his body outside and threw it into the river Volga. As he floated downstream, he raised an arm and shook his fist at them, yet they said there was enough poison in each cake to have killed ten men instantly. But, as Charles remarked, 'It's my bet they'd told that story for meals and drinks so long that they began to believe in it.' I've never found out whether what they said was the truth or not.

After a few years with the Prince, Alice Astor divorced him and married Raymond von Hofmannsthal, son of the poet Hugo. Raymond was a bit of an actor and he had a small part in the production of *The Miracle* when Lady Diana Cooper played the part of the Madonna, so of course again there were parties every night after the theatre, and even when he was 'resting' these went on. He had a liking for the ballet and as Sadler's Wells was beginning to show the way at that time, Frederick Ashton and Robert Helpmann were frequent late-night visitors. Many years later Mr Dean met Sir Frederick Ashton – it was probably when he was at the British Embassy in Washington – and Charles was astonished that he not only recognized him but that he said, 'You know, Mr Dean, you used to terrify me, in fact I think I was more frightened of you than any man in London, when you were butler at Hanover Lodge.' Charles tells the story with astonishment but secretly I think he's rather pleased.

After a spell with von Hofmannsthal, Alice Astor married yet again. Mr Dean was in New York with her while the divorce was going through. One day, when he was buying flowers, the shopkeeper said, 'Hello Mr Dean, nice to have you back. I hear your lady is getting another divorce.'

'Is she?' responded Charles.

'Didn't you know?'

'British servants, ma'am, are like the three monkeys: they see no evil, they hear no evil, they repeat no evil.'

'Is that so?' replied the shopkeeper, and added slyly, 'another thing about you Britishers that I've noticed is that while your ladies often change their husbands, they never change their butlers.'

In the event Mr Dean did leave Alice Astor shortly afterwards, to take up service with Mrs Bouverie, and so he came into closer contact with the Royal Family than he'd ever been before.

As I've already hinted, Ascot week was the period of the most intense activity at Cliveden. Outside his family, farming and politics, the breeding and racing of horses was his lordship's main interest. Ascot's unrivalled supremacy as the chief racing social event of the year and Cliveden's proximity to the course gave her ladyship the excuse for really going to town. It was the annual jewel in her crown as a hostess. Yet in fact she didn't enjoy horse-racing and she would only attend one day, sometimes coming back early from that. But even without the races Ascot satisfied her lust for hats. I remember one week I had to produce forty-five for her to choose from and she'd wear two or three each day. 'I don't know why you don't wear one and carry the other,' I grumbled at her, when she couldn't make up her mind between two. 'Shut up, Rose,' was the inevitable response.

Yes, Ascot week was really hectic. Every guest-room

would be occupied. The kitchen and stillroom staff had prepared the cold meats days before for the buffet lunches, for although most of the visitors went racing, some stayed behind to keep her ladyship company. Breakfast was served at eight-thirty and there'd be a dozen hot dishes to choose from. Before this the footmen would have been scurrying along the passages with early morning tea and brass jugs of shaving water. Then downstairs to clean shoes and iron the laces. Some of the ladies' maids, like me, would even wash laces before ironing them. Then there were the breakfast trays to be prepared and carried to the ladies who couldn't face other people at that hour of the morning.

Frank Copcutt would be in very early to replace flowers and plants, and to rearrange the many vases and bowls. Later he would reappear with a tray of buttonholes and sprays for the racing party to choose from as they assembled in the hall to be escorted to their cars. There would be a large selection so that the ladies could choose those that went with their colour scheme for the day. The carnations for the men were again of different colours and sizes. As Frank said to me, 'His lordship always chose the smallest he could find. On the other hand, the Duke of Devonshire wanted the biggest. One day I took along a huge red one and as he went to the trays I handed it to him. "Who do you think I am, Frank, a blooming poof?" he retorted.'

At around six o'clock the racing party would return, in what kind of spirits depended on their success with the horses. Frank drew my attention to something rather extra-ordinary. 'You know, Rose,' he said, 'I could nearly always tell the winners from the losers by the state of my button-holes when they came back. Flowers seemed to reflect the feelings and expressions of people.'

At seven forty-five the gong would sound in the hall, which was the signal for all the guests to go to their rooms and dress for dinner, though I'd be lucky if I got her lady-ship up on time.

The grand finale of Ascot was the Royal Ball at Windsor Castle. This my lord and lady always attended, as did many of the guests. It meant, as can be imagined, a busy and worrying day for me. Once again I'd put all the clocks on in her room. 'Is that the time, Rose?' she'd say as she came in to change.

'Yes, my lady,' I'd lie. 'You'll have to hurry and get ready.' And of course it was kitchen stove night; fixing the Astor tiara was a business with a bobbing excited figure; and I'd have been having kittens all day with the thousands of pounds'-worth of jewels in my safe. I practically lived in her room. When I'd thought we'd finished her ladyship would examine herself inch by inch. She was particular when she was entertaining in her own house, but when she was going out she was obsessional. Eventually, when she was satisfied, she'd rush to the door, say 'Good-night, Rose,' and down she'd run to the hall, like Cinderella after the ball, thinking she'd only got seconds to spare. Either his lordship was always early or Arthur Bushell told him about my ruse with the clocks, anyway she never tumbled my deceit.

All the servants, and I think his lordship as well, used to heave a sigh of relief when Ascot week was over. For most of us it had been eighteen hours a day for the past fort-night, no time off, and none of us had been out of the grounds, and so it happened year in, year out. There was one exception, though it was before my time. Mr Lee re-calls it as if it were a nightmare. 'Freddy Alexander, my under-butler at the time, was what I can charitably describe as a seasoned drinker, Miss Harrison. As he told me, he not only wanted a pint, he needed it. So I made an excep-tion in his case. "You can go to the Feathers" – which as you know is the pub at the end of the drive – "but you can only leave while the guests are changing for dinner, and only so long as you are back on duty in time. But take care you are not seen by other members of the staff, and in particular not by her ladyship." I didn't need to tell him to take the smell of drink off his breath, he always carried a packet of cloves in his pocket and generally reeked of them. He promised this, and was duly grateful.

'One day he must have left it a bit late, so he took a short cut under the front terrace. It would have been all right if her ladyship had been changing as she should have been, but she was on the terrace, talking to that other woman Member of Parliament, Mrs Wintringham. "Where are you going, Frederick?" she shouted.

' "Not where you think, my lady," was his reply.

'Well, she did continue to think, and I don't know whether he considered he might as well be hung for a sheep as a lamb, but he was missing throughout dinner. After the meal I was keeping an anxious eye open for him and eventually saw him weaving his way back, again in front of the terrace.

' "You blithering idiot," I thought. So did Lady Astor. I got him as he came through the back door and ordered him into his room, and told him to stay there. But her ladyship had got the bone in her mouth, and she was determined to shake it.

' "Where's Frederick?" she demanded when I returned.

' "He's unwell, my lady."

' "You mean he's drunk, Lee."

' "Yes, my lady."

'She turned away angrily. She didn't tell me to dismiss him, but I had no option. Things are a deal easier today, but discipline then was tight; so, for that matter, was Freddy,' Mr Lee allowed himself to quip. 'He didn't make it hard for me. "Of course I've got to go," he said, "you've no option." I was sorry to lose him but was able to see he got a reference.' That all-important document; a reference.

So, as I hope I've shown, entertaining for the Astors wasn't just something that they did, it was indeed an industry. Now there will be people who will criticize them and talk about poor people and the unemployed. But this was the accepted way of life at that time, people spent where it gave them the most pleasure. They also provided employment and kept money circulating. Workmen and tradesmen alike were grateful to them. And they also gave enjoyment to their own class. And why not? Comparisons are supposed to be odious: I think that they can also point the truth. I've never heard of anyone today who won half a million on the pools giving the money away for the betterment of mankind. It's not in the nature of things.

7 *The Astor Family*

As I was afraid I would when I began, I have given the impression that we served only one person, Lady Astor. This isn't true and I must try and explain why. In fact the standards of service and behaviour were set by his lordship, reflected on to Mr Lee and in turn from him on to us. Mr Lee had joined as a footman in 1912. A few years later he became valet to Lord Astor and was therefore very close to him. He liked and admired everything that he saw of Lord Astor and tried to emulate him either consciously or unconsciously. And not only outwardly. He caught a lot of the inner man too, so that when he came to a position of authority he was able to command us in the same way as his lordship had, through example. Everyone is the better for having known a good person. Mr Lee was in a way an intimate of Lord Astor's and later a disciple. A good commander, a man of real worth, delegates authority. He doesn't keep running around to see if his orders are being carried out – he doesn't need to. He has trust and gives it; the moment that trust is abused he knows it and takes action, but he's also aware that the more that he gives the greater will be his return. That was his lordship and that was Mr Lee. It wasn't Lady Astor. It wasn't her fault, nor was it true all the time, but she had to interfere; it was in her nature, and she had to test from time to time to make sure that even those to whom she had seemed to have given the most trust were not taking advantage of her, but responding to her with loyalty. She did this with me almost to the end of her life.

Lord Astor was a good man of great stature. When you read about such men they seem dull, but to be with they are not, nor are they to remember. Without his lordship I am certain that a small part of history would be changed. Her ladyship would not have been the first woman Member to take her seat in Parliament, she would not be famed as a hostess; for one thing she would never have kept the staff to do it. His presence provided the stability and the permanence that was necessary for her to dance her life around. Having said that it is almost all there is to say. He had chosen a political life, it was cut off through no fault of his own and inherited by my lady. He continued to devote his time and money to helping the less fortunate, but in this world it seems to me it's words not deeds that count, or at any rate it's words that keep you in the public eye. His relationship with Lady Astor was one of a young love which had matured over the years into a lasting deep affection. To those who didn't know him there were no outward and visible signs of emotion. It wasn't the fashion of the time to show them. I've asked Mr Lee if he saw any but as he said, 'Good servants at the sight of any emotion turn away from it and make an opportunity to absent themselves.'

Her ladyship's attitude towards Lord Astor was one of easy acceptance; she took without question or appreciation all that he gave her. Of course, she loved him, if ever she'd thought about it, but she didn't give herself time. She mimicked him as she did all of us, sometimes cruelly. She was impatient if ever he was ill. She would blame it on to his lack of faith. If she'd given to him a tenth of the time she gave to her religion, Christian Science, he would have been a much happier man. I remember when I was in hospital, and his lordship came to see me, I was trying to express my gratitude towards him and I said, 'It's at times like this that you need all the kindness and understanding that you can get.'

'Understanding, did you say understanding, Rose?'

'Yes, my lord.'

Then he seemed to speak to himself. 'Yes, I know just

what you mean.' And I think we both knew what he meant. Then the shutters came down.

Once again it seems I'm criticizing her ladyship. I'm not, for while to some extent it was in her nature, there were also circumstances which kept her away from him. She had a busy political life which he could only share in the shadows. She had this passion for entertaining people which early in his own political life he must have encouraged, so when it became a near-fetish it was to some extent his fault. He could also have tempered it, but it seemed that everything that gave her ladyship enjoyment gave him happiness. Perhaps after the war, when her ladyship gave up her seat in Parliament, he hoped that they would settle more together, but it was too late. He by then was a sick man; sickness was something that Christian Scientists have to ignore and my lady was impatient with her new life. 'What shall we do with her, Rose?' his lordship would say to me, and we'd set forth on a succession of travels to try to soothe her itching spirit. In a way, my lady was like a man who has devoted his whole life to his work, has found no time to interest himself in anything outside, so when he retires he finds he is lost. When she left Parliament she found herself in a similar predicament. She still had people and friends to interest her, but it was a long time before she was able to come to terms with herself.

His lordship had a hobby, racehorses. He was an owner-breeder. Now I don't know anything about horses and I didn't get the opportunity to find out much about them while I was at Cliveden, even though the stud farm was on our doorstep. When I saw them I thought they were very beautiful creatures, but while owning them may have been a profitable hobby for Lord Astor, backing them would never have been for me. I tried betting once when I first joined Miss Wissie. She said to me, 'Daddy's got a horse running to-day which I believe is going to win.' She told me the name and when I went down to the servants' hall I got one of the footmen to invest a shilling on it for me. It didn't come up to Miss Wissie's expectations and no more was said about it except under my breath.

Some days later she said, 'Daddy's horse Penny Come Quick is expected to win today, Rose.'

'I've learned a lesson after your last try, Miss Wissie. It seems it's Penny Go Quick with me.'

This time of course she was right, it won. It didn't make any difference to me though; I reckoned I was a bad chooser and so was never tempted again.

Mind you, I don't think that Lord Astor backed horses. He bred and ran them for the love of it. Mr Lee and Arthur Bushell, his one-time valets, had hoped that he would occasionally give them a winner, but he never did. He said to them, 'I will never give a tip to anybody. If I think my horse is going to win, and say so, and it doesn't, I feel I've done people a disservice.'

Sometimes his lordship would take Mr Lee with him racing. He recalls one Derby: 'Despite the fact that his lordship discouraged betting I couldn't see the point of going racing without having a little flutter. He'd got a horse running called St Germains, and even if he was saying nothing, the stable seemed to think it had a good chance, so I had a nice each way bet on it. I was going back to the grandstand when I met Lord Derby's valet. "What do you fancy, Astor?" he said to me. (We always called each other by our masters' names.) I told him what I'd done.

' "I've heard a bit different," he said, "and that is that my lord's Sansovino can't be beat. Let's go down again. I'll cover myself with an each way bet on your lordship's horse and you do the same with a win on mine."

'I did that, Miss Harrison, and he was right, Sansovino won and St Germain was second. It helped us to enjoy a very good day out.'

To his disappointment Lord Astor never won a Derby, though he was second four times. One of my favourite pictures at Cliveden was one that Alfred Munnings did of him amongst his horses. There's no doubt that they were a great relaxation for him. Racing people were continually on at Mr Lee for tips, but as he said, he couldn't help them as his lordship never told him anything. This didn't stop them though. When Mr Lee had given his usual reply to Sir Harold Werner, another owner, Sir Harold said, 'Well, what are you backing yourself, Lee?'

'Nothing sir, I never bet off the course.'

Sir Harold laughed and said, 'You're a damn sight different from my bloody butler, he's never off the phone to his bookmaker.'

According to Mr Lee some servants of racehorse owners gave tips for money, which again struck him as a betrayal of trust.

His lordship also took a pride in the gardens and greenhouses, and was a great friend of Frank Copcutt's. 'The difference between him and her ladyship, Rose,' Frank said, 'was that if he wanted anything done in the gardens he asked if it was possible to do it, whereas her ladyship demanded that it be done.'

According to Frank he was a generous employer, he paid ten shillings a week more than the going rate and provided cottages or accommodation as well. He started a social security service after the First World War with sickness benefit for the wives and children on the estate, and a pension scheme for the men. He was fond of sports of all kinds and engaged cricket and tennis coaches for his children in the holidays. George Fenner was the cricket coach. He was popular with the boys and the staff alike, particularly with Mr Lee, who was good at cricket and often played for the Cliveden side.

Above all else Lord Astor's interest was in his children, and from an early age. Mr Lee recalls the time when he was valet to his lordship. 'He was an early riser; a call with coffee at 6.30, a bath, then I would shave him. It was always about this time that the children, knowing he was awake, would come rushing down, and he would have one on each knee while I tried to control the razor. I was scared that I would cut either him or the children, and times out of number I've had to restrain myself from putting the shaving brush in their mouths.'

As I've said, when I arrived at Cliveden in 1928, Mr William was twenty-one and the youngest, Mr Jakie, was nine, so I saw nothing of any of their early lives or their relationships at that time with their parents. Mr Lee, Arthur Bushell, Gordon Grimmett and Frank Copcutt would often talk about them and their growing up. For them it seemed they were very much part of the vitality of the house; they made it more real, gay and happy, a place with a purpose. The children caught from their father the way to behave with servants and sometimes it seemed from what they said that they and the other servants got more enjoyment out of them than their parents did.

Cliveden was of course a wonderful place to be young in. It had everything. Theirs was a traditional upbringing: the nursery, governesses, preparatory and public schools and university. It was inevitable from the moment they were born. Let me begin with the nursery and Nanny Gibbons. She had joined the Astors when Mr William was born and she lived the rest of her life there. Now even nannies who are good with their children can be very unpopular with the rest of the staff. They are neither fish, flesh nor good red herring. By that I mean they are not servants, neither are they masters, they are in-betweens, in limbo as it were. In smaller households than ours they often dined with the master and mistress of the house and afterwards sat with them. They had the ear of their employers and could, and sometimes did, speak of things that went on below stairs. They could make demands, particularly of the kitchen staff for special food for their charges, at inconvenient times. They could also be toffee-nosed and hoity-toity. Therefore to servants they were suspect. Not Nanny Gibbons; she struck exactly the right balance. She had made her requirements plain from the moment she'd arrived, had seen that they suited and fitted in with everybody else's and was always friendly though not familiar with the staff. Never, according to Mr Lee, had she made complaints about the servants to anyone but him and when she had they had always been justified, so the staff respected her. The children showed her great affection, and did till the end of her life. In that she was clever, too. Some nannies tried to get too much from the children they looked after. They attempted to become the mother-figure. This could cause great emotional problems with both children and parents. As it was, the Astors as children adored their mother, but I think looked on Nanny Gibbons as a warm and friendly grandmother.

In stature Nanny Gibbons had a figure similar to her ladyship's, short and slimly built. In the morning she wore a white blouse and grey skirt and changed into a darker grey dress for afternoon and evening wear. She was devoted to her children, she studied all their interests and looked after their diet, their clothes and their money. She was very painstaking with the repairs of the boys' clothes, which were handed down as they would have been in any poor family, often I think to the annoyance of the recipients. She didn't like waste of any kind.

One of the rituals for the younger children was a drive in the pony cart every afternoon regularly at two-thirty. That way I think the children must have got to know every blade of grass for miles around. I understand that one way the boys relieved the monotony of these daily drives was to wait for the pony to make a rude noise, and then stare at Nanny Gibbons until her stern set features dissolved into a smile. She was perhaps a little prim. It was the mould of nannies of that time.

Arthur Bushell told me about an evening when some of

the staff were giving an entertainment in the servants' hall. Nanny and the children had been invited. Arthur as usual was dressed up as a woman and, as was his custom, sailing near to the wind with his jokes and behaviour. The broader these got the more the children laughed, and the more set became Nanny's expression. The next day Arthur asked her how she'd enjoyed it. 'The children seemed to be amused, I found your dress left much to be desired.'

'Oh, Miss Gibbons,' he said, 'what did it leave you desiring?

She swept off: and for a week when she saw me she only sniffed.'

When Nanny died and she left £7,500 everyone thought she had saved it from her salary. It got them all wondering how she could possibly have done it. She couldn't. In fact £3,500 had been left to her by her sister, and I know that the children gave her £2,000, though they won't thank me for saying so.

Assisting her was a nurserymaid, whose job it was to clean the nursery, do the washing and ironing, lay the tables and serve the food, wheel the babies in the pram or, when they were older, take them for walks round the gardens and play games with them. Nurserymaids wore print dresses with starched cuffs and collars, and when they were out had grey felt hats and coats. Then there always seemed to be a French or sometimes a German governess around the place so the children learned languages from a very early age. Finally there was the nursery boy, more commonly known as the hall boy, who carried the food trays from the kitchen and did any of the harder rougher jobs that were necessary.

The day nursery was a large, comfortable, light room. In the centre was a table and there were cupboards and bookcases all around the walls where the toys and books were stored. These were plentiful and watched over religiously by Nanny Gibbons, and the toys were kept under lock and key unless they were in use. From time to time my lady would have a blitz, take what toys she thought the children no longer wanted and see that they were given to less privileged children. There was a large comfy couch and easy chairs; a sideboard decorated with flowers and never without fruit on it, so the nursery was the essence of comfort, and of course of cleanliness.

Nanny slept in the night nursery with the children in cots or beds until they were old enough to move into their own rooms. I have spoken of the nursery as if it belonged to the Astor family, but it was often shared with visitors' children. It was in this way that nannies became well known among the aristocracy; our Nanny Gibbons had a great reputation. There was another such at Hatfield House. Although Nanny Gibbons's affection was visited mostly upon the children she was devoted to the Astors and particularly to his lordship. It was he who as it were ruled over the nursery, and it was to him that she went for help or advice if ever she needed it, though this was rare as they seemed to think and behave as one.

His lordship, while wanting his children brought up in the pattern of the time for his rank and position, was determined that they should not be spoilt. For example, he limited their pocket money. Indeed Mr Lee has told me that at times he and other of his men have slipped them a few pence on some special occasion, such as the annual fair on nearby Woburn Green. I suppose too Lord Astor wanted his children brought up in his own image. If this is a fault it's one that is in most of us. We want our children to do at least as well as, if not better than, we have done. We think we can show them the way and we get offended or hurt if they rebel against us. It is something in human nature that is hard for parents to deny or escape from if they think about their children at all. In my day 'the sins of the fathers were visited on the children'. Today it seems that the sins of the children are visited on the fathers. In looking for an excuse for misbehaviour children are encouraged to blame their parents by doctors, lawyers, schoolteachers, and their likes.

Having got that off my chest let me hasten to say that this feeling about their mother or father is not one shared by any of the Astor children, though it may have been in the minds of others when considering the occasional misdemeanours that they consider have been committed – 'poor little rich children' is an easy gibe and one which cannot be applied to them. I'm sure they are today as proud of their parents as I am and would never attempt to use them as whipping-boys for anything wrong that they may have done. There are problems about growing up rich. Perhaps rich people are encouraged to think they're different from others, but in the Astor home they were taught that this difference brought with it responsibilities to others that poorer children don't have. Example and leadership are two such things. Unfortunately the slightest lapse from either in this day and age brings down the wrath of people who have few if any qualities themselves. But I'm getting ahead of myself.

The big moment of any day for the children when they were little was when they went down from the nursery to join their parents after tea, whether there were guests with them or not. Her ladyship was at her gayest at this time and this gaiety pervaded the room. She would turn anything into a laugh. It was as though she was an actress; she turned her charm on, it flowed like water from a tap and she gave a different performance every night. These were the people with whom she was most at home, the young and innocent, and as I found out during the war years it was not reserved just for people of her own kind. She was as easy with a child from a slum and so he was with her. I used to envy the boys these times with my lady. It was only occasionally I had glimpses of them. Even more I loved the other evenings when she would tell her 'Nigger' stories, with their mixture of the comic with the melancholy, acting the various parts and reverting continually to her Deep South drawl. Of course the children didn't always find it beer and skittles, there were times when her gay mood could change to gall and she'd be her other self, sarcastic and mocking.

Of the boys' school-days I knew little. They all went away at about the age of eight to their preparatory school. I've later gathered that it was selected because the headmaster admitted pupils who were Christian Scientists. Not I think that they could have had much idea at their age of what this was all about. Apparently they didn't suffer from going there. They retained the charm they'd cultivated early. There was no religious compromise over their public school, they had to go to Eton. Again to the best of my knowledge they enjoyed it and it seemed Eton enjoyed them, judging by the attitude and number of friends who came to visit Cliveden. Mr Lee paid several visits to the school, taking fruit and serving picnic luncheons on the Fourth of June.

The only person who didn't care for the school was Gordon Grimmett. 'I had good reason not to, Miss Harrison,' he told me. 'It was during Mr Billy's first term. Mr Lee came to me one day after he'd been there about eight weeks and said that according to Nanny Gibbons someone, and that on this occasion that someone was me, had to go to Eton to examine his suits and shoes to see if any repairs were needed. Any shoes which wanted heeling – and I was informed that there was some sort of competition as to who could first wear them down to the soles – were to be taken without argument to Ganes, the old-established cobbler in the High Street, and any clothes that required mending were to be returned to Nanny Gibbons.

'I was driven by Bert Jeffries, then his lordship's second chauffeur, in the Daimler to Mr Conybeare's house. It was a rambling old place. Outside there was a group of boys, top-hatted and all carrying badly rolled umbrellas. "Could they," I asked, "inform me which room the Honourable William Astor occupied?"

' "Try the top floor and knock on every door until you come to his," was suggested.

'This I did. Grinning faces appeared and I received comments like, "Go away, you annoy me," "Your looks revolt me" and "Never heard of him, my good man."

'Finally by threats and perseverance I found the room and achieved the purpose of my visit, leaving with a pair of trousers and two pairs of shoes. On my return, half-way down the passage, doors suddenly opened and I was ambushed by a dozen boys who chased me downstairs with a rain of blows from hockey sticks, cricket bats and umbrellas. When at last I reached the car I explained to Bert Jeffries what had happened. Unsympathetically he roared with laughter. "You were lucky," he said, "they usually de-bag outsiders like you who come on a clothes and boots check."

'When I returned I reported the incident to Mr Lee and told him that never again would I venture near the place. He too was unfeeling: "You'll be all right next time, you won't have to make inquiries, thereby finding it unnecessary to knock on the boys' doors and advertising your presence."

'I stuck to my guns though and when the next visit came round another footman took my place. Like Bert Jeffries, I saw no reason to inform him what to expect. He gave a better account of himself than I did, however, and gave as good as if not better than he got and returned to Cliveden with nothing more than a badly battered top hat.'

It was after her children had reached the age of puberty that Lady Astor seemed to lose her understanding and with it her affection for them. Although, as I've said, she disliked 'yes men' among her friends and servants, she seemed to expect complete agreement and obedience from her children in thought, word and deed, and when she didn't get it was indignant and angry. She made no attempt to see their point of view. It's a difficult time for children of either sex, but she only saw it as difficult for her. Nor did she attempt to use love to keep close to them. She couldn't. She tried to hold them through religion, but adolescence is an age when most children are more interested in Mammon than God. The temptations of the flesh seem very attractive, the more so if you know you can afford them, and this my lady didn't seem to realize. The strange thing is she only hurt herself; the good thing was that she eventually got back their affection and respect and nobody was permanently hurt.

To a lesser degree his lordship was the same. He expected them to grow up like him and to take the road he planned for them, but the boys had different ideas and this puzzled and disappointed him. By nature he was philosophical, he'd had to learn to be, so it didn't come quite so hard to him.

As for the children, well they, like most, learned to adapt themselves. Theirs was a fascinating, changing world and there were plenty of other things for them to think about. Anyway they each had a small fortune to look forward to at twenty-one which meant freedom for them. I'm glad to say that by the time they got it they had learned not to abuse it, and weren't so keen on breaking adrift as they might at one time have been. Perhaps they were like that boy of sixteen who thought his parents were dull, stupid and old-fashioned and who, when he was twenty, was amazed how much they'd learnt in the last four years.

I suppose really that the Astor children–parent relationship was little different from that of the majority of families. It was just that with me being so close to her ladyship and liking the boys so much, that I was critical of her behaviour towards them and wanted so often to tell her where I thought she was going wrong. I couldn't, of course, it wasn't my place, but I did give some very strong hints at times! In any case it's always easy to criticize when you are watching from the wings and without any real personal involvement; just as it's also easy to be wise after the event.

The children's holidays were times to look forward to, times when Cliveden became a home. Then there were also visits to Tarbert Lodge on the island of Jura and to Rest Harrow at Sandwich. These holidays meant a deal of packing for me because we went for weeks at a time and had to cater for all weathers. I must say I didn't care for Jura, though it was ideal for children, with fishing, swimming, climbing, walking, shooting and deer-stalking, but none of these things interested me. I went fishing once or twice and caught quite a few, but it seems to me that once you've done it and got over the excitement, it becomes a nasty, monotonous, slimy business conducted in the cold and the wet, and can be downright dangerous. Then again while I like fresh mackerel I don't want them for breakfast every day of the week and apparently it's a crime not to eat what you catch. I also found I'd grown out of the taste of venison since my childhood.

The lodge was in the middle of nowhere and I missed the excitement of London and the companionship of Cliveden. There wasn't anyone I could really talk to. The housekeeper and her husband were nice enough people if I could have understood a word of what they were saying, so was the kitchen-maid, but it was difficult to carry on a conversation with someone who'd never been off the island until we visited there and took her on an outing, and who had never even seen a railway train. Neither did I have enough to do. My lady insisted on my packing all her oldest things which when she discarded them would be thrown or given away, and this included her undergarments, so there was no pressing, washing or mending and of course she rarely changed during the day. Once I even found myself scrubbing my bedroom floor out of sheer boredom!

I don't think her ladyship enjoyed it either although she used to pretend she did for the sake of the children. She too was bored and therefore short-tempered which didn't help matters. She used to give vent to her feelings by knocking golf balls about the place. I remember once, she must have been particularly frustrated, she was putting on the grass in front of the lodge and she suddenly turned and fired four balls at the house; two of them went through the glass of the windows. I think I know how she felt.

The first time I went to Jura (and I saw to it that I only had to go once more), I was treated to one of my lady's bouts of petulant unpunctuality. The day of our departure came and the two boys, Mr Michael and Mr Jakie, were to return to school the following day. I was down at the quayside near the ferry with the boys and their luggage, waiting for the Astors. His lordship had sent me ahead while he hurried my lady up. Apparently she didn't care for the way he did it, went into a tantrum and refused to budge. I guessed what had happened and did my best to persuade the ship's captain to wait for them, but either the Astors' name meant nothing up there, or he was one of those sailors who'd heard of her temperance drive; anyway he sailed bang on time. When the flustered couple arrived some minutes later there was a deal of sorting out to be done. Eventually a small boat was hired and I and the boys and their two trunks were dispatched to the mainland, where I was to do my best to get them to Glasgow, put them on a train and wait at the station hotel until the others arrived. I was unable to hire a car so we had to go by bus, and a comic journey that was with two large trunks and a couple of boys who didn't mind in the least if we missed the train, and they missed school. Anyway we made it and with time to spare, though I must say I was relieved to see my employers the next day as the hotel management were giving me a few sidelong glances as if they knew I hadn't enough money to pay for my room.

Although as I say we took a lot of luggage on these visits to Jura or to Sandwich, there was always a special piece that came with us; a cow, which was in a truck attached to the end of the train. His lordship was very particular about the kind of milk the children drank and so this cow and a cowman from the Home Farm were detailed to travel with us. I remember her being milked on the station and thinking it all a bit extraordinary, but you get used to anything and I grew to accept her as the right and proper thing to accompany us on our journeys.

I really enjoyed our holidays at Sandwich. Rest Harrow was a civilized house and her ladyship found plenty to amuse her while we were there. I could also catch up on my sewing and sleeping. We still entertained there of course, but it was more family and al fresco. Although we only used the house for about two months a year at the most, Lady Astor was very generous with it and would often lend it to her friends. There was one romantic occasion before I joined her that caused particular excitement. Gordon Grimmett recalled it to me in detail, and with some relish. 'One morning Mr Lee sent for me and told me that her ladyship had loaned Rest Harrow to Lady Louise Mountbatten, Princess of Battenberg. She was to spend her honeymoon there with Gustavus Adolphus, Crown Prince of Sweden. "Naturally," Mr Lee said, "as always on these occasions their whereabouts are a secret, so you will use your discretion and not mention it to any others of the staff. You will be going there to prepare for their arrival. I shall join you later and together we shall attend on them during the two weeks they will be in residence."

'Well, Miss Harrison, I thought at the least it would be a change from polishing silver, and I looked forward to it. I did a bit of research before I left and discovered that Lady Louise was thirty-four, and the Crown Prince forty-nine. "Left it a bit late," I thought, and comforted myself with, "Perhaps they'll be making up for lost time so there won't be too much for us to do."

'The marriage took place on 3 November and the happy couple arrived, in what I learned later was a specially built

Daimler with a high body that had been selected because
the Prince was six foot six tall. I blenched a little when he
jack-knifed out of the car. I hadn't seen the bridal bed, but
it seemed to me that he was likely to have some uncomfortable nights. Mr Lee showed no similar reaction. He quickly
took over, escorted the couple into the house and returned
to attend to the luggage. As you know, Miss Harrison, he
had little time for chauffeurs, and since this one had made
no attempt to unload, he waded into him. "What's your
name?"

' "Erb."

' "Well Mr Erb . . ."

' "No, no, Erb is short for Herbert. You know, it's my
Christian name."

' "I know nothing of the sort, but what I do know is that
you're an idle fellow and that you've been sitting here
wasting valuable time. Now get that luggage off, give it to
Gordon here and then take yourself off, and quickly."

'Herbert moved as Mr Lee had suggested, fast.

'Travelling with their Highnesses were Mr Neilson, the
Prince's valet, who knew not a word of English, and Lady
Louise's personal maid. I asked Mr Lee how I should
address the royal couple. "Your first greeting in the morning will be, 'Good morning, your Royal Highness,' and if
you have cause to speak to them further it will be Sir or
Madam." '

Gordon Grimmett continued: 'That night dinner was
served just for the two Royals, with Mr Lee and myself
waiting on them. The atmosphere was a bit subdued. They
conversed in whispers with the occasional giggle. Mr Lee
was ready for the occasion. "Gordon," he said, "though it is
the custom for us to remain in the dining-room throughout
the meal, tonight we will break with it and retire after each
course is served."

'Hovering outside the dining-room was the resident Rest
Harrow housekeeper, Mrs Avery. "Whispering Avery", the

under-staff called her on account of her habit of putting her
mouth up against your ear when she had something she
thought important to say, and then when she'd finished of
bringing her elbow smartly into your ribs as if to say, "Just
between you and me, eh?" Since she did it with all of us it
seemed she was full of open secrets. On this occasion it was
apparent that she had something to communicate to Mr
Lee, but since he refused to bend from his lofty height, I
got the message too. "How many hot water bottles shall I
place in the royal bed?" she inquired.

' "I'm afraid I don't know and I've no intention of hazard-
ing a guess," replied Mr Lee. "I suggest you ask Lady
Louise's maid."

' "I've done that and she says that up until now she always
had three."

' "Under those circumstances I suggest that tonight one
will be sufficient," said Mr Lee, with great authority, though
how he arrived at that figure I was unable to conjecture.
Mrs Avery seemed satisfied and, giving Mr Lee her customary dig in the ribs, retired.

'I must say that those days in Sandwich, Miss Harrison,
were delightful and leisurely. And what a friendly couple
they were, no airs and graces. It was please and thank you
for everything that was done for them, and when they left
Mr Lee was given a sizeable envelope of money which he
shared amongst the staff. On our return to Cliveden I was
greeted as I'd never been greeted before. Everyone wanted
to know how the royal couple had got on, particularly the
maids. Naturally I knew little, but to have heard me you'd
have thought I was a proper Omar Khayyam.'

There was another adventure later when I was at Sandwich with the family. Lord Astor's sister, Mrs Spender Clay,
owned the house next to Rest Harrow and Tommy Phipps,
my lady's nephew and Joyce Grenfell's brother, was staying
with her. He'd been over in our house during the evening
larking about with the boys, but had returned with Mrs

Clay. We had just gone to bed when there was the sound of a shot and shortly afterwards I heard Tommy Phipps shouting from downstairs. The whole house turned out in their dressing-gowns. Mr Tommy was trembling from head to foot and stuttering and spluttering; eventually we gathered that a man had appeared at his door demanding his money or his life. He'd given him a pound, which was all he had, the man had taken it from him, fired at him, missed and run out into the night. It was like a scene from a murder play. The footmen seized whatever weapons they could from the kitchen and rushed outside, the housekeeper fainted, Mr Billy called his dogs and went off with a knife, and his lordship followed with a golf club, leaving Mr Tommy helping himself to a brandy and her ladyship to phone the police.

I stood and waited for something to happen. Eventually two carloads of police arrived and our gallant men came wandering back looking rather comic with their various cudgels and things. After a brief talk with Mr Tommy the police left to take up the search, while an inspector was left behind to cross-examine us servants. To everyone's utter amazement John, a young footman, suddenly burst out that he was the villain of the piece. Well, that got everyone clucking with curiosity. It was not to be satisfied. John, his lordship, Tommy and the inspector went into another room and we were told to get back to bed.

Next morning to my surprise John was still with us, but he refused to say anything about what had happened. It was several days before we were able to put the pieces together. Apparently Tommy Phipps, who was unpopular with the staff anyway, had been getting at John, taking advantage of his position to tease him out of his wits. So John decided to get his own back. He'd used a toy pistol and was eventually going to reveal his identity. He hadn't expected Mr Tommy to get so scared. His lordship, although he reprimanded John, was also extremely angry with Mr Tommy, and he held him responsible for the whole incident. The police inspector apparently mumbled something about arresting John for pretending to use a firearm, but his lordship had already tried the case and administered the sentence so he was quickly silenced. In those days even the police knew their place.

Mr Jakie, the youngest of the Astor boys, and therefore the one to whom I probably felt the closest, was also the most witty and amusing. He'd either inherited or copied this trait from his mother. Whichever it was, his wit didn't include her wicked bite or will to hurt. One quick remark of his which probably sums up his mother's attitude towards her children is contained in a skirmish of words they had when my lady was considering writing her autobiography. 'You can't describe yourself as you really are, Mum,' Jakie said. 'The result would be too horrifying.'

'What a wretched thing to say about your mother. Anyway, why would it be horrifying?'

'Because you're so possessive,' said Jakie. 'That's why all your children are cases of arrested development – though I must say,' he added, 'that Bobbie is the only one of us to have actually been arrested.'

He is referring here to his half-brother Bobbie Shaw, and it brings me to the first experience I had of her ladyship in grief. Mr Bobbie was apparently a bit of a wild one as a young man. He had gone into the army, as an officer in the Blues, and developed a taste for the drink. This had led to his having to resign his commission, a disgrace that probably drove him even closer to the bottle. He became reckless and was caught by the police committing a homosexual offence. Then, there was none of the understanding of such matters as we have today. To be honest, at the time I knew nothing of it. I remember Mr Lee assembling the whole staff and speaking to us. He explained in vague terms what had happened and then said, 'After you leave the servants' hall no one will speak about the matter. Anyone heard or suspected of doing so in or out of the house will be instantly dismissed.'

I was again told about it by her ladyship; she was in such sorrow that it had to come out. I remember it was so hard to comfort her, not fully understanding what it was all about.

The police I gathered were doing their best to help. They pointed out to his lordship and to Mr Bobbie that a few days would elapse before they issued a warrant, which meant that if Mr Bobbie left the country and stayed away and out of mischief for a year or so nothing further would be heard of the matter. He refused to budge and decided to face the music. Her ladyship was nearly out of her mind with worry. The timing couldn't have been worse. She and his lordship, together with Bernard Shaw and a few others, had accepted an invitation to visit Russia. It was one of the first such visits since the Revolution and therefore had aroused a lot of public interest. As was obvious from Mr Lee's talk with the servants, the main object now was to avoid publicity over the case. I don't know how it was done, but not a word was published in any newspaper. Of course his lordship owned the *Observer* and his brother *The Times*, and in those days dog didn't eat dog, but there must have been a deal of string-pulling behind the scenes. It meant of course that Lord and Lady Astor had to keep their appointment in Russia; if they hadn't there would have been public speculation as to why and this would undoubtedly have given the show away. Nobody could be really sure what was likely to happen and the case wasn't to come up until after the Astors had left, so my lady was in a constant state of turmoil. 'I wish you were coming too, Rose.' she kept saying, and I believed her. She needed someone uncomplicated in whom she could confide, and she tried up to the last moment to get visas for both Arthur Bushell and myself. When she said good-bye to me she was in tears and as I tried to comfort her she said, 'If I can get over this,

Rose, I can get over anything.' She did get over it, and so nearly did Mr Bobbie, but it's my opinion that no one ever really gets over a prison sentence – even of only three months.

To me one of the greatest and most lovable qualities of my lady was her ability to forgive people who had, in her eyes, done wrong. Drink and sensuality were the two big ones in her sin book yet in London and Plymouth she's brought back drunken servicemen rather than let them get caught by the military police, and the compassion that she showed to Mr Bobbie was by any mother's standards remarkable. If only she could have left it at that it would have been better for him. Unfortunately she couldn't leave religion alone and exhorted him too much in that way. It took the gilt off the gingerbread. The children too were wonderful to him then, and for the rest of his life. To hear them speak of him today is to listen to nothing but praise for his charm, wit and courage. There's no question but that he was devoted to his mother, though they were constantly at cross purposes and many's the tear I've helped mop up after he'd been with her. In her later years, he was particularly attentive and seldom a day passed when he didn't telephone or visit her.

Yet somehow I couldn't like him in the same way that I did the other children. He was too changeable for me. He'd come into his mother's room, sometimes he'd be pleasant and delightful and others he'd try and corner me in conversation and make me say something indiscreet about my lady or the other servants. I always felt on my guard when I was with him. It may have been something to do with a happening very soon after I joined her ladyship. I was waiting outside her room on the landing near a bathroom at Sandwich while she was dressing, and he came along and started talking to me. Suddenly from out of the blue he said, 'I bet you were glad to leave Lady Cranborne, weren't you, Rose?'

'No, Mr Bobbie, I wasn't,' I said after a moment's bewilderment. 'While I was with her I was very happy and she was always kind to me.'

He smirked at that and went away. A few seconds later the bathroom door opened and out walked Lady Cranborne. He'd known she was in there and had tried to make me say something that would have caused her a hurt. I took the incident as a signpost of the direction his mind worked in and was ready for the other occasions as they happened. Poor Mr Bobbie though, he had more than his share of misfortune; two bad riding accidents that cracked his skull, badly bombed while serving during the war (ironically enough he was in a pub when they fell), and an attempted suicide. He's a person I've grown to admire more since his death. His will was the answer to a servant's prayer. He left his money and his house to his housekeeper, Lottie Moore, to whom he'd given the job out of kindness when she had to leave Cliveden where she had been head housemaid. It was a small fortune, about a hundred thousand pounds in all, and was given providing she looked after his three dogs. Unhappily though there wasn't a fairytale ending for Lottie. She died a year later and had little time to enjoy the money.

Mention of dogs brings to mind the place of dogs in society. In most of the houses that I visited it was little dogs allowed in the house and big dogs outside in the kennels. If my memory serves me aright the Tuftons didn't keep dogs either in London or at Appleby Castle. The Cranbornes kept two constantly with them, and they had working dogs as well for shooting. I particularly liked Lord Cranborne's yellow labrador and he took to me. He'd try to sneak into my bedroom at night when his lordship was away so that he could sleep under my bed. Her ladyship had a greyhound. Whether this was because she liked them or she knew what a graceful pair they made when she took him for a walk, I don't know. Dogs and people can complement each other I've found. Many an ugly man can look quite handsome alongside his bulldog.

When I first went to Cliveden Lord Astor's Peke was the only dog allowed in the house. 'Peeky' slept in his bedroom and wandered around everywhere with his lordship. When he was away Mrs Ford the housekeeper looked after him and Peeky was still given the run of the place. During his lifetime his lordship had a number of Pekes. They weren't a breed I'd been particularly fond of, but I grew to like them, and I've found this with all types of dogs, it's just a question of getting to understand them.

All the children had dogs. I remember Mr Billy's black labrador, Mr David's spaniel, Miss Wissie's miniature poodle and Mr Michael's and Mr Jakie's terriers. As for Mr Bobbie, I reckon he ran the gamut of Cruft's. I think I saw him with every breed under the sun. He was constantly changing them. If a friend admired one he'd suddenly find himself the owner of it. This way Lady Astor acquired one, another Peke, Sue-Sue she was called. It was after the war; before that her ladyship had always said she was too busy to keep a pet. It was obvious from the start that she didn't know how to treat it. She didn't attempt to earn Sue-Sue's affection by exercising her, talking to her and giving her her food. We were at Sandwich when Mr Bobbie presented Sue-Sue to her. When the time for her to drive back to London I brought the dog down to the car. 'What on earth are you doing with that, Rose?' she said. 'You don't think I'm going to drive back to town with a Peke to keep me company. What sort of fool do you want me to look?'

'Well, it's your dog, my lady, and Mr Bobbie gave it to you to look after.'

'Well I'm not going to have it in the car with us, so you can shut up, Rose.'

'Very well, my lady, then what do you propose I should do with her?'

'You can have it, Rose, as a present from me,' she cried, slammed the door and drove off to London.

At the time I was rather pleased. I'd never had a dog of

my own and I'd grown fond of little Sue-Sue. My pleasure
didn't last long when I rejoined her ladyship. Talk about
the eternal triangle! She was jealous of Sue-Sue. She was
always getting at me now through that dog. 'You do more
for her than you ever do for me, Rose,' became a constant
cry. 'I suppose you've been with that dog,' whenever she
rang for me. The last straw came one night when I was at
the front door of Hill Street and her ladyship came to let
me in. 'What sort of maid are you to me, Rose?' she cried.
'You think more of that dog than you do of me.'

That was it. I went home the next day on some pretext
or another, and gave Sue-Sue to a friend whom I knew
would care for her as I had. I can report that she had the
drawing-room for the rest of her life.

I don't want to give the impression that Lady Astor disliked dogs. She didn't. She liked to see them around and she
encouraged her children to keep them. It's just that she
didn't have the patience or the inclination to understand
or look after them herself.

After my experience with Sue-Sue my feelings can be
imagined when once again her ladyship accepted the gift of
a dog, while she was at Sandwich. This time it was a corgi,
christened Madam. She'd been a present from Mr Bobbie
to Mary, the housekeeper at Rest Harrow. Mary couldn't
cope and offered it to my lady who accepted it. Now of
course, she was very much older, it was about three years
before her death, so I hoped she would have mellowed a bit
in her attitude. At first too I tried to ignore the dog. This
got me into trouble. 'You don't like Madam, do you Rose?
Why? She hasn't done anything to upset you, has she?' I
couldn't win. Then as someone had to feed her, Madam
developed at least a cupboard love for me, and so it went
on until soon she was scratching at her ladyship's door when
she heard me coming.

Then came the inevitable, 'That dog belongs more to you
than it does to me.' I didn't bother to reply. I know when

I'm beaten. I must say she really got my rag out one day though. I'd gone into her ladyship's bedroom to change her. 'Where's Madam?' I asked. 'I don't know, Rose,' she replied.

About two seconds later I heard a muffled woof and a scratching. I went to the wardrobe, opened the door and let Madam out. Her ladyship was speechless and uncomfortable, so was I for a second or two, then I let her have it.

'That, my lady, was downright cruel and you ought to be ashamed of yourself. If you ever do it again I shall tell the boys that you're not fit to look after a dog.' Oh, I was angry! Of course I got a 'Shut up, Rose', but it was a quiet and rather ashamed one. I must say Madam was more affectionate towards her ladyship than Sue-Sue had been. Perhaps that was because she was constantly giving her chocolates; perhaps it's worth comment that she didn't even bite into them before offering them to her either!

I also showed the whip hand a bit over Madam. I remember once when we were staying with my lady's niece, Mrs Lancaster, at Haseley Court, my lady decided to take her for a walk in the fields. Well I knew the dog's habits, so I said, 'Be careful with her, the fields are full of sheep. We don't want her rolling in their dirt otherwise she'll come home and smell the place out.'

I probably shouldn't have said it. It was a challenge to my lady. I reckoned she must have encouraged the dog if she didn't actually put her among the sheep's dung and roll her in it, for Madam came back covered and stinking to high heaven. Her ladyship had a sort of little smile of triumph on her lips as she saw me. Battle commenced. I got a bowl full of water, set it on a towel on the floor, handed my lady a piece of soap and a brush. 'There,' I said, 'I asked you particularly to watch her, and now look what she's done. She's your dog, she's got to be cleaned so get on with it.'

She set to without saying a word. That did it; of course

169

I couldn't watch her so I took over, admonishing her with every rub of the soap and scrub of the brush. Eventually we both ended up roaring with laughter. Madam was the only one who didn't see the joke.

There was another habit of that dog's which had a comic twist. William, our odd man when we lived in Eaton Square, often used to take her out at night for a walk. Like all odd men William enjoyed his pint of beer, so she was taken into the various pubs in the neighbourhood where she was given potato crisps and bits of cheese while William took his drink. She became a sort of regular, popular with the landlords and the other drinkers, and a bit spoilt by them. So when my lady came to take Madam out for a walk, and she got near a pub, Madam would tug at her lead and try and pull Lady Astor into it. Then when they came to the door of the bar she'd sit back on her haunches and whine, and wouldn't budge however hard she was tugged. This didn't please Lady Astor, but it amused the passers-by, particularly those who knew who she was, because though all her other political beliefs and actions might have been forgotten, her prohibitionist views were always remembered.

Cats were something never seen in any of our houses; strictly taboo they were. Her ladyship could not tolerate them. I can bear witness to the fact that she was terrified of them, because when during the war we rented Bray House, Rock, Cornwall, after Elliot Terrace, Plymouth, was bombed, a cat was as it were let with the house, and it was my job to look after it and see that it was kept out of my lady's way. It was such a beautiful happy creature that I couldn't believe that she wouldn't like it if she saw it, so one evening I carried it down to her room. If I'd had a bomb in my arms it couldn't have had a more startling effect. She went as white as a sheet and started to tremble. 'Get that creature out of here,' she shouted. I did, and fast. It was then that I could understand why the gamekeepers at Cliveden had orders to shoot any cat that came on to the estate.

Let me now go back in time to the outbreak of war. Like almost all children of their kind the boys immediately became involved. Mr Billy went into the Navy. Mr David was commissioned into the Marines. Mr Michael came back from America to join his Yeomanry Regiment, the Berkshires, and Mr Jakie was already an officer in the Life Guards. Mr Bobbie was in a bit of a fix, his head injury from riding seemed to keep him out of everything, but he was determined and eventually served with the Home Guard, and then later with the ambulance service.

Both his lordship and my lady accepted the boys' loyalty as a matter of course, but like any other parents were always anxious for them. It was so good that they all came through and a matter of great thankfulness to my lady, who for the rest of her life remained conscious of her good fortune, and never ceased reminding herself of it. Her pride in her boys manifested itself in the most extraordinary way. She began knitting socks for them. I was sent out to buy the most expensive wool and then had to cast it on to the knitting needles so that she could begin. I suppose she'd learnt the rudiments as a child, but that was some time ago. She was hopeless at it, it was comic to watch her. I got a number of 'Shut up, Roses' for doing just that. When I remonstrated by saying I hadn't uttered, she said, 'It's the vile expression on your face that I can't stand.'

Give her her due, she persevered with them. Came the day when they were finished and she handed them to me to press. I held them up to look at. They were ludicrous; one had a long leg and a short foot and the other a long foot and a short leg. 'I take it one's for Mr Michael and the other for Mr Jakie,' I said.

'Mind your own business, do as I tell you and parcel them up. I'm going to send them.'

'They won't get past the censor,' I said as I went out of

171

the door. Eventually there was a family conference about them and it was agreed that a mother's love could be taken too far. Nanny Gibbons was commissioned to unravel them and knit them up properly.

By the end of the war all the Astor boys were married, Mr Michael in 1942, Mr Jakie in 1944, and Mr Billy and Mr David in 1945. Perhaps it was as well there was a war on because it allowed for the minimum of interference from her ladyship; there were plenty of other things around for her to think about. Mr Jakie married the daughter of the Argentinian Ambassador, Chiquita she was known as. She was of course a Catholic, which was as a red rag to a bull to her ladyship. She wouldn't attend the wedding, nor did his lordship. Again I couldn't interfere, but I rumbled a lot. The absurdity of putting a human relationship at risk on account of religious bigotry just beggared my belief.

My lady's attitude to wives was predictable in view of the possessiveness she'd shown towards all her boys. She was critical; this was a fault she readily admitted, but knew she could do nothing about as it was in her nature. I remember her once saying – it was after his lordship's death – 'I'm inviting all my sons to lunch, Rose, but I'm going to tell them they can't bring their wives.'

'Now there's an absurd thing to say,' I told her. 'You can't possibly do it. The child leaves his mother and cleaves to the wife. That's the nature of things. They won't come and it'll only cause trouble. Suppose someone had done that when you married his lordship saying, "He can come but you can't," what would you have said and done? It's stuff and nonsense!' It was one occasion when she took my advice.

Miss Wissie, who was the first to rebel against her mother's domination, was also the one to grow closest to her as the years went by. She put herself out to try and understand and help her, and well she succeeded in the later years.

Hers was a marriage which her mother had been unable to fault. To begin with she and Lord Ancaster were what society would call the ideal match, but that apart he was a man of great distinction, a gallant soldier, gentle, kind and thoughtful of others. He and Lord Astor were men of similar quality. I've never heard a word spoken against him, either above or below stairs. But although my lady left Lord Ancaster alone, even after Miss Wissie's marriage she continued to treat her as if she was a child. I remember once when Miss Wissie had come to see her in her bedroom, just before dinner, her ladyship looked at her and said,

'You're not coming to my dinner table in that dress, go and change it at once.'

Well, naturally, if Miss Wissie had been in sackcloth she'd have stayed in it after being spoken to in that way, so she refused, forcibly. Then the feathers flew and the tears began to fall. I waded in and separated them getting some 'shut ups' and 'don't interferes' for my pains. Eventually Miss Wissie stormed out leaving me with a tigress. All this over a dress! I busied myself for a bit tidying up, and then went to see Miss Wissie. 'I'm not changing it, Rose, if that's what you've come for.'

'No, it's not that, Miss Wissie,' I said. 'I've really come to apologize. It's my fault her ladyship's in such a state. I rubbed her up the wrong way earlier on and you got the stick that I should have had so it's a bit silly to ruin your evening on my behalf.'

'No,' she said, 'I won't do it.'

'Do it for my sake, otherwise I'm going to feel responsible.'

She thought about this for a moment and then said, 'All right, Rose, but I shall tell Mother I did it for you.'

Well, I wasn't going to protest about that, so I went back to my lady.

'I shall not be going down to dinner, so tell Mr Lee to inform his lordship.'

173

'Very well, my lady,' I said, 'but it's a pity as Miss Wissie has gone to the trouble of putting on a new dress.'

It was a Pyrrhic victory. She looked at me suspiciously and said, 'You didn't apologize for me did you, Rose?'

'No, my lady.'

'Then what did you do?'

'Never mind what I did, you just go down to dinner,' I said. But she didn't care for it and kept sniffing around like a bloodhound to find the reason. Servants mustn't be allowed to win. In a way it's a footling story, but attitudes are built up by a series of petty incidents in all walks of life.

Now I come to something which I don't really want to write about, because in all conscience enough has been told already, and it's best forgotten. Yet to ignore it would only be to draw attention to it. I refer of course to the Profumo Affair and Mr Billy's part in it. It all came to light in 1963, a year before my lady died. She was eighty-four at the time and though in many ways she was as bright as she'd ever been, her memory was beginning to go. We were living at Eaton Square, and Charles Dean was her butler. Mr Lee had stayed on at Cliveden after his lordship died and had enjoyed serving the now Lord Billy. He was in on the beginning of what was later to become a *cause célèbre*, though he retired before the scandal broke.

Lord Billy had had an accident on the hunting field and he was attended by a physiotherapist, Doctor Stephen Ward, who aided his recovery. A riverside cottage was vacant on the estate around that time and Doctor Ward and his brother, an army colonel, took it as a weekend retreat. After a time, according to Mr Lee, it was noticeable that the Colonel didn't come down so often and in retrospect he thinks this was because his brother started bringing girls with him. Doctor Ward and the girls made very occasional visits to the house. Mr Lee liked him: 'An affable and friendly gentleman.' It may have been forgotten that Doctor Ward had talent as an artist; he persuaded Mr Lee to sit for him and did an excellent sketch. I wouldn't have seen it had it not been for a perfectly splendid mistake someone made. At the height of the scandal six of these drawings were published in the papers. Mr Lee's was among them, but under his portrait he was described as 'Lord Astor'. He dined out on the story for weeks from his home in East-bourne, and many others of us had a good laugh. It was about the only one we did have during the whole sorry affair.

The girls Doctor Ward brought with him seemed 'well enough behaved' to Mr Lee. He thought they were Wind-mill girls. 'I treated them just as I would any other guests and, as far as I know – and I should have known if they hadn't – they conducted themselves properly when they were in the house. I didn't meet Mr Profumo and his wife, they were visitors after I left. I honestly believe, Rose, that his young lordship was just an unfortunate victim of cir-cumstances, as indeed were many others who were con-cerned in the case.'

At Eaton Square Charles Dean was the butler and Mrs Campbell-Grey, one-time Lady Boothby and later Lady Gage, was companion to her ladyship. Our job was to ensure that she saw or heard nothing about the business. It wasn't easy. The newspapers had to be spirited away or doctored. The television was put out of order. The radio was more difficult to deal with without arousing my lady's suspicions. It was arranged that every day a little before one o'clock in the afternoon and six in the evening, the times the main news bulletins of the day were read, some friend of her ladyship's would ring her up and keep her in con-versation until they were over. Once, whoever's stint it was, forgot. Charles Dean was ready for the occasion. Just as the news was being announced he came into her boudoir and switched the programme over to another station. 'Why have you done that, Dean?' my lady asked.

'Well,' he said, 'it just happens that they're playing a

series of tunes from the American South, your favourites,
on the Light Programme. I know you'll want to hear them.'
They weren't of course, but by the time her ladyship and
Charles had argued it out between them, the danger was
past.

Visitors were warned to keep off the subject. We only had
one big scare when Mr Bobbie appeared one evening a little
the worse for drink. 'I think Mother ought to know and I'm
going to tell her.' Within the limits of our position, which
were a lot wider now, we did our best to dissuade him. I
don't like imputing motives to people but I think he felt
that since his own misdemeanours had become common
family knowledge, that Mr Billy's should be too, that he was
a bit lonely being the only black sheep in the fold and
was looking for company. He must have said something
to her because she rang for me and said, 'Get Pover [the
chauffeur] and put your hat and coat on, we're going down
to Cliveden.'

'What for?' I asked.

'All this trouble going on and no one telling me about it.'

'What trouble?'

'I don't know and that's what we're going to find out.'

'Whatever trouble there was happened three weeks ago.
Lord Astor is now in Ireland.' I posted him there quickly.

'Are you sure?' she asked.

'Of course I'm sure.'

'Well then, get Cliveden on the phone. I want to talk to
someone there.'

I spoke to Charles. There were two telephone lines in the
pantry; he dialled his own line, naturally got the engaged
signal, and put it through to her ladyship. 'Keep on trying,'
she said. He did, using the same ruse, until we were able to
get her mind on to other matters. By the next day it was
all forgotten. I am firmly convinced that she never knew
anything about what had happened. If she had she would
most certainly have spoken to me about it. I was by then

her confidante in everything. So she was spared what most of the rest of the country revelled in.

Today attitudes have changed. People are ashamed of how they behaved at that time and look for a scapegoat. They blame the Press. It's nonsense. The Press give the public what it wants. If it wants a campaign against fox-hunting, it gets it. If it wants a man-hunt, it gets it. It's the law of supply and demand. It was the sanctimonious Members of Parliament that were responsible. Spare me from them! I admit to being a prude; a Yorkshire prude at that. I don't swear, I don't drink much, I'm unmarried and I like it that way, I've a code of behaviour over sex and I've lived by my rules. Come to my flat. You'll find it spotless. Everything in its place, that's me. It's my nature. That's the way I like it. But that doesn't mean that I expect everyone else to live in the same way, or would want them to. Please yourself, get on with it, I won't interfere with you so long as you don't interfere with me. Nor am I the sort of person who goes around saying, 'Isn't it awful? How disgusting! She ought to be ashamed of herself.' The trouble with people is that they worry too much about what other people think of them, and the reason they do that is that they're worried about what other people think and do. I believe if you leave people alone they'll leave you alone. And I mean this on the big scale. Why do we have to gloat when things go wrong for others? Why do we enjoy destruction? Only because we are not prepared to live and let live.

My Lord Billy was a victim of the Profumo Affair and was tried, judged and sentenced by the public on no evidence. My last words on the subject are that I am a better person for having known him.

8 A Family in Wartime

There is a saying that 'no man is a hero to his valet'. Arthur Bushell would give the lie to it on behalf of his lordship, and if it can be taken to apply to a lady and her maid, so would I. This may come as a surprise as I don't seem to have given any heroic impressions of my lady as yet, but heroism requires the occasion and it wasn't until the war that this came. It gave her what she wanted, the opportunity of doing things for people, for individuals, and of being able to see the results of her actions. I suppose I must have listened to Chamberlain's speech on the radio when he announced that we were at war with Germany, but I don't remember where I was. I know it caused both Lord and Lady Astor a lot of distress, because up until the last minute they believed that war could and would be avoided. People now blame them for this and call them appeasers, singling them out as if they were the only ones who didn't want war. They seem to forget that only a few months earlier most people in the country didn't and for the right reasons. The Astors stuck to their guns to the last and, though they may have been wrong, they too did so for the right reasons. Once we were committed, no one could have fought more strongly for their country.

Like everyone else when war came I and the rest of the staff expected things to happen quickly and that there would be big changes. Changes indeed there were: some of the men were called up, others enlisted, and some women went into the Services or industry. Although there was still entertaining it was not on the same scale, so that at the beginning anyway there were fewer people to do less work. Rest Harrow was closed for the duration, but 3 Elliot Terrace, Plymouth was now more our regular home. The city had broken with tradition and had elected a man from outside, his lordship, to be their Lord Mayor, so with her ladyship as one of their Members of Parliament and Lord Astor as the head of civic affairs, both felt it right that they should be down there as much as they could. Her ladyship had to attend at the House of Commons regularly, but she would travel up and back by sleeper whenever possible, so conserving her days. This for a woman in her sixties showed the kind of stuff my lady was made of. It was strange, and I know it gave them both joy that they, Americans by birth, should hold positions of stature and authority in the city of Britain that had closer ties to America than any other. Later, when the port was so much used by the American Navy, they were able to act almost as ambassadors to the frequent and changing visitors; from seamen to admirals – from G.I.s to generals. Another way in which their American birth was of advantage to Plymouth was that, as Lord and Lady Mayoress, the Astors behaved more like their American counterparts and were involved in the government of the city in every way, not, as had been the custom here, just as figureheads. In ordinary times this might have been resented, but in the war as it developed it was so much appreciated that his lordship remained in office for five years.

In the grounds of Cliveden the hospital was reopened and a wing of the house was given to the doctors and nurses. His lordship offered the whole place to the government, but it was considered unsuitable in construction for any particular use. American diplomats and friends visited there and Mr Lee remained in charge if the Astors were away. He was not liable to be called up because of his age. He had served as a sergeant-major in the First World War, which any servant who was hauled over the coals by him recognized and referred to in uncomplimentary terms.

I got used to being a sort of yo-yo. Up in London, down in Plymouth, and occasionally in between at Cliveden. I got blooded in the London air raids when they started, but since there was no point in staying at St James's Square overnight when we were safer just outside London at Cliveden, I didn't see a lot of them. Plymouth had twenty-odd small raids during the first year, but compared with what was to follow, these were of little consequence except to those who were directly affected. All that really merits reporting of our first year of the war was that my lady busied herself sixteen hours a day, seven days a week, and therefore so did I.

We were first directly affected in October 1940 when some incendiary bombs hit 4 St James's Square. It was the same night that Mr Bobbie was injured during an air raid in Kent. It was the first of four hits that the house was to receive. Fortunately it only affected a top corner. Lord and Lady Astor were both away at the time so Mr Lee and I went down from Cliveden to help. Her ladyship's and my bedrooms were both badly burnt. I managed to salvage a few things, but she lost everything. As often happens when there's a fire, it's the water that puts it out that does the damage. Lady Astor's boudoir was swimming in it. We salvaged whatever we could; fortunately there was nothing of great value there since the best things had been moved to Cliveden and stored in the stables. Shortly after this, the Free French Forces took over the house as their head-quarters in London. We still retained the offices at the back and made them into a small flat where we could sleep from time to time. This had its own front door in Babmaes Street, a cul-de-sac near Jermyn Street. Although this wasn't part of the history I learnt at school I understand that Jermyn Street was, during the eighteenth and nine-teenth centuries, a place where gentlemen had their little love-nests and accommodated their mistresses. I was further given to understand that in this century the mistresses were disposed elsewhere, but ladies who entertained gentlemen more by quantity than quality had moved in and personally

At Lord Mildmay's when Queen Mary went visiting.
Here I am amongst the men. We had been out for a drive.

This is when Lady Astor sent
us out in a boat fishing. I am
sitting at the end

With the ghillie at Jura, 1931.
This was a splendid sporting
place for the gentlemen, but
very boring for Lady Astor
and me

My sister Ann as
'Washing Day'

'Eliza Comes to Stay'

My brother-in-law Cyril
Price, as 'National Health'

My sister Olive won first prize
as Nell Gwynn

At the Hotel Astor with a stewardess and a hairdresser from the *Media*.
Lady Astor treated us to a dinner with cocktails and all the trimmings.
This photograph was taken to show we had really been there

In Tucson, Arizona. Arthur
Bushell, Lord Astor's valet,
was having a joke on me

Mirador, Virginia : a home from home. I saw the most wonderful sight in my life there when the fireflies lit up the trees like Christmas. It was one of the seven wonders of the world to me

Lady Astor and Mr George Bernard Shaw on the terrace at Cliveden, 1945, with the blue cedars in the background

On the rocks at Georgetown, Bermuda. I had just seen a huge stinging jellyfish in the sea. I never went in again

Lady Astor dancing with a sailor on Plymouth Hoe, 1942. She was full of fun and ready to join in anything

LIST OF JEWELS IN LADY ASTOR'S
MAID'S CHARGE.

Items on In Policy

No:on Insurance.
Policy.

BROOCHES.

✓2. Diamond Bow Brooch. Silver set, gold back.

✓3. altered in to 2 earrings
March 1938 4. 1 Pearl is the clip
Pearl and Diamond Bar Brooch. 2 Brills, and three pearls. Ear 330

Diamond & Aquamarine Brooch set in platinum, gold pin. *Treasure Sale* the square one with drop.

✓ Not insured Given to Miss Marylin CRN 1936.
Antique Filigree gold oval brooch set with white sapphires.

✓ Not insured. Gold & Enamel Flying Duck, Safety Pin Brooch.

✓ 5. Given to Lowie Manning
Coral, Onyx & Diamond Square Brooch, open centre set in Platinum. (4) 225

✓ 6. Emerald, Turquoise, Moonstone & Diamond Brooch, in form of two pear shaped pieces put end to end. Diamonds & Emeralds at intervals round gallery. Platinum Set. 5 150

✓ 8. snap on diamond necklace.
Diamond Rectangular Brooch, made up of two rows of diamonds, and in centre a row of two brilliants and one brilliant set separately at intervals, the whole set in platinum. 50

✓ 9. A plain diamond brooch in form of three oval double rings. Given to Mrs Grenfell Xmas 1945. 75

✓ 11. Diamond Bow Brooch platinum set - blue white diamonds.

✓ 12. Diamond Oval platinum set brooch. ✓ 10 300

✓ 14. Sold to Biggs 1953.
Emerald & Diamond Flower Brooch. (Emerald about 12 cts.) altered. Emerald & sapphire brooch. 99. 150

✓ 15. Given to Lady Mueller 1952
Rose Cut Diamond & Pink Tourmaline Brooch. (Outside border with leaf collets, surrounding tourmaline.) on handbag.

✓ 16. Turquoise & Diamond Gold set Antique Brooch. 13. (9 Turquoises).

✓ 17. Diamond & Green Enamel Circle Brooch. (Centre Daisy Circle Rose Diamond - Diamond and enamel entwined & outer circle of diamonds.)

✓ Not insured missing
Antique Rose Diamond Circle Brooch (Half Pearl centre.)

✓ 18. Diamond & Emerald Bar Brooch in form of a centre emerald with 2 rows of diamonds round on a diamond set bar. 75

found R.N. /19. Missing Diamond Fox Head Mask on a safety pin, gold set.

R. Harrison aug 6th 39. Fur Boxes April 10th 1929 ✓ W. B.H. Browne March 20th 1929.

Charles Dean the butler, Otto the chef, two French dailies and me

This is a page from my own record of the jewellery that was handed over to me when I went to Cliveden. I kept the book up-to-date as Lady Astor had pieces altered or gave them away. This was my protection against losses: I could account for the whereabouts of everything

With Otto the chef; setting off from Eaton Square for a month's holiday in Vienna, 1961

Lady Astor in her last years . . .

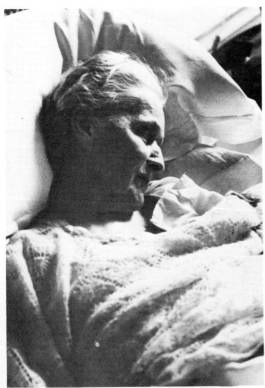

. . . and a few weeks before she died

advertised their wares on the street corners. If I hadn't have learned it I would have soon discovered it when we lived there. Her ladyship must also have found out because the nearest she ever came to a sexy joke was when she would announce to her friends to try to shock them that she was the most important woman in Jermyn Street, the queen of the tarts. One night when she was coming to the house she saw a young American soldier lying drunk on the pavement. She helped him to his feet and as he staggered up she said, 'Come on get up, you're coming home with me.'

'Oh no I'm not,' he said, and he slumped down again. 'My mother warned me against women like you.'

'Women like me?' she screamed at him, 'I'm old enough to be your grandmother.'

Eventually she got the protesting soldier into the flat, and had him put to bed. The next morning she gave him a lecture on the evils of drink and a five-pound note, and sent him packing. She loved drunks, they gave her a chance to preach what she practised.

Babmaes Street as the war progressed became a proper sort of courting place. It was not far from Rainbow Corner, the American Forces Club near Piccadilly Circus, though I think it was used by all nationalities. It was embarrassing for anyone coming in at night, and according to William, our odd man, it was the same in the morning when he went out to scrub the steps. I remembering him complaining, 'I don't mind them feeding on the fruits of love but I wish they wouldn't leave the skins around for me to sweep up.' We were all of us to suffer from the wretched things. A few mornings after William's complaints he came into the kitchen grinning all over. 'It was his lordship,' he said. 'He went off early this morning and I hadn't had a chance to do my sweeping. It had been a particularly bad night and as he came to the step he couldn't help but see them. He stopped in his tracks, sort of shuddered down his back and then walked off with his head held high as if ignoring them. This was a pity because one stuck to his shoe. He couldn't ignore that. He removed it with the ferrule of his umbrella and moved off, but it had now stuck to his brolly. He stopped again and trod it from there with his foot. "Here we go again," I thought. "It's a sort of perpetual motion." Well, he made certain he got rid of it this time. Then he turned round and he must have seen me grinning at him. "I shall report this to the police," he said, as though it was all my fault, and then he stalked off.'

As I've said, I've suffered from one and so did her lady-ship. I was embarrassed but she apparently wasn't. I was astonished that she told me about it. She'd always been so squeamish over such things, but somehow she became more tolerant during the war. I suppose we all did.

The unexpected was something I learned to expect from my lady. One evening, quite early on in the war, when Jim Brand her nephew was spending part of his leave with us at St James's Square, she suddenly said to me, 'Get your best bib and tucker on, Rose, Jim's taking you out to dinner.'

'That's news to me my lady, because he hasn't asked me,' I said.

'No, quite rightly he asked me, but let's have none of your North Country stubbornness, go and get changed.'

Off we both went and had a whale of a time. As we left the restaurant he said, 'Let's go to a nightclub, Rose.' Since her ladyship had given her permission I agreed, but like Cinderella my eye was constantly on the clock. Jim was in no hurry to go home. 'But your aunt will be waiting on the doorstep for us,' I protested.

'Nonsense, Rose, she'll have been in bed hours ago.'

'Like to bet?' I said, and we settled on a five-shilling wager, a fortune for me, but I had no worries about losing it. We rang the bell and within seconds there her ladyship was at the front door and it was one o'clock in the morning!

Nowadays people get the key of the door at an early age, but it wasn't until my lady was eighty that I was allowed one.

After the Free French took over, a kind of plague hit St James's Square – rats. With the bombing they'd been disturbed in London. Whether it was that they liked French food or what, I don't know, but they invaded us. They were everywhere, under the floorboards, running along the gutters, in amongst the garbage cans. It was like living in Hamelin. If only I'd had the courage I'd have introduced a cat into the house, but I knew what it would mean if her ladyship saw it. The rats were worse at night. At around midnight, when the streets had quietened down, I'd hear them scuffling to get outside like a regiment on the move, then at about four in the morning they'd pour back in again. I used to nearly suffocate with my head under the bedclothes. As far as I'm concerned I class rats with creepy crawlies, I can't abide either.

The war really began and ended for me at Plymouth. It began on 20 March, 1941. I had been down there for some days beforehand with my lady getting ready for a visit of the Royals. Although such visits were informal, obviously certain preparations had to be made, since his lordship and my lady as first citizens of Plymouth would have to escort the King and Queen around the city and to entertain them. The day was a success; their Majesties were given a great welcome and were obviously impressed with what they saw. I remember Lady Astor telling me some time later that a matron at one of the hospitals told the Queen that she thought they were ready if the hour ever came. By the following morning she'd given living proof that they were and she was to be called upon to do so constantly for many months afterwards.

Their Majesties had tea with us at 3 Elliot Terrace. Just as they were leaving the sirens sounded. Nobody took any particular notice as daylight raids were very rare at that time, particularly so far from the French coast. Although we weren't to know at the time it was a reconnaissance plane. The King and Queen left by train and on the Astors' return from the station, dinner was served.

I remember Mr Ben Robertson, the American journalist, was staying with us. He was one of the brave band of newspapermen from the States who reported on how Britain was taking it and he felt that he'd got to be in the front line where the trouble was. I don't know whether he was looking for trouble when he came to Plymouth but he certainly found it. Just as they were having coffee the sirens sounded and within seconds the anti-aircraft guns were in action. Then it seemed as though all hell was let loose. I said to myself, 'This is it, my gal,' and as I was a member of the fire-fighting team for the Terrace, got my tin helmet on and saw to it that we had buckets of water and stirrup pumps on all the floors. Every available vessel was called into action. The bombs and the incendiaries started raining down, though fortunately not on us. Her ladyship was nowhere to be seen. Foolishly and fearlessly she and Mr Robertson were standing outside in the street watching it all happen. I called her in, but she took no notice. I persevered and over the noise of the bombs and guns I heard a few, 'shut up, Roses.' What a time and under what circumstances to hear that, I remember thinking.

I don't know whether it was my voice that summoned him, but after a while an air raid warden came along and ordered them both into the house. It was just as well he did because as they came into the hall a stick of bombs fell nearby and blew the glass of the front door out. Both Mr Robertson and my lady had the good sense to throw themselves on the floor as they heard them coming down. I helped my lady up and we went to the shelter in the basement with Mr Robertson sensibly following. As we were going down she was reciting the 23rd Psalm: 'The Lord is my shepherd: therefore can I lack nothing . . .', and when

we were in the shelter she began on the 46th Psalm, 'God
is our hope and strength: a very present help in trouble. . . .'
She seemed serene as she sat there and quite without fear.
She chatted about her childhood days in Virginia as though
she was trying to put the fear out of our hearts. I occupied
myself picking the bits of glass from her hair which had
lodged there as the door pane smashed. She started talking
to Mr Robertson about me and my time with her, how we
had worked together for thirteen years. I loved her for using
the word 'together' and not 'for'; it made it seem like a
partnership, not a job. Then she went on to say that I was
the only woman who would put up with her and she was
the only woman who would put up with me. I thought it
was time I said something. 'Mr Robertson, her ladyship is
the kind of woman who takes a lot of understanding. It
took me nearly three years.' Bombs or no bombs, her ladyship still had the last word. 'There, Rose,' she laughed, 'you
have the advantage of me because I've never got to understand you.'

During this time Plymouth was being subjected to a
bombardment comparable only with that of Coventry. The
house constantly trembled and the noise of the guns and
bombs was terrifying. Then young Jim Brand, my lady's
nephew (later to be killed in a tank in Germany), who was
staying with us and was with Arthur Bushell (who had been
an officer in the Machine Guns in the First World War),
fire-watching on the roof, ran down to tell us that an incendiary bomb had gone through the slates and set light
to a beam. Up we all went with buckets of sand and water
and eventually got the fire under control. There were four
more incendiaries in the street which had to be dealt with.
By the time we had done this the raiders had gone, leaving
the city burning and in ruins. I eventually got my lady to
her room. She wanted to be out in the street, but as his
lordship and I told her, her work would begin the next day
and she must be ready for it. Thank God she was able to

get some rest and we could clear things up a bit before snatching a couple of hours in armchairs.

We were all of us up and about early the following morning. Before breakfast my lord and lady went walking the streets, and came back looking very sad and strained. They had a big day in front of them: Mr Menzies the Australian Prime Minister was visiting Plymouth, and as well as looking after him there was the tremendous job of assessing the damage, reviewing the efficiency of the services, rehousing, feeding, clothing and comforting. It seemed an impossible task but they set about it sensibly and efficiently. There were no theatricals from my lady, just confidence and strength. His lordship was authoritative and efficient, a great organizer. Mr Menzies fell in step with them, his schedule of visits was cancelled, he was content just to go along. He was to have been entertained at Elliot Terrace, but that was out of the question now so he dined at the residence of the Admiral.

We servants spent the day clearing and cleaning. We could have saved ourselves the trouble, as events turned out. Almost to the minute of the night before, the sirens sounded and, what seemed only seconds later, we were showered with incendiaries. Arthur Bushell, Florrie the housemaid and I rushed upstairs making for the roof. As we were nearing the top landing there was a scream of bombs falling. Fortunately the landing windows had been left open to get rid of the smell of burning, because as we reached them we got the blast of bombs which knocked us against the wall. We were out of breath, but we must have found some from somewhere because the next thing I remember was being down in our basement shelter. There was just nothing we could do, the onslaught was too terrific. If the house was burning over our heads it would have to. If we went up there we were likely to be blown to bits anyway. It was the feeling of helplessness that got me down, not being able to do anything but just wait, hope and pray.

But what a comfort prayer is at such a time. I don't think it was just selfish prayer either. I found myself thinking of all sorts of people and of course I was desperately worried for my lady. It didn't seem possible that people could live through what was going on outside. The raid continued for about three hours, then just as suddenly as it had started the noise ceased, but the comparative silence was punctuated by the crackle of the fires and the occasional burst of a time-bomb.

We went to look on the roof. The incendiaries there had burnt themselves out and by some miracle we had escaped once again from the high explosives, but as I looked over Plymouth it seemed as though nowhere else had. It was a horrifying yet magnificent sight, like a gigantic volcano crater, a city on the boil. All immediately around us had been destroyed. No. 1 Elliot Terrace had been hit, though much of it was still standing. A house at the back had been completely destroyed and the whole street seemed in ruins. There was nothing for me to do so I turned back and went to see what damage our house had sustained. I looked into my lady's room and when I saw it with windows shattered, walls cracked, part of the ceiling down, glass splinters everywhere, I couldn't help thinking about the useless work I'd done the day before. I got a broom, swept up a bit and got my lady's bed sleepable in, but by now I was worried out of my wits thinking that something must have happened to her. I went down to join the others. Just as I got to the foot of the stairs her ladyship came rushing in, she looked frantic. 'Rose,' she screamed, 'thank God you're safe,' and she flung her arms round me. 'I'll never leave you again,' she sobbed. My tears started to flow too though I was astonished at her outburst. It later transpired that as she approached the house she saw the shells of the buildings at the back of us and thought that we had been hit too. It was an astonishing show of emotion, particularly from my lady, but they were emotional hours when we were all on the brink of eternity.

My lady was completely exhausted. She and Lord Astor had been on duty all day and had been out with the services during the raid. His lordship was little better, but having delivered Lady Astor into my hands, he set off walking the ruined streets. We tried to stop him. We told him it was foolishness, but he wouldn't listen, or rather didn't seem to hear. He was like an automaton, all feeling had drained from him. After I'd got her ladyship to bed fully clothed, since her room was freezing, I thought about sleep, there seemed to be nowhere for me except the basement, and I felt claustrophobic after the hours I'd spent there during the raids, so I made for the roof again and joined Arthur Bushell. We stood there watching the city burn, seeing the flames from one house moving to the next and demolishing that, and eventually the whole row. There was nothing we could say about it, we'd said everything and seen everything.

Arthur eventually decided to walk along the roofs of the terrace to check that all was right with the other houses. I just stayed and watched. Suddenly I saw a huge black mass rising from over the road. I don't know whether I threw myself down or was blown down. A time-bomb had exploded in a nearby garage. I lay on my face deafened by the explosion, but not so much that I couldn't hear the rubble falling around me. One or two bits hit me. Luckily I had two coats on so I got away with a few bruises. Arthur at the time was behind a chimney-stack on the roof of No. 8 and escaped everything. He came running to me and picked me up. 'I thought you were a goner, Rose,' he said as we staggered together downstairs. 'No,' I replied, 'I'm a cat, I've got nine lives.' Her ladyship was none the worse for the explosion, but claustrophobia or no claustrophobia, I spent the rest of the night in the basement with the others because though I'd boasted of having nine lives, I wasn't sure how many I'd got left.

Though it hadn't seemed possible, the next morning was

worse than the one before. I went out at daybreak to see the devastation around us. Somehow it looked worse in the daylight: skeletons of houses, twisted girders, wrecks of cars, the rubble that was once a home and possessions strewn across the streets; pathetic things like children's dolls, lying dirty and lonely. I saw a wounded spaniel dog with a little boy standing guarding it, and then eventually the R.S.P.C.A. men who came and lifted it tenderly away. People were standing around helplessly; exhausted, dirty and apathetic. I couldn't watch, I felt I was intruding on their private grief.

I made my way back to the house and tried to rouse myself to start tidying and cleaning it up. My lady had left. There was no routine now, no ringing of bells, no 'Where have you been, Rose?' It was all for one and one for all. Only our French chef Monsieur Lamé kept to his place, the kitchen, and he was hard put to it because there was no gas now or electricity. He found an oil stove somewhere and worked a few miracles with that. 'We must eat to beat the Hun,' he said to everyone, as a sort of personal slogan. Then he would go into a string of expletives about the Germans as though they were his own particular enemies. I had to remind him that we British weren't feeling too kindly disposed towards them either. I must say Lamé worked wonders in the kitchen throughout the war and was particularly good to me. 'Eating keeps your strength up,' he would say when I protested he was giving me too big a portion.

I felt a bit lackadaisical all that morning as I and the other servants got some order out of the chaos. We were beginning to see the results of our labours when at one o'clock her ladyship turned up with a party of air raid wardens. 'We've all of us got to get out, Rose,' she said. 'There are six unexploded bombs surrounding the house.' If ever I felt like swearing it was then. All that hard work and now we'd got to evacuate the place. I don't think I was worried about the bombs even after my experience with the delayed action one the night before. I packed her ladyship's things and my few bits and pieces, grumbling all the time. We were separating: Arthur Bushell and I went to a hotel in Ivybridge, a nearby town, and the Astors went to stay with some friends.

Once we'd arrived in Ivybridge I stopped moaning. It was wonderful to see a fresh clean bedroom again and think there was a possibility that I should sleep between sheets that night. Even so, I was keeping my fingers crossed. We weren't far from Plymouth and the surrounding area had already suffered some damage. In the event we were lucky, but every day I was reminded of what the city had been through, since Arthur and I travelled to Plymouth to help the Astors in any way that they wanted. It was now that I saw the great work that my lady was doing. She was in her element: she was helping people. Arthur and I ran messages for her and distributed clothes where they were needed, many of which had been sent earlier from the States having been collected by her ladyship's friends and relations there. How wonderful America was in that way. There's a story of how forty children arrived at school barefoot holding their shoes in their hands and saying, 'Give these to the children of Plymouth, they need them more than we do.' And of another school that raised a thousand pounds in a few days when they heard of the bombing. Lady Astor was proud to be able to speak of her country's sympathy and help. Then we'd be running backwards and forwards from the various emergency centres reporting their requirements. We were always told to look for cases of individual hardship, for people who were too proud to ask for help, or who didn't know what was available for them. Nor did his lordship or my lady leave this to other people: every evening when they weren't directing or administrating they'd be on the streets to see for themselves.

I remember once her ladyship was going round a hospital

chatting up the patients and seeing what they needed. She came to one bed where there was a young boy of about sixteen who looked very poorly. 'He's suffering from pneumonia and shock,' said the nurse. 'He's very unhappy but we don't know why, he's French and no one in the ward can talk to him.'

In an instant my lady was rattling away at him in his own language. 'He wants to get near his brother in Liverpool. Is he fit to travel?'

A doctor was called. 'It's a risk,' he said, 'he'd have to go in an oxygen tent. It would mean travelling first-class and he hasn't any money.'

'That's no problem,' replied my lady. 'I have. Get him ready and I'll be in touch with you.'

She rang Ellen Wilkinson, a local Member of Parliament, who arranged a hospital bed there and the boy was on the train within hours. It's a small incident but typical of so many. His lordship, while he wasn't so communicative, did things his own way. It was said at that time about the Astors that, 'She found out what needed doing, and he saw that it was done.'

Another big job that she attended to was seeing that those who were away in the Services were kept informed about their parents' welfare and whereabouts; a special bureau was set up to deal with phone calls and written inquiries. It wasn't an easy job but she knew from personal experience how necessary it was. In between times she'd be popping backwards and forwards to London to attend to her Parliamentary duties, and what she'd seen that had gone wrong at Plymouth during the raids made her critical of the government. She became unpopular with the Churchill administration. She and the Prime Minister had never been exactly bosom pals anyway. However since she was as usual speaking the truth as she saw it, it worked, and things were either done or changed.

This then was the time when a lady became a heroine to

her maid. Previously I had had a deep and growing affection for her despite – and sometimes even because of – her faults. Now in battle her qualities were shown. Her courage, not the 'backs to the wall' stoic kind of British courage, but the flashing tempestuous rousing roistering courage of the Virginian exemplified by the way she would turn cartwheels in air raid shelters to cause a diversion when things were at their worst. Not your sixty-one-year-old Nancy Astor, Lady of Cliveden, hostess to the aristocracy and Member of Parliament, but Nannie the wild-eyed girl who rode unbroken horses. And along with this went the softer, compassionate creature; the voice behind the sad Virginian songs, that would comfort a mother whose child had been killed while her own heart was grieving for the mother, yet hardening against the Whitehall officials who in their shortsightedness had not declared Plymouth an area for the evacuation of children. Then catching the night train to London and the next day telling Parliament what should have been done and being accused that by saying what she had, she'd given information and help to the enemy. Yet still not giving a tinker's cuss. This was a woman I could idolize.

Still, at times her waywardness showed through. While the raids and the danger seemed to increase her strength, they took their toll of his lordship's. Tramping around in all weathers he got a chill which, ignored, became a fever. It was obvious he had to rest, but he refused to return to Cliveden, because he wanted to be near Plymouth. It was decided that he should go and stay at a hotel near the little town of Rock in Cornwall, and that I should go there with him as a kind of nurse/valet. Her ladyship was to accompany us there and spend a day or two with him. The day we were leaving there was a lunch party at Elliot Terrace for some of the local dignitaries. The house had been repaired quickly for use as the mayoral offices. It happened that on that morning some chocolates and sweets had arrived from

America for the people of Plymouth. After lunch my lady asked his lordship to get some of these for her. He explained that they were not intended for her, but for others whose need was greater. She straightaway went into a tantrum, was rude and spiteful to him in front of the guests, and told him she wouldn't now go to Rock with him. His lordship left the room. I didn't know about this at the time, I was told about it later by Florrie the housemaid who came with a message from her ladyship that I was to unpack her things as she wasn't now going away. I started emptying her cases, then in came Arthur Bushell with a summons from his lordship. When I went to his office I could see at once that he was in a dreadful state: he had difficulty with his breathing and his face was high-coloured. I thought he must have had a stroke, and to this day I'm convinced I was right.

'Rose,' he said, 'Lady Astor has upset me badly. She now refuses to go to Rock. She must go and I need your help to see that she does.' I was moved by what he said and very worried at his condition.

'Very well, my lord, I'll see to it.' I waited for the guests to leave then went into the drawing room. 'I hear from Florrie, my lady, that you're not going to Rock.'

'No I'm not,' she said, rushed out of the room and up the stairs. I was ready for her and caught her on the landing. I got hold of her by the shoulders and shook her.

'Listen to me,' I said, 'I don't know what you've done to his lordship, but he's now very ill indeed. You'll go with him to Rock and if you don't I'll write to all the boys and tell them that his condition is your fault because you were greedy and selfish over a few miserable sweets.' Then I threw her away from me in anger and waited for the storm to burst over me. To my astonishment she looked at me meek and ashamed.

'All right, Rose, I'll go,' she said. At that moment it was hard to believe that this sorry-looking person was my heroine of a few hours before and would be again a couple of days later.

During the next six weeks at Rock I got to know his lordship more intimately. I think I rather enjoyed having a man to look after and spoil. I did all I could for him, though it's difficult nursing a Christian Scientist because you have no doctor's orders to go on. Once he was over the chill and the effects of the row with my lady I tried to get him to continue to rest. It wasn't easy. When he and Lady Astor had seen the damage inflicted on Plymouth after the first two terrible raids, they said publicly, 'We will rebuild it again,' which those who heard it thought was meant to apply to them and the other citizens, as I'm sure it was. But by the way his lordship began to work now it seemed as if he meant it to apply personally and he saw this period at Rock as an ideal time to get things started. The government had other things to think about, so he worked without its help, and it was during this time that the new foundations for Plymouth were laid and the great work was conceived that Professor Abercrombie later carried out as the planning consultant. If the Astors loved Plymouth when it was whole they loved it more now when it was so badly wounded. It was at this time too that a codicil was written into their wills saying that in the event of them being killed during a raid, they wished to be buried in a common grave with the other casualties.

So it was that much of my work was answering the phone, taking and giving messages, sending telegrams and generally acting as a sort of secretary-cum-mouthpiece. I remember one day, while I was fumbling over the reading of some message to him, his lordship said, 'Give it to me, Rose.'

'No, my lord, it's not meant for you to read.'

He roared with laughter. 'Don't you think I'm old enough, Rose?' he said.

'It's not that, my lord, it's written in my particular brand of shorthand.' This seemed to amuse him even more. Still, as he had to admit when he was well enough to return to Plymouth, it had worked.

Almost exactly four weeks after the first two appalling raids on Plymouth the Germans struck again, and the night attacks of 21, 22, 23, 28 and 29 April, were as ferocious as the earlier ones had been. Now their main target was the Devonport area, the dockland. By the end of the month the city had become the most heavily bombed of any in the country. There was hardly a building that had escaped some damage. His lordship and I were safe at Rock I'm grateful to say, but her ladyship was often in amongst it all.

My stay in Rock with his lordship had an eventful ending for me. I received from him the first tip I had ever been given during my time in service. I'd had presents, of course, from my lady and others, but those came as it were in the line of duty. When we left Rock he handed me an envelope containing money. I took it as I'd seen other servants take such things and regarded it as a tip, something given for that bit of extra service. I was quite thrilled and excited about it.

I remember shortly after speaking of it to Mr Lee and we got on to the subject of tipping in general. 'You know, Rose, there's a mistaken idea among some people that we behave as we do in the hope of getting a financial reward, and particularly do they think this is true of menservants. How wrong they are. I can't recall in the whole of my service ever doing anything because I thought there would be something at the end of it. Naturally when I was a footman and I was asked to valet for a visitor I expected to be given something for the work that I'd put in, but my opinion or respect for him was never formed or changed by the amount he gave me. Most gentlemen work on a given scale, just as you and I do with porters and taxi-drivers and the like. Nevertheless I never could like the person who rushed about as he was leaving, sort of not seeing you so as to save himself a sovereign, neither did any of my men, and strangely enough that kind of behaviour generally came from those whom we knew to be loaded.'

From now on my lady and I went backwards and forwards like shuttlecocks between London and Plymouth. We rented two different houses in Rock, Bray House and later Trebetherick. It did mean that after either of them had finished their work in Plymouth they could be sure of a reasonable night's sleep. Some people may criticize them for leaving the battleground when others couldn't, but commanders have to if they're to be in a fit condition to direct operations in the future, and in these circumstances I looked on my two as generals. From May onwards, we were lent a house, Bickham, on Dartmoor. It was easier and quicker for us to get in and out of Plymouth. I don't know whether someone told Hitler about our move, but the moment we got in there the bombs began to fall around us again.

By now of course our jobs had ceased to have any definition, we just did whatever needed doing. Cleaning up seemed to be my main occupation. Since we'd left Cliveden for Bickham in something of a hurry, I'd only packed a few things and the frock I'd got on at the time was the one I had to work in. Whether it was a bit worn or whether it was the effort I put into my work, it eventually split, making a big hole underneath my arm. As Arthur Bushell was going into Plymouth with her ladyship, I asked him to get me an overall for decency's sake. He returned with a parcel containing a maternity smock. He pretended to be very penitent when I opened it so I couldn't be sure whether he'd done it on purpose. Anyway it protected my anatomy, so I put it on.

That evening when I went in to dress my lady she took one look at me and screamed, 'Oh Rose, I didn't know you were in that sort of trouble.' I tried to explain. 'It's no use trying to blame that on enemy action,' she said.

196

In exasperation I pulled the smock up. 'It's only a hole I'm trying to hide.' We both of us ended up screaming with laughter. His lordship popped his head round the door and said, 'Oh it's you two, I thought it was the air raid sirens.' He eventually ended up in stitches too when the situation was explained to him. I never found out whether Arthur had done it purposely or not. If he did it was one of the best jokes he ever perpetrated.

I won't say that bombs in the country are better than those in town, but they're different. To start with, when you hear a stick of them coming down you don't find yourself wishing them on your neighbours by praying that they'll miss you. To find the next morning that they've hit a sheep or a cow and made their craters in a field brings only a sense of relief, it doesn't trouble the conscience. But while they're actually falling the country has its hazards. We seemed to attract incendiaries and as Arthur and I continued our fire-watching at Roughborough we were kept very busy. Baskets of the wretched things were dropped over and around us. It's one thing putting one out on a roof or a pavement, but we were kept running around the grounds and the fields with our buckets of sand and water and our hoses and stirrup-pumps.

Now, in normal circumstances I'm fond of roses, but their bushes at night are a hazard, and if there were any around I seemed to find them in my chases to put out incendiaries. I'd study the garden in daylight to make sure that I wouldn't make the same mistake again, but there is something about the dark that makes me lose any sense of direction. Then often Arthur and I would be out in the fields, and though I may not have shown much sympathy for cows and sheep earlier on, I felt even less as I skated about in their pats and droppings.

Eventually Arthur and I struck a bargain. I'd do the near incendiaries and he would tackle the more distant ones. There's a saying 'He travels fastest who travels alone,' and that was certainly true of Arthur one night when he ran to put one out. One moment I saw him silhouetted on the skyline, and the next moment he wasn't there. I thought I heard a cry from his direction but I couldn't be sure so I busied myself putting some earth on a nearby incendiary. When it was out I called into the direction in which he'd gone and got a muffled response. I went to look for him, picking my way carefully, which was just as well because I found myself on the edge of a small sandpit, and from the noises that came from below I realized that that was where Arthur had disappeared into a few minutes before. I eventually worked my way round it and rescued him. He was none the worse for his fall, but was covered in sand and mud. 'Perhaps you'd like to borrow my overall,' I said to him as we went back to the house.

I also found that bombs can have some funny effects on people. One night Arthur and I were outside the house, we thought that incendiaries were raining down on us. Well, it's one thing to put them out, it's another to be hit by them, so we made for the house. In the hall were my lady and his lordship, looking somewhat startled. 'Where did they drop?' she asked. Both Arthur and I tried to reply. We must have looked very comic because although we mouthed the words no sound came out, we couldn't utter. We were later told that three bombs had dropped some way beyond the house and that what we thought were incendiaries was in fact the earth and stones from the craters they'd made, and that the blast had in some way stopped us from speaking. 'I want to get a supply of them,' her ladyship said, somewhat cheekily, I thought, when we'd recovered, 'then I might be able to get a word in edgeways.'

One of the more pathetic sights around this time was in the evenings when people were leaving the city on foot for the comparative peace of the countryside. They would sleep under hedges, in barns, out on the moors, anywhere where they could feel safe from the bombs. If a car of ours was returning from Plymouth it was always packed with these nocturnal refugees. Then from time to time her ladyship would ask friends to stay the night. We always had to be ready to receive them and, more difficult still with the rationing, to feed them. I remember one evening when she turned up with three sailor boys. 'They're hungry and need a good rest,' she said as she put them in my charge in the servants' hall. We gave them eggs and bacon, our personal rations, and prepared beds for them. Then the sirens sounded and soon our peace was shattered. There was a lot of activity that night and the sailors were kept busy putting out fires and running down to the village where help was needed. At about four in the morning all was quiet so we made ready for bed, only to be told that the sailors had to rejoin their ship at six o'clock and that they were hungry again. So we cooked them more eggs and bacon – this time it was her ladyship's rations though she never knew it – and saw them on their way, eventually thumbing a lift for them on a passing lorry. About a week later her ladyship got what she described as a lovely letter from them, thanking her for all she had done. 'We gave them a good time, eh, Rose?'

While we were on Dartmoor Mr David spent part of his leave there, looking very splendid as an officer of the Marines. He saw some action while he was with us. One night we were standing together on the lawn when I heard a bomb whistling over. I went to ground. He stood his and when I'd recovered myself said somewhat patronizingly, 'Only a bit of shrapnel, Rose.' I was convinced it was a bomb that hadn't exploded, but couldn't argue with an officer who spoke with such calm authority.

The following morning there was an explosion which could only have come from a delayed action bomb. I was in the sitting-room at the time with Lady Astor and her son. 'What on earth was that?' said her ladyship.

'That,' I said, 'was Mr David's bit of shrapnel going off.' I'm glad to say he had the decency to wince.

Nineteen forty-one was Plymouth's most terrible year and probably my lady's greatest. It wasn't that she'd changed – she just had the opportunity of showing her real quality. I was rewarded too. It made the years I'd spent with her so very much more worthwhile. Service is something you give without expecting anything in return. When you get it it somehow has a purpose.

By the end of the year the raids had decreased. Indeed in 1942 nothing of importance in the way of air action was recorded. Now America was in the war so the Astors, on top of their other duties, became unofficial ambassadors to our friends who had now become our allies. They were of course ideally suited and not only because of their birth. My lady revelled in it and she became almost bilingual, reverting constantly to her Deep South drawl. We had moved back to Elliot Terrace and a part of the house next door had been incorporated in ours as offices. We were entertaining again and having visitors, many of whom now were Americans, officers from all the services. The G.I.s and other ranks were not neglected by my lady, as she superintended the opening of canteens and clubs for them. I particularly remember General Lee staying the night with us. I went up to his room after he'd left to make his bed, and had the surprise of my life. The bed was laid out as if for a kit inspection; it was impeccable. I ran and fetched my lady so that she could see it. She was as delighted as I was and as we left the room she turned and saluted the bed, American fashion, 'Thank you, General,' she drawled.

The year may have been peaceful, but it was busy. There was one event which caused my lady a great sadness. The death of the Duke of Kent, who with his wife Princess Marina had been a regular visitor to Cliveden before the war, and whose visits to us at Plymouth had been even more frequent because he always stayed with us when he inspected R.A.F. airfields in the district. His plane crashed in Scotland during August 1942. It was only a day or two after he had been with us with his pilot Squadron Leader Fergusson and his batman John Hall. John had been his valet before the war. Charles Dean and he were great friends, and Charles was also well acquainted with the Duke and always used to look after him when he and the Princess went to stay with Mrs Bouverie, for whom he was then butler and was a regular visitor to Coppins, the Duke's country place, always spending Ascot week there. Such was their relationship that whenever John Hall knew that the Duke was to be anywhere where Dean would be he took the days off, telling his Highness that Charles would be a more than adequate substitute. The Duke must have been of the same mind because perhaps Charles's most treasured possession today is a cigarette case which was given him inscribed 'George and Marina'. Even the Royals don't give that sort of thing easily.

The mention of Mrs Bouverie brings to mind a conversation I had with Charles Dean recently. I asked him why she had been such a friend of the Royals. It appears that her mother, Mrs Willie James, was perhaps the most famous or notorious of all King Edward VII's mistresses. I couldn't see this as a reason for giving her the entreé to Buckingham Palace. Charles then muttered something about blood being thicker than water, and when I asked him to explain, he said that in Edwardian times the children often took after the men that their mothers most admired, like people take after their dogs and cats today. It was all in the mind, he said. His Mrs Bouverie must have been hot-blooded like her mother, because she married three times.

While the war gave some women the chance of not having to worry about their appearance, if possible my lady became more particular. She was not one for dressing up to look like the working classes so that they would feel she was one of them. She believed it boosted people's morale to see her smart and well turned out, and it gave the impression that come what might Hitler wasn't going to get her down, or change her way of life. Also I think it helped her to keep going. It was a challenge to me with clothing on coupons. Fortunately she had a large wardrobe and by my cutting up and restyling I suppose you could have said when you looked at her, 'You wouldn't think there was a war on.' Like many others she did fiddle a few coupons. I've got letters from her to prove it, and of course I gave her what I could spare from my ration. Friends in America also sent her things. All very reprehensible you may say, but it's very human, and feminine. It got her into trouble. In the summer of 1943 she wrote to a Mr Yandall, a friend of hers in the Red Cross, and asked him to bring stockings and clothes over for her when he next flew to Britain. The letter was opened by the censor, proceedings were taken against her and she was summoned to appear at Bow Street Magistrates' Court. Some of the newspapers took a 'holier than thou' attitude against her, but she herself made light of it. She was speaking in Parliament the same morning that she had to appear and when the time came for her to leave she said a sort of 'Toodle-oo, I'm off to Bow Street,' to the Members and nearly got a round of applause for it. Apparently the people who administer the laws in this country are not so light-hearted as those who make them. She told me that the magistrate was not in the least amused, ticked her off as if she was a naughty schoolgirl and fined her £50. It was water off a duck's back and as a punishment definitely backfired. When her American friends heard about it she was flooded with nylons.

While the latter years of the war when the tide turned in our favour were not uneventful and often exciting, there is little to record from a servant's point of view. The old order had changed. Mr Lee and the housekeeper, with a skeleton staff, many of them dailies, the older married women, kept Cliveden running remarkably smoothly. The chef managed with little help in the kitchens, but then there wasn't the food available and the amount of entertaining was comparatively negligible. The gardens and greenhouses were just maintained.

It was a period of stagnation for town and country houses. It was also a time of enlightenment, too, for in many places where for years scant attention had been paid to kitchens and the servants' quarters below stairs, mistresses were now paying the penalty. They were having to work down there themselves and, with the bombing, suddenly the basement rooms became the most important in the house – and the most lived in. Yet many of them were damp, dark, poorly heated and their cooking and cleaning facilities were old-fashioned. For the Astor staff, and particularly the old faithfuls of whom I had now become one, the most striking change was in relationships. No longer did the distinction of servant and master apply. We were family. We'd soldiered together, looked death in the face and suffered the loss of many friends. We'd been shown qualities which no other circumstances would have demonstrated to us, and had shared emotions that would otherwise have remained hidden. We'd liked what we'd seen and these things were now ties as strong as those of class and birth. They are bonds that few if any will ever know again. They have given my life a purpose.

By the end of 1944 when victory in Europe was assured, two decisions were made which were to change the shape of our lives. His lordship, partly because of ill-health and partly because of political pressures in Plymouth, decided not to stand again as Lord Mayor. It grieved him I know because of all the work that he had done for the reconstruction of the city and which he now very largely had to hand over to others.

Her ladyship also decided not to stand as a Member of the Sutton Division of Plymouth at the next general election. I say she decided; this is a distortion of the truth. It was decided for her by his lordship, with the support of the family. She was against it and gave way only under pressure, then spent years resenting it and showing her resentment to those who had pressured her. Particularly was this true of her attitude towards his lordship. It meant that at a time when the two of them could have been expected to come closer together, and when he needed love and kindness to compensate for his illness, he got only contention and mistrust. Nor did she see, when the election results showed that his lordship had been right, that the country wanted a change and new faces, that she would almost certainly have lost her seat.

So the war, during which she'd given such a sparkling account of herself, ended in what she would have called her defeat. As, in a way, it did for Churchill. Though in so many respects they were opposites, they had similar natures. I remember her saying, 'Only I and Mr Churchill enjoy the war, but only I admit it.'

9 Achieving My Ambition

I began my working life with one ambition, to travel. I achieved it beyond my early dreams and in the grand manner. For me the saying might have been written, 'We haven't much money but we do see life'. For this I have to thank her ladyship because she didn't just take me with her and forget about me. From the moment she realized I was an avid sightseer – and I made this plain from the start – she either took me around with her or else arranged and paid for me to go on coach tours. I remember the first time I visited the Continent with her, she saw me buying some picture postcards. 'What are you getting those for, Rose?' she asked.

'Well, my lady, none of the people I know are going to believe me when I tell them where I've been unless I can show them proof. These are the proof.'

From then on she always bought my cards for me. I've still got them. I could give a travel talk with lantern slides that would last for several days. I could write a book on the places I've seen, but I'm not going to. There have though been certain incidents on our journeyings that I think are worth the telling which show the kind of things that servants have to be ready for, and which illustrate my lady's character and behaviour.

The United States of course was her second home, if you can say that about someone who already had four in Britain. I visited there with her over twenty times, mostly, I'm glad to say, by sea. I loved the luxury of the great liners and enjoyed the opportunity to catch up on my sleep. I've stayed in the best hotels in the world, and in many of the greatest houses. Even the grandest though can hold surprises. I remember in 1932 we were staying with Mr Thomas

Lamont, the famous banker of the House of Pierpont Morgan. I was given a charming room, and spent what I thought was a comfortable night. The following morning while I was attending her ladyship she said, 'What's the matter with your arm, Rose?' It was covered in bites.

'It seems as if the mosquitoes have had a meal out of me, my lady.'

She looked at them and then stepped away from me as if I'd got the plague. 'Those aren't mosquito bites, they're bug bites. Go and see the housekeeper at once, there must be bugs in your bed.'

Well, away I went and saw the housekeeper and very unpleasant she was too. 'You must have brought them with you from the ship,' she said. I wasn't going to take that.

'Lady Astor does not travel on buggy ships, it's your buggy bed. Let's go and see.'

We did, and her ladyship was right, the mattress was alive with them. I went back and reported, 'They want to put me in another room, but if you don't mind I'd rather go to the Westbury Hotel where Arthur Bushell is staying. You know the old saying, my lady, "Once bitten, twice shy".' That started her laughing so I got my way. There was a tremendous fuss about it all. Mrs Lamont apologized to me personally, and the housemaid was sacked. When I got to the Westbury I put all my clothes out on the balcony that night. It was freezing hard and I thought it would get rid of those that there might be in them. I'd never seen any before and I've never seen any since, I'm thankful to say. The trouble with the mention of bugs is that it sets people off itching. I noticed her ladyship scratching herself during the rest of our stay with the Lamonts. I'm sure both she and his lordship were glad when we left.

A disadvantage of our American trips was that her ladyship was asked to make public speeches wherever we went. Indeed I suppose that that was sometimes the purpose of our going there. Unfortunately she was very outspoken and would take the opportunity of criticizing either the government of the country or some of the people, such as the Irish or the Roman Catholics, and of course she was always on about strong drink. Freedom of speech is all very well, but there's also freedom to write, and the newspapers took full advantage of it. Also the day after she'd spoken she seemed to get a sackful of abusive letters. It was my job to separate them from the ordinary mail, to go through them and to read some of the ruder ones to my lady. It used to upset me that people could write such terrible things, but she would only laugh. 'You worry more about them than I do, Rose.'

Miss Wissie and the boys were travellers from early ages, at first mainly to Europe. We paid annual visits to Switzerland for the winter sports, the South of France and Italy. Mr Jakie was being introduced to the Continent when I first joined her ladyship, so he and I were constant companions and great fun he was, amusing and witty from an early age without being smart or precocious. He enjoyed doing battle with his mother. I remember once when we were in Brioni in Italy, he and I hired a couple of bicycles and rode around sightseeing. I thought I'd go native so I bought a beret. When my lady saw me in it she shrieked, 'Take that off, I'm not going to keep a maid who wears a thing like that on her head.' Rather shamefacedly I pulled it off.

'Put it back on, Rose, I like it,' said Mr Jakie, 'and since it's me you're going out with I'm the person that matters. I'm going to photograph you in it and I'll give you a copy and I'll give one to Ma.'

True to form her ladyship loved someone standing up to her, and she roared with laughter and sent us on our way with her blessing, both on us and the beret.

A trip I shall always remember was one we took in the 1930s. Her ladyship was attending a women's international convention in Istanbul and was travelling there with Dame Edith Lyttelton. Well, I thought my lady was forgetful, but it seemed these intellectual women were worse. We went by train from Victoria station. We were to be travelling for three nights and two days and I looked forward to a peaceful and interesting time. All was well till we got to Dover. I went to collect the two ladies, to find the carriage in an uproar. All Dame Edith's luggage was opened and her things scattered round the place. She'd lost her passport.

Well, I helped in what I knew to be a fruitless search. She hadn't lost it, she had just forgotten to bring it with her. Eventually we gave up, packed up and with her ladyship pulling a few strings and judiciously disposing of a few pound notes, we were allowed on the boat with instructions to get a temporary passport from the British Embassy in Paris. When we got to the Gare du Nord I took the luggage over to the Gare de Lyons while the ladies sorted things out at the Embassy. They arrived back with not a lot of time to spare before the train left. We got to the ticket barrier. 'You've got the tickets, Edith,' said my lady.

'Oh yes,' she said, rummaging in her handbag.

'Oh no,' I thought, with a sinking stomach, and I was right. 'What on earth did you give them to her for?' I whispered fiercely.

'Shut up, Rose,' my lady replied in defence.

We were at our wits' end, the train was almost due out, there was no time to do anything. Suddenly up someone rushed calling out, 'Lady Astor, Lady Astor.' It was a messenger from the Embassy with the tickets in his hand. Dame Edith made to take them, but I got there first. 'Oh no, from now on I'll take charge of these,' I said, and her ladyship agreed.

Well, by the time we got to Istanbul we were all exhausted, and Dame Edith nearly penniless. Nobody on any of the frontiers we passed through liked the look of the passport, and a lot of money was needed for the necessary visas. In a nasty way I rather enjoyed it, watching my lady get more and more testy. I thought it would show her how easy she had it when all she had to do normally was to rely on me.

The hotel in Istanbul looked comfortable enough when we got there, but I got a horrid shock when we were taken to my lady's room. I went over to the window as I always did to check on fire precautions. When I looked out, there below was a pile full of refuse, covered in scavenging cats. If she saw them I knew there'd be fireworks, and I wasn't in the mood. I drew the curtains.

'What are you doing that for, Rose?'

'I thought you'd want a bath straight away,' I said, and ran one for her. This and dressing filled in some time, but I was still afraid I was merely putting off the moment when she would see what was going on below and we'd have to pack up and find another hotel. I got her into the corridor and on her way down to luncheon and popped back into the room for a quick peep out of the window. To my astonishment the cats and the refuse had all disappeared.

With the ladies occupied listening and talking at their convention I had most of the days to myself. I spent one of these at the Sultan's Palace where I saw treasures that reminded me of my childhood image of Aladdin's cave. I went up to the Golden Horn and looked over to Constantinople, drank Turkish coffee and visited the mosques, exchanging my shoes for the little mule things they give you. I think my description of my travels must have excited Dame Edith, for the night before she was to return she went missing. We discovered her absence at half past ten.

'She's never gone out on her own in the dark, Rose,' said her ladyship. But when we checked with the porter, she most certainly had. 'We'll have to go and find her.'

I didn't like the idea one bit, but I had no option so off we trudged. I must say the streets didn't look the same at night and men's faces took on a villainous expression.

'Perhaps she's been kidnapped for a harem,' I ventured, voicing my own fears.

That made her ladyship's night, she didn't stop laughing for the rest of our search. It was miraculous, but we found Dame Edith wandering down one of the side streets, and gazing up at the houses. She didn't seem the slightest bit put out at the trouble she'd caused us. 'Wretched conditions they live under here, Nancy. It's quite encouraging, it makes our slums in Britain so much better than we think them to be.'

My lady and I bustled her back to the hotel and both breathed a sigh of relief the following day when we saw her on to the train. We stayed an extra two days. The excuse my lady gave was that she wanted to go sightseeing, but as she said to me as the train steamed out, 'I couldn't have stood the journey back with her. Enough is enough.'

In 1936, shortly after Lady Astor and I had returned from America, she and his lordship were invited to Yugoslavia by Queen Marie. Arthur Bushell and I helped to get them there. On the boat out we travelled with the Duke and Duchess of Kent and made friends with her maid and the detective who was going with them. They too were bound for Yugoslavia, but were travelling by a different route. Ours was another long train journey. For me, familiarity by now was beginning to breed contempt.

We were met at Belgrade by diplomats, a fleet of cars and an army of soldiers. Arthur and I had a limousine to ourselves, with an officer in front travelling with a chauffeur as our escort. Arthur began playing it up, acting like the Royals.

'Well, Rose, my queen, this is better than the bloody milkfloat.' I of course screamed with laughter, which must have alarmed our officer because he looked at Arthur as though he thought he was trying to do me in. We were driven to the palace outside Belgrade. Arthur and I were given rooms in a cottage. The gardens around were some of the most beautiful I had ever seen, though we found it a little strange that the gardeners were working under

military supervision. Directly it became dark we were confined to barracks. We were told that anyone seen in the
grounds after dark was shot. That was enough for me, I
didn't even go near the windows. We used an underground
passage to get to the palace, all very eerie with a soldier
with fixed bayonet on each corner.

The men and women servants were segregated for meals
and I expect in most other respects. On both the nights we
were there there was a film show in English. The servants
sat downstairs. We all had to wear black dresses and white
gloves, and the Royals and the notables sat in the gallery.
While we were there there was quite a party of them, Queen
Marie of Rumania, the Queen of Yugoslavia, a German
princess, the Duke and Duchess of Kent, Prince Paul and
Princess Olga, Prince Nicholas of Greece, and of course our
two. When they came in we were ordered to our feet, did an
about turn and bowed low. On my way up I looked at her
ladyship and without moving a muscle she threw a big wink
at me. The film was Harold Lloyd in *The Milky Way*. I
remember thinking how incongruous it was in the setting
in which we were watching it. The next day Arthur and I
were taken on a tour of Belgrade by the palace housekeeper,
and a military guard of course. Then the same routine at
night, and another film. Theirs was a lush life, but it must
have become very boring.

From Belgrade we went to Budapest and stayed beside
the Danube opposite Marie Theresa's palace. It was a beautiful hotel, I would have liked to have stayed there for
weeks, but we'd more Royals to visit, Princess Ileana and
Count Anton of Hapsburg at Schloss Sonberg near Vienna.
It was a comfy enough place, again with beautiful grounds
and gardens, but both Arthur and I were a bit put out by
having to clean his lordship's and my lady's rooms. The
strange thing was that ours were cleaned for us. Some sort
of protocol I suppose. The Count's hobby was aeroplanes
and he and his valet, who was probably chosen for his

engineering qualities, seemed to spend most of the day tinkering about with them on the airfield which was part of the grounds. I don't think the Prince and her ladyship had a lot to say to each other. We finished this trip with a few pleasant days at the Hotel Bristol in Vienna.

It seemed her ladyship had itchy feet this year because almost immediately after our return we were off to Biarritz. In July we went to Paris, the George V Hotel. My lady was the guest of the Canadian Government at the unveiling of the war memorial on Vimy Ridge by Edward VIII. Although we were only to be there for a few days, from my point of view it was the full treatment. Clothes galore for every type of party and of course a lot of the valuable jewellery. I didn't expect to leave the hotel so I didn't worry about my things.

The big morning came and when I'd finished getting her ladyship ready she said, 'Now you go and get dressed, Rose.'

'What for, my lady?' I asked.

'You're coming with me of course.'

I hadn't expected there would be any of course about it and I told her so. 'Anyway I've nothing to wear.'

'Put your hat and coat on, that's all of you that will be seen,' she said, and away we went.

Now my lady had a strange mistrust of hotel safes and would never allow me to deposit her jewellery in them. 'It's safer in your hands, Rose,' she always said, and that's where it was on this outing. 'Don't ask me where your sparklers are, my lady, because they're in my handbag,' I said, as we sat in the train to Arras. I'd visions of it being snatched in the crowd, but I needn't have worried, she took me on the dais with her. I had a wonderful view of it all and in the greatest possible comfort. When I got back to the hotel I related the scene to Lady Byng's maid. She was furious. She hadn't even been in the crowd. According to her Lord Byng had commanded one of the armies there and this gave her precedence over me. I suppose it did, but as I said to her it wasn't my fault her lady hadn't asked her.

In a way I suppose her ladyship's generosity and thoughtfulness were rewarded, because during her later years we were able to recall the many interesting, happy and amusing occasions that we'd had together. Of course this could never have been in her mind at the time. No one, least of all my lady, ever really thinks about growing old.

In September off we went again to America. It was the one and only time I stayed in the Waldorf Astoria, which might seem a bit strange as the Astors had once owned it so everything there was for free, but with really rich people money ceases to mean anything in certain terms, particularly when it concerns themselves, their own happiness and comfort, or if they're generous as my lady was if it concerned those in her immediate thoughts. In any week of our travels, I was probably costing her twice my yearly wages, yet if I'd asked for a rise in salary of only a few pounds, she would have become suspicious and avaricious. It's hard to understand. I gave up trying early on. As I've said her ladyship carried very little money with her, she didn't need to.

I must say Arthur Bushell and I enjoyed ourselves hugely at the Waldorf. We were given the same V.I.P. treatment as our master and mistress. We weren't sorry to leave though, because we were both looking forward to our first trip to the West Indies, to Bermuda. We sailed on the *Queen of Bermuda*, which seemed a comfortable and solid enough vessel, and were particularly looking forward to the Thanksgiving Day party on board. Arthur promised as a special treat that on that day he would bring me my tray of early tea. The morning dawned, but no Arthur. It didn't take me long to realize why. As I tried to get up I was thrown all over the cabin. Eventually I found my way to Arthur whose appearance was rougher than the seas. He was busy over the washbowl.

I staggered to my lady and tried to get both her and his

lordship their coffee, but it was impossible. Like the early American pilgrims, our day was spent praying for a safe landing. All of us, that is, except Arthur, who told me later that he was praying for a quick and easy death! The storm blew itself out that night and we had our turkey the following day. It didn't seem the same though.

Bermuda in 1936 was a heavenly place. It hadn't been so developed then. We stayed at Mr Vincent Astor's home, and had what I can only describe as a glorious country holiday. Arthur and I found bicycles and toured around on those when we weren't working, and we were allowed the use of the swimming pool and tennis courts. Formality was forgotten. No, that is not quite true: Arthur was there to act as butler/valet. On our first evening he changed into a tail coat, stiff shirt and winged collar. He came down to show me the result. 'Whatever shall I do, Rose?' he said. He was the most pathetic figure; it looked as though he'd fallen into the swimming pool. His shirt-front had disintegrated and his collar was like a bit of soggy paper. He was drowning in a bath of sweat.

I suppose I shouldn't have laughed. 'Talk about mad dogs and Englishmen,' I cried. Her ladyship heard me and came rushing in. She collapsed too. Poor Arthur! He could have dealt with me on my own, but with her ladyship there he could only get redder and redder with pent-up rage. It was shirt-sleeve order for him that night and a light tuxedo and a soft shirt from then on. Like a number of our trips this one ended abruptly. Mrs Brand's son Winkie, my lady's nephew, was killed through falling from a window of a New York hotel.

We were again in the States later that year at the time when Edward VIII abdicated. My lady had of course known about the scandal, as it was thought of at that time, from the beginning, and had tried to dissuade Edward from marrying Mrs Simpson. Her attitude in a way I found difficult to understand. She had divorced Mr Shaw and re-

married and had become a member of the British aristocracy. Yet she was vehement that Mrs Simpson, an American
divorcée like herself, should not become Queen. She was
very upset when I broke the news to her: I'd heard the
paper-boy shouting it in the streets. She cried bitterly. It
must later have been some consolation to her that her
greatest friends amongst the Royals, the Duke and Duchess
of York, acceded to the throne.

The next two and a half years, the years before the war,
followed a similar pattern, though I think 1936 was probably our most hectic travel time. We continued to go to
St Moritz, the South of France and Biarritz regularly, and
to the States fitfully. We visited Palm Beach, staying at the
Breakers Hotel, the millionaires' paradise, but only for one
night though because my lady was chastised by the management for walking through the hotel in her bathing costume
and wrap on the first morning. Up we had to get, pack and
move to the Delray Beach Hotel, where the rooms had doors
like horse-boxes, opening both top and bottom. Arthur was
very disdainful about Palm Beach. I didn't care for it either.
I was bitten by sand-flies and spent much of my time with
my feet in a bath of hot water and Epsom salts to get the
stings out. Then I had toothache and the dentist caused
me so much pain I nearly floored him. I think everyone
was happy when we moved away from there.

On another trip – by this time we were taking internal
flights in America – our plane was diverted and we stopped
off at Savannah. Since we were in for a longish wait my lady
hired a car and we took a trip round the town. Somehow
she got hold of a reporter; she was disgusted by the litter she
had seen on the streets and she described Savannah to him
as 'a beautiful lady with a dirty face'. Apparently it made
the headlines the next day and within twenty-four hours the
place had been cleaned up. Which showed that sometimes
Lady Astor's outspokenness was accepted in the spirit in
which it was given.

It was shortly after we returned from this trip that I went with my lady to stay with Lord Mildmay of Flete. Other guests were Queen Mary, Lady Cynthia Colville, Lady Lansdowne, Lady Fortescue, Admiral and Lady Plunkett-Ernle-Erle-Drax, Sir Reginald Seymour, Sir Raymond Green, Lord Mount Edgecumbe, to name a few. I remember one of the valets saying, 'Not a bad field, quite a few thoroughbreds amongst them.' It was on this visit that I realized the quality of Queen Mary. It was as she came down the staircase for dinner. She seemed to become aware that the staff had assembled, though not by general design, to watch her entrance. She stood perfectly still, then moved slightly from side to side as if embracing us all into her sphere. You could almost feel the warmth of her personality and you remembered the smile on her lips for a long time afterwards, and yet it seemed unconscious – there was no feeling of performance about it. She's the only lady I ever came near who gave this overwhelming sense of presence and this aura of majesty.

I've spoken about my lady's unpredictability. On one occasion his lordship rivalled her. She was going to Copenhagen for another of these women's conventions. She decided to fly there. On the morning of her departure and when I'd finished her packing, Arthur Bushell came into my room and said, 'His lordship's compliments, Rose, but you're to travel with her ladyship to Copenhagen.'

Well, I just thought it was another of his pranks and told him so in a few well-chosen words, but then he handed me the tickets. I'd just half an hour to get ready. I think it was the shortest notice I'd ever had and all the time there was something in the back of my mind that I was determined to do. When we got to Croydon airport I found time to do it. We had an enjoyable trip and as you will have gathered nothing untoward happened. A day or two after our return her ladyship was going through some papers and she suddenly said, 'What's all this, Rose, you've cost me twenty-four shillings for insurance. What's the meaning of it?'

'Well, my lady,' I said, 'I've got good reason for doing it. I've now got responsibilities.'

That set her back on her heels. 'Responsibilities, what responsibilities?' and she started to laugh.

'It's no laughing matter, I'm now a woman of property, the same as you,' I said. And I explained to her that I had just bought a bungalow in Walton-on-Thames so that my mother could have a permanent home near my sisters, that it was on a mortgage and I wanted to make sure that the mortgage could be paid if anything happened to me. As I was saying this a change came over her. She couldn't have been more pleased if I was buying the bungalow for her. She put her arm around me and promised that if ever anything happened to me my mother would be looked after. I never had to bother about insurance after that.

The war put an end to any thoughts of travel. If my lady missed it she didn't mention it to me. If she was homesick for America it was compensated for by the presence of so many of her countrymen over here and the use that she could be to them. The moment peace came though she was anxious to be over there again. So anxious in fact that she settled for a banana-boat, and I mean just that. *Eros*, the ship was called, a Fyffe's banana-boat, though what connection there was between love and bananas I didn't know and I said so when I got on board.

We sailed from Tilbury and we expected to be in New York in seven days. It took us fourteen. The ship did everything but sink, yet I don't think any of us ever had a happier voyage. It didn't start too well. Her ladyship had insisted that we should bring along three dozen eggs, and I was sent down to the chef to deliver them. He wasn't in the least grateful. 'I've got three thousand in the fridge, we don't need them so you can take them back to whoever it was who sent them.'

I explained it was her ladyship. At the mention of her

name his face darkened but he didn't comment. 'Just take them back up to her,' he said.

'They'd better go back home then, Rose,' said her ladyship when I rejoined her. 'They need them there.'

Well, of all the absurd remarks to make in mid-channel.

'What do you want me to do, throw them there?' I asked.

'Shut up, Rose,' she responded, 'and take them back to the chef. He must be able to make some use of them.' Down I went again.

'Oh, it's you back. What is it this time?' Ungraciously he took the eggs. 'I'd like to throw these at your Lady Astor,' he said, 'She's the one that tried to get our rum ration stopped during the war.'

'Did she?' I said.

'Yes, she did.'

'Well, it was none of my business,' I replied. 'I'll get her to come down and answer for herself.'

'If you do that I won't hold myself responsible for my actions.'

I knew how he felt. Chefs are notoriously hard drinkers. I believe it's the only way they can keep their sanity.

I told her ladyship about what he'd said. 'I must go down and see him,' she answered, and she did.

I don't know how the conversation went but that evening when I was in the galley filling the hot water bottles the chef said, 'Great lady that Lady Astor of yours. One of the best.' And he sang her praises for the rest of the voyage. So did the crew from the Captain downwards. I must say my two did behave well under the worst possible weather conditions. They were a contrast to some of the other passengers, always praising, never complaining.

When at last we docked in New York we were the first off the ship because Lord and Lady Astor had the courtesy of the port. As we reached the gangway I looked round and there were the crew lined up on the top deck in their mess jackets, and they began singing 'For she's a jolly good

fellow.' When her ladyship reached shore and turned round
to wave at them, she was crying her eyes out. It was a
wonderful moment for her, particularly as she was stepping
on to her home ground for the first time in six years.

We stayed at the Ritz Carlton, their hotel. We were all
given the best of everything. Never have I had a room to
equal the one I slept in. Her ladyship's suite was like a
florist's shop. All her friends must have sent flowers, and
fruit too. There was a wonderful hand of bananas; I hadn't
seen any for five years, for although the *Eros* was a banana-
boat, it had came out to collect, not to deliver. My lady
caught me eating one. 'You can have the lot, Rose,' she said
as I was about to apologize. She was in the seventh heaven
of happiness.

So many people came to visit both her and his lordship,
they hardly had a spare moment, but they didn't forget the
crew of the *Eros*. Two days later his lordship gave a luncheon
party at the Hotel Astor for them. Everyone was there. I
sat between John, our steward, and the chef. They had the
time of their lives. The chef took a bit of a shine to me I
think because he asked me out the following evening. It
seemed all right to accept while we were having lunch, but
I got second thoughts the next day. My lady had got wind
of it, and insisted that I went. I must say we had a good time,
but when I found myself in a nightclub at midnight and
was watching the chef sink rum and Coca Cola as if Lady
Astor was likely to ban it the next day, I thought enough is
enough and made my excuses and returned to sanity.

About a fortnight later we went to Florida, at the invitation of Mr Clarence Dillon, a banker friend of the Astors,
to cruise on his yacht. I viewed the prospect with some
qualms. I've never been one for small boats. Small boat! It
was like the *Queen Mary*. We wallowed in luxury, travelling from Miami up the east coast then inland to Lake
Okeechobee and across to the west coast, down to Key West
and back up to Miami again. We were certainly making up

for the austerity of Britain during the war. As if this wasn't enough we left Florida for South Carolina, another million-aires' paradise, staying at Mr Thomas Lamont's house, with its own private golf course, set amid masses of camellia bushes, and for a change of diet a splendid Norwegian chef. Her ladyship's grand-niece Elizabeth Winn came here to stay with us and we formed a friendship which has endured. We'd go into Charleston together, some eighteen miles away, and as a contrast to the rich food we were now accus-tomed to would always lunch simply at Woolworth's, and enjoy it.

From South Carolina we went to Washington to the house of Mr William Bullitt, staffed with French servants whom he'd recruited when he was Ambassador in Paris. More rich cooking and plenty of wine for all including the staff. Knowing her ladyship's antipathy to alcohol he was for ever having a dig at her. One evening he came to her room and seeing me said, 'Oh Rose, you'll be glad to know there's the usual bottle of whisky on the table by your bed.' I curtseyed and thanked him kindly, while my lady snorted.

From Washington back to New York and the Ritz Carl-ton, then home to England on the *Queen Mary*. She hadn't been fully converted from her role as a troopship, but was nevertheless quite comfortable. Before Arthur Bushell and I left the hotel the manager asked to see us. He thanked us profusely, and we asked him why. 'There have been no complaints, not one single word of criticism. When you go on board you will find an expression of my gratitude in your cabins.'

We told him we'd only done our jobs and that it was he who deserved the credit. He'd have none of it. So in a haze of mutual congratulation we left to board the ship. The manager had been as good as his word: there were baskets of fruit and large food parcels waiting for us in our cabins. As Arthur said as we stood by the rails waving good-bye to

New York, 'It's a wretched menial job being in service, eh Rose?'

During 1947 we renewed our friendship with the Continent and listened to many tragic wartime tales of hardship and deprivation. At the end of the year his lordship rented a house in Tucson, Arizona from a Mr Thomas Hardy. There we really came up against the colour problem. Going with the house as it were was a coloured cook, Birdie. Now, while Birdie didn't mind cooking meals for our two, she did for Arthur and myself, so it was arranged that we should eat at the Arizona Inn opposite the house. Nor was there any accommodation for Arthur. He was not permitted to use the coloured servants' quarters so he had a room over at the inn. It was all very complicated. I remember remarking that the colour question was more difficult for servants than for masters. Anyway I soon saw that I wasn't going to be able to tolerate this eating out business. It meant changing before each meal and changing back afterwards. Arthur felt the same. Nor could I see why we shouldn't help Birdie in the kitchen, so gradually we came to take our lunch with her. At first it wasn't exactly with her, she sat at one table and we sat at another. It was ridiculous, so after a couple of meals that way I laid the table up for three, and she joined us. We eventually ended up by eating off the fat of the land. Like us she hated segregation. Her ladyship didn't appreciate what we were doing, and said so.

'My lady,' I replied, 'you have been brought up differently. I have been taught to think that all men are equal in the sight of God, and what's good enough for God is good enough for me. I shall continue to go on the way I've learned.'

Mention of God always quietened my lady down. She respected my God as I respected hers. She said no more. It ended up with Birdie, who had a little car, driving Arthur and me around sightseeing. We became firm friends and corresponded for some time afterwards.

During her stay in Arizona we went to a rodeo in Tucson. It was boiling hot. I remember getting my behind scorched on the seats which had been frying in the sun before we sat on them. I was thrilled with the bucking broncos, but when they started lassoing the steers and nearly strangling them, it was time for me to leave. Her ladyship felt the same so we all went home. The sight of the broncos must have done something to my lady because the next day a man turned up at the house with a performing horse. He did all sorts of tricks on it and then she decided to ride it. She went through the same routine as he had, making it rear up on its back legs while she held on like grim death. My heart was in my mouth, and when I looked at his lordship his face was ashen with fear for her. She was now approaching seventy and was behaving like the wild Nancy of her youth. Guts and courage she had till the end.

Travelling in America blew like her ladyship, hot and cold. We left the sunshine of Arizona for Des Moines in Iowa where my lady was a guest at a farmers' dinner, with General Marshall and her as the main speakers. Within forty-eight hours I was in danger of losing my ears in the intense cold. This was the thing that made packing so difficult, with clothes at the ready for all seasons. The dinner must have been an organizers' nightmare because our train got stuck in the snowdrifts and had to be dug out, and General Marshall was caught in the floods at Tennessee. So neither of the main speakers got there on time. After this fiasco my lady and I set off on a whistle-stop tour and when finally we arrived back at New York and were ready to return home she had the news that her sister Mrs Flynn, who had been very ill, was at death's door. The trunks were on board so had to be offloaded. This was the first and only time I collapsed from nervous exhaustion and had to take to my bed for a day. I was very thankful when two weeks later we were really on our way back to England.

The travel pattern continued much the same over the

next year or two. His lordship's death in September 1952, though not unexpected, was a very great shock to Lady Astor, and the readjustment of her life when Mr Billy came into the title and took over Cliveden, though made as easy as possible for her by the children, was difficult for her to accept. Travelling she found made a diversion so February of the following year found us in America once again. This was the occasion of her personal attack on Senator Mc-Carthy, at a party given by Senator Taft. She and McCarthy were introduced. She must have been waiting for the moment. 'What's that you're drinking?' she asked.

'Whisky,' he answered.

'I wish it was poison,' she said loudly, so that all around could hear.

And they did. The next day I was busy sorting out the mail again. This time she was called a Communist! It seemed to me now she had been called everything in the political dictionary. Some of the papers demanded that she be flung out of the country. She loved every minute of it.

Once again we travelled everywhere. I marvelled where she got her energy from. I was a bit astonished where I found mine because I was no longer a chicken. It was in May just as we were leaving Washington station that a message came over the loudspeaker for her and her ladyship returned waving a cable and saying, 'Get the things off quick, we're going back to England.'

I remember I didn't feel particularly shaken, I was re-signed to this sort of thing, and while I was unloading she explained that she'd had an invitation from the Queen Mother to sit with her in Westminster Abbey for the Coronation. Previously she'd been told that she couldn't go because dowager ladies were not being invited since there was insufficient room. Home we went, with not a lot of time to get ready for this big occasion.

I had thought to get a long rest after the Coronation for my lady had been invited to Southern Rhodesia for the

Rhodes Centenary there and was going to take the opportunity to tour Africa. She decided she could manage without me and I was not in the least bit offended or disappointed. I made arrangements for a holiday with my family and to spend some time with my mother, who was very unwell.

I should have known better. A few days before her ladyship was to leave, which was the day after the Coronation, I had a phone call from Miss Wissie saying that there had been a family conference and the children had decided that I should accompany their mother and had bought my ticket. They didn't actually force me to go, they said the decision must be mine, but they made it pretty nearly impossible for me to refuse. Whoever made that remark about flattery didn't know me! I couldn't go on the same flight as my lady to Rhodesia, there wasn't room. I went the day before, on a Comet. At this time there had been a bit of fuss about the Comets being unsafe, and with the words of a few Job's comforters ringing in my ears, I boarded the plane feeling like a sacrificial lamb. Whatever it cost I was determined to have a brandy the moment I got on board. It was free, so was the champagne I had later.

I had the most perfect flight. Whatever my lady said about the horrors of drink didn't apply to me on that trip. We were staying at the Livingstone Hotel by the Victoria Falls before going to Bulawayo. I had a day in hand so I took the opportunity of visiting the Falls, a trip I repeated the next day with her ladyship with me acting as a know-all guide. When we arrived at Sir John and Lady Kennedy's for the Celebrations I was given a little house in their grounds, a rondavel, all the visiting maids and valets had one. They were built specially for the occasion. We ate in the house, where they had a full staff, English fashion. The Queen Mother and Princess Margaret were the guests of honour and of course I had a grandstand view. Lady Kennedy was especially nice to me. I had known her when she was a young girl and a friend of Miss Wissie's. She saw to it that I was invited to all the cocktail parties that were given. I remember her ladyship catching me with a glass of sherry in my hand. 'You're not going to drink that, Rose, are you?' she said. 'I don't want to keep a maid who drinks.' I suppose I must have been with her then some twenty-five years, and yet here she was playing the martinet and pretending to threaten me with dismissal. I loved her for it.

Later we moved on to Salisbury where we stayed with Sir Robert and Lady Tredgold: he was Chief Justice of Rhodesia. Here we ran into the same colour trouble as we'd had in Arizona, so I was put into a hotel. This didn't suit me, but this time I had no option but to conform. It meant travelling backwards and forwards by taxi for my meals. My lady must have seen that I didn't like it because on the second day when it came to lunch-time, she had a little table set on the veranda and personally came and served me with each course. She did the same with every meal while we were there. 'Rose, my gal,' I said to myself, 'food tastes a lot better when it's served by a viscountess.'

One afternoon I went shopping with the two ladies. Hats of course. They bought one each, which showed great restraint on my lady's part. As we were going home she said to me, 'What a pity, Rose, we haven't a chiffon scarf to match her ladyship's hat.' As she said it I remembered that I'd brought a square with me that exactly suited it. That evening I roll-edged it and gave it to Lady Tredgold. If I'd given her the moon she couldn't have been more grateful. It did something to her. From then on we were friends and corresponded regularly until she died, and although Sir Robert is ninety he still continues to send me a card every Christmas. We travelled around Rhodesia in what I call a butterfly plane, a flimsy-looking thing with room for only four passengers. I noticed it carried guns, ammunition and food in case we had to make a forced landing. Not a very reassuring sight. One house we visited which I particularly remember was in the middle of nowhere and belonged to Sir Stewart Gore-Browne. He'd had it built in stone on the lines of a Hollywood villa. It was a splendid place. While I was there he gave me into the charge of a chieftain's young son, who did everything for me and followed me wherever I went. I suppose he was instructed to see that no harm befell me. He did his job well and we became friends, even though we had difficulty in communicating.

Sir Stewart had a house in England, in Weybridge, which adjoins Walton-on-Thames where my family now lived, so we had something in common. He visited Lady Astor and stayed the night in Hill Street shortly after we'd been with him. When he left I gave him a colourful Fair Isle jersey to take back for my young chieftain's son. I got a lovely letter back written in English, and I've kept it to this day.

It seemed that for the next few years we were continually on the move. Backwards and forwards to and from America and the Continent. One visit I particularly looked forward to was to the King and Queen of Sweden in Hälsingborg. We took a plane to Copenhagen in Denmark, were met at the airport by the royal car flying the standard and driven to the ferry. We were given precedence everywhere. I enjoyed imagining myself royalty, and so I'm sure did my lady. I didn't feel so sunny when we were on the ferry and one of my shoes caught in the deck and practically broke my ankle. I was out of action for the entire stay. I remembered the old saying 'pride goes before a fall'.

In 1956 we visited Lady Astor's elder sister, Mrs Dana Gibson, in Virginia after receiving an urgent message about her health. It was a sad reunion for this once beautiful witty woman was now senile and her mind was going. After a month, during which there was little my lady could do for her, we flew to Nassau. Mrs Hobson, the school-friend of her ladyship's, joined us there. When the time came for her to leave it was suggested that I should fly with Mrs

Hobson to Miami, spend the night there seeing the sights, and return the next day. I looked forward to this, but had my usual worry of what to do with my lady's jewellery. We were travelling with quite a small fortune. 'What about the sparklers?' I asked her.

'I'm not looking after them,' she replied, 'you'll have to take them with you.'

We got to Miami and to Mrs Hobson's surprise when we arrived at the customs, they asked her to open her cases. 'I'm an American citizen,' she said, 'you've never before examined my luggage.'

'Special check, lady, we're looking for drugs and jewellery.'

I felt my stomach hit the floor. I just opened my case and waited to be arrested. The customs man fumbled around quite a bit, but only on the side where the jewellery wasn't. He closed the case, made the little chalk sign and I was through. If he'd only looked at my face instead of the case I'd have been in real trouble!

That trip was fated. We must have spent three hours and a lot of money touring around in a taxi to find a hotel room for me. Everywhere was full. Eventually I arrived back at the airport. There was nothing for it but to return to Nassau. Fortunately nobody seemed to worry if I took drugs and jewellery there with me. I arrived back shaken and tired to face the merriment of my lady and her friends at my plight.

The following year, 1957, we went again to Nassau. We sailed on the *Coronia*. Sir Humphrey and Lady de Trafford were travelling with us and so was the Marquesa de Casa Maury, who was at one time Mrs Dudley Ward. It was worse than our voyage on the *Eros*, the banana-boat. King Neptune threw the book at us. One morning as Lady de Trafford's maid and I were sitting on the sun deck, pretending to ignore the elements, a wave hit us and smashed the windows as if they were paper. Wringing wet we went below to find that Mrs Dudley Ward's (as I shall always think of her) portholes had blown in and her cabin was awash. It wasn't exactly all hands to the pump but pretty nearly.

When I went to report to my lady, there she was lying in bed as if nothing had happened. She looked like Cleopatra reclining in her barge on the Nile. When I told her about Mrs Ward's troubles she phoned the Purser and used her influence to get her a cabin near to us. Later that day those of us who could walk there assembled in the ship's cinema to be told by the Captain that we were riding one of the worst storms in his experience, which didn't strike me at the time as particularly reassuring. Still there's something about the confident calm of sailors that makes even the worst situation bearable.

The following year it was Nassau again. By now I'd forgotten what an English winter was like. This time we stayed at Mrs Winn's house, my lady's niece. She had bought it that year from Lady Kemsley, wife of the newspaper millionaire. It was a lovely place with a splendid patio. We were not alone in thinking that. Every dog in the neighbourhood assembled there our first night and serenaded us. Her ladyship nearly went mental. Those dogs got more 'shut ups' in a few hours than I did in a lifetime.

I got up, put on a dressing-gown and went down to try and disperse them. Now there's a saying that dogs by their nature know who likes them and who doesn't: it's nonsense. I was hating those animals that night, yet as I tried to shoo them away they came running up to me wagging their tails and jumping to lick my hands and my face. 'Come back in, Rose,' my lady screamed at me. 'You're encouraging them.' Eventually Mr Winn phoned the police and they were taken away in vans. They didn't come again. I wish they had, I had nightmares thinking about what the police might have done to them.

After we'd visited Nassau the following year, we sailed

back to France and had a few days at the Ritz. Miss Wissie joined us there and we flew to Casablanca en route to Marrakesh. Her ladyship had the habit of taking my hand from time to time. She did this on the plane and as she was doing so I twisted one of her rings straight. When I looked up I saw Miss Wissie had gone quite white. She put her fingers to her lips when she saw that I was concerned for her. We made an early opportunity of speaking together. 'Rose, I've left all my jewellery in my room at the Ritz. Whatever happens Mother mustn't know.' I knew how she must be feeling. The Ancaster gems may not have been quite as valuable as my lady's at that time, but she had a beautiful collection.

At Casablanca I held my ladyship's attention while Miss Wissie phoned Paris. They were safe. The chambermaid had handed them in to the office. We collected them on our return. Yet another example of the honesty of servants, I thought.

After a long car drive we got to Marrakesh. Now I'm sure a lot of people would have found Marrakesh a very nice place – not me. It gave me the creeps and the smells turned my stomach over. Rug and carpet-making is interesting to watch for ten minutes, but when you've seen one person doing it, you've seen the lot. I was amazed to see a donkey and a camel drawing a plough together, but once I got over the shock, my interest went. Then one morning as I was putting on my shoes, a large brown creature jumped out of one of them. I went demented and rushed to Miss Wissie. All right, she said it was a locust and harmless, but I thought I was going to die from the bite of some poisonous creepy crawlie.

I was glad when the time came for us to leave. It seemed as if the country didn't want to lose us. On our journey to the airport I saw a wheel hub fly off our cab as one of the tyres blew out. Then Miss Wissie had a parcel to collect at the airport which nobody seemed to know anything about, and finally I heard her ladyship going hammer and tongs at the passport examiner who either didn't like the look of her passport or her ladyship, for which at the moment I couldn't have blamed him, and was purposely holding her up. Eventually we got in the plane in a heap, and with just seconds to spare. Whenever I see Marrakesh in a holiday brochure today I quickly turn over the page.

It was in June of that year, 1959, that I had one of the most amusing trips ever, with her ladyship. She had asked her niece, Mrs Nancy Lancaster, to join her on a visit to the Swedish Royals and to meet Queen Ingrid of Denmark and her three daughters. Before we flew over Mrs Lancaster came to Eaton Square to spend two days with us. When I saw her luggage I thought she'd come for two months. It transpired that the impending visit had gone to her head. She expected to be wearing four or five dresses a day and had brought hats, jewels, coats and furs to match. Well, I did my best to disillusion her, but was only partially successful. Her complaint I found was catching. Her ladyship, who should have known better and have explained to her niece that the Scandinavian monarchs behaved simply, merely tried to go one better and despite my protests I found myself in charge of a mountain of luggage. It cost a fortune in overweight at the airport.

We had a perfect flight and the now customary royal drive in a beflagged Cadillac to the palace. That drive was the only formal part of the visit. King Gustav met us in an open-necked shirt and a pair of flannel trousers, the two queens were in plain summer frocks, and the Danish princesses were running around like urchins. I felt embarrassed as I unpacked the two ladies' clothes. I had a cup of tea in the Pugs' Parlour where I made discreet inquiries into what my two should wear for dinner. Dinner! It was served at seven o'clock, about the time we have high tea in Yorkshire. I must have looked astonished when I was told because the housekeeper explained that there was some rule in Sweden now that servants had to get away by a certain time, that most people dined at six and the palace was only able to have the extra hour by paying the servants more.

My ladies were not impressed by the circumstances in which they found themselves. Mrs Lancaster was particularly disappointed, and waxed vocal in showing her feelings. Then they started giggling together like two schoolgirls. By the following morning they were hysterical. They decided they couldn't see their stay out. We had a conference as to how they would get away and where they were to go. Paris was decided on. I had to do the dirty work, which was to go into Hälsingborg, cable Miss Jones, her ladyship's secretary, who in turn was to cable us to demand our return on the following day. I also had to book our flights to Paris and the hotel accommodation there.

I returned to find my two stretched out in deckchairs with the others, looking utterly bored. Everything I'm glad to say worked to plan. I'm not sure the Royals weren't glad to see the back of us because the night before we left, though truthfully it was more the early hours of the morning, Mrs Lancaster woke up wanting a glass of water. She got the taps mixed up and started flooding the room, called for my lady, the two of them panicked and rang every bell in sight. Down came the King and his aide-de-camp and the four of them ended up on their knees mopping up the floor with towels.

It all seems unlikely I know, but I have the letter still which I wrote to Mrs Hawkins, the housekeeper at Eaton Square, and I've copied the events that I've described here from that. I called the visit 'All dressed up and nowhere to go'.

Although I didn't know it, neither did my lady, we'd now made our last journey to the States. Continental visits were frequent, but were comparatively uneventful. They continued to be enjoyable with her ladyship relying more and more on me. I don't say this boastfully, after all these years together it was inevitable. In a way I enjoyed it. Many servants I knew had outlived their usefulness and had to retire. I was able to be of service to the end.

So this chapter has described the fulfilment of my ambition. Much I have had to leave out, but I think everyone will agree that the dreams of a poor callow Yorkshire girl were realized beyond any of her expectations. As I've re-lived these travels I've been reminded of something that Mr Bobbie Shaw said when I'd only been in my lady's service for a few years. He was trying to draw me out in front of her. 'What would you like most in this world, Rose?'

And I replied, after a moment's hesitation. 'To live my life over again.' Today my answer, without any hesitation, would be the same.

10 Religion and Politics

Religion for a servant could be hazardous. Even at the time I was in service there were many big houses where family prayers were still the order of the day, where servants were marshalled to church twice on Sundays, where tenant farmers, their labourers and those villagers in tied cottages were counted and where absentees could jeopardize their livings and their homes. It was still a time too when the remark in the vicar's reference that you came of 'God-fearing parents' carried more weight in some places than your education, experience and ability to do your job, and when employers were more worried about the care of your soul than that of your body. The kitchen staff were generally the exception for these people. The chef or cook and their minions were either given some sort of divine absolution or else it must have been accepted that their souls were past redemption for the traditional Sunday lunch was sacrosanct. I know of this kind of attitude by hearsay, not from personal experience.

My childhood religious upbringing has been the rock on which my faith has been built. For me religion is a personal thing and not something I display or discuss. I think it is necessary for me to declare it now since it affected my relationship with Lady Astor. My daily life is the outward expression of my religious feeling. Through my behaviour, my approach to my work and my relations with other people I try to show an inner grace. I try to be good, do good and think good. Of course I don't always succeed, but I find it a simple creed and one that I can follow without the worry of doubts or dogma. I'm also a believer in faith through prayer and I think there have been occasions when through my prayers I and others have been touched by God. Having said that let me say that I don't expect other people to think the same way any more than I expect them to question my belief.

When I went into service with the Tuftons I found that while they would have allowed me to go to church, my absence would have dislocated the running of the house. Even more would this have applied at the Cranbornes'. I had to content myself with occasional visits on my Sundays off. I discovered the beautiful sung evensong at Westminster Abbey and I enjoyed the services at the Guards Chapel, but my church attendances were irregular and I was driven to recalling my childhood experiences at the village church for consolation. I have done that throughout much of my life because when I began to work for the Astors, going to church was almost out of the question. I complained about it once or twice to her ladyship. 'If you really wanted to you'd find a way,' she said.

'And if I did you'd find a way of making things awkward for me, my lady,' I replied. So in service I learnt to rely on my own prayers, and they have never let me down.

I've already mentioned my experience when my work and my lady's attitude towards it and me made my life unbearable and how I was given strength to endure and to win through. There were two similar occasions that are easy for me to recall and relate, and others which are too personal for me to write about. The first was when I was in Germany near the town of Garmisch before the last war. We were staying with a millionaire friend of her ladyship's, in a vast bungalow. We'd come there from Munich where we'd stayed a few days at the Continental Hotel. During the first day there my lady decided to catch up on her mail, but by the time she'd finished writing she found she had missed the local post. Since some of her letters were urgent I was asked to go by train to Garmisch with them where I would be able to catch the post. I was driven to the station, had some language difficulty at the ticket office, and eventually settled for a single ticket to Garmisch. I found the post office and posted the letters.

When I got back to Garmisch station I couldn't remember the name of the place I had to book to, nor the name of the house or person we were staying with. I searched my bag for some clue but found nothing. I panicked. I then remembered that the name of the station ended in . . . grinau, but discovered that there were two places, Untergrinau and Obergrinau. I decided to settle on the latter. When I got there it meant nothing to me. I tried talking to the passengers who got off the train with me, but they didn't understand a word I said, and eventually I found myself on my own outside the station. I felt very small and lonely as I stood there with the mountains of the Austrian Tyrol looking down on me. I was alone and lost. I was like a little child. I wished myself back in my friendly Yorkshire village with my mother to care for me. I called for help. It came. I was suddenly warm inside and carefree, no longer alone. A fresh strength had entered my body and my mind. A spirit touched me. I allowed the sensation to take over. When it had passed my mind was clear, I knew what I had to do. I found the station phone box, telephoned the Continental Hotel in Munich where we'd been staying, got someone who spoke English and asked if they knew where Lady Astor was now. They did but wouldn't tell me. I explained who I was and asked them to ring Lady Astor giving my whereabouts and to tell her, 'Rose is lost'. They did this, for in minutes a car arrived for me, with my lady. I was a little girl again. I flung myself into her arms and said, 'Whatever you do don't scold me.' I then told her my story, leaving out the prayer bit. 'But whatever made you ring the hotel at Munich?' she said. Then I explained about my prayer. She put her hand in mine, saying nothing, but I could sense her understanding and love at that moment. 'Stuff and nonsense! You're imagining things,' I can hear people say, but

I know the truth of what happened as my lady did, as anyone else will who has had a similar experience.

The other occasion I am able to recall was when I was called before a tribunal who were to decide into what wartime job I should be recruited. On the face of things as a lady's maid I stood no chance of exemption. My lady had asked me if she could send a letter. I refused. I wasn't ungrateful to her but something in me thought it would be wrong. I had to appear at Slough in Buckinghamshire. On the train down I dismissed all thoughts of what I was going to say from my mind. I thought about my lady, the times we'd had together and the work I was doing for her and the country. Her ladyship had one of her secretaries meet me at the station to escort me to where I had to go. 'She didn't want you to be alone in your ordeal.' 'What ordeal?' I thought to myself. When my time came to appear I was ushered in front of five ladies in uniform.

'What is your present employment?' one of them asked.

'Lady's maid,' I replied, and I could see from her and the other faces that they thought I was an easy one.

'What would you like to do for the war effort?'

'Stay where I am.'

'Why?'

Then I told them. I think it was the greatest speech I'd ever made. I told them about her ladyship's work as a Member of Parliament and Mayoress of Plymouth. How it was my job to see that she was fit to do hers, and simply and truthfully I said how I'd been able to assist both her and his lordship. 'Where are all these words coming from?' I asked myself as I said them. It was as if it was not me that was speaking.

I must have gone on for about five minutes. The chairman looked flabbergasted. Without even consulting the others she said, 'Thank you, Miss Harrison, we shall not be requiring your services. Please continue in the good work that you're doing.' And the others murmured their agree-

ment. Then I was outside telling the good news to the
secretary, who fled to telephone Lady Astor. Again I was
sure that someone else had taken over. So was her ladyship.
'I was praying too, Rose,' she said, though how she knew I
was remains a mystery.

I've already said that Lady Astor was a devoted Christian
Scientist. Now having said that I don't question other
people's beliefs, let me say that neither did I question her
ladyship's. I fulfilled to the letter everything she asked me
to in the practice of her faith. It never entered my head to
influence her in any way. I never called a doctor. Only one
stipulation did I make, that if I thought she was seriously
ill I would get in touch with Miss Wissie or the boys and
hand over the responsibility to them. This was made of
course after his lordship's death, though since he too was a
Christian Scientist I would if I had thought it necessary
have gone over his head to the children, while he was alive.

My lady went to church every Sunday and on Wednes-
days when she was in London. She read her books and the
Bible every morning and every evening. So did his lordship.
They had not always been Scientists, my lady was the first
to change from the Protestant religion at the beginning of
the First World War. Her great friend at that time, and for
the rest of her life, was Philip Kerr, later Lord Lothian,
who was to be our Ambassador in America shortly after the
beginning of the Second World War. He was born a Roman
Catholic, but as a result of my lady's conversion, he was
persuaded to read *Science and Health*, was impressed with
it, and after a little time renounced Catholicism. His lordship followed their example shortly afterwards.

While I am sure all three got help and consolation from
their faith, and although I met many good men and women
who were Scientists, particularly the practitioners whose
lives were a living example of what their religion should be,
in my experience of watching it I believe it to be harmful
not only to its followers but to people around them. Here I

am not just referring to Scientists' attitude towards doctors and medicine. It teaches people to think far too much about themselves, their own bodies and souls. So long as they are in good health they're unsympathetic and impatient. Other people's sickness is their own fault. If they were better spiritually they wouldn't be ill. I've never heard of a Christian Science mission to help the sick, undernourished and deprived. It lacks what is to me the cornerstone of any faith: charity, and to a greater or lesser extent this is reflected in the actions of the people who follow it.

Yet you will say this often belies the picture that I have painted of Lady Astor. It does and it doesn't. She was a creature of instinct and I believe that when she allowed her true nature to take over she was a fine person. It was when she harnessed herself to her religion that things went wrong with her. Despite the work that she put into it I don't think Science ever really satisfied her, and I believe that towards the end of her life she realized this. Mr Lee said to me once, 'Lady Astor is not a religious woman, she's all the time looking for a light she can never find.' Christian Science though suited her way of life. It had no dogma and could be twisted and bent to excuse her faults and actions. It made her smug and sometimes self-righteous. It was as though she had invited Our Lord to one of her parties, he had accepted and sat at her right hand. It encouraged her to hate groups of people, Roman Catholics – 'Red Cherries' – as she called them, the Irish, the anti-prohibitionists. Yet perversely, among her greatest friends were Hilaire Belloc, a bigoted Catholic and Jew-hater, and two godless Socialists, Sean O'Casey and Bernard Shaw. The latter, with Lord Lothian, could without any doubt be called her two closest friends. Again Christian Science is only for the rich or the middle class. You can't get a practitioner on the National Health, nor do you find one of their churches in a poor area. You buy your pardons. It cost the Astors plenty.

The Astor children were brought up on Christian

Science, though I don't think they ever understood it, let alone practised it. It's my opinion that they looked on it as a bit of a joke. It was the only way they could tolerate it. Though I wasn't there at the time there's a family story about Mr Billy who when he was at Eton coxed a boat for the school at Henley Regatta. His crew got through the first heat, but was beaten in the second. Mr Billy was given a dressing-down by her ladyship. Their first victory, according to his mother, was because he had done his Christian Science lesson on that day, but his defeat, and that of the eight men whose boat he was steering, was because he hadn't done it on the subsequent day. If that interpretation of religion is given to a young man he can only despise or laugh at it.

If good health is proof of a religion then my lady was a saint. There were only two occasions when she had anything really wrong with her, until her final illness. The common cold and the odd dose of flu is not supposed to count with Scientists. Once she had a bad boil under her arm which was causing her great pain. There came a time when I said to her, 'If you'll allow me, my lady, I think I can shift it.' She was playing according to the Christian Scientist's rules when she agreed. 'It's going to hurt,' I told her. It must have done, but she gritted her teeth and no cry came from her. I was able to get the thing away and she was grateful. She showed great courage.

The second occasion was more worrying. She had a quinsy in her throat, though I was not sure what it was at the time. She took to her bed and was unable to eat anything. She got thinner and thinner until finally the quinsy burst. I felt I could no longer take the responsibility for her so I phoned Mr David, and he arrived with a doctor. She recovered fast, though she was then nearly eighty. I think that most of us would be happy if we thought that those two things were all that was to be wrong with us during our last thirty-five years of life.

Much as she may have deprecated the medical profession in its attitude towards ordinary illness her behaviour towards the doctors, surgeons and nurses at the Military Hospital at Cliveden, and to the hospitals in Plymouth, was one of admiration, courtesy and kindness. She was a constant visitor. Her ability to cheer people up was welcome medicine.

Once again there is the other side of the coin. The first occasion came shortly after I'd ceased serving Miss Wissie and had joined her ladyship. It was in the December of 1929. Miss Wissie had gone hunting in Northamptonshire with the Pytchley and had taken a very bad tumble. She was carried on a gate to Kelmarsh Hall where she was staying with her cousin Nancy, wife of the Master of the hunt, Ronald Tree. Doctors were summoned and so was my lady. Fortunately someone also called a radiologist who brought along portable equipment. The doctors found nothing radically wrong, but the radiologist did. Miss Wissie had badly injured her spine, and he told my two so when they arrived with the Christian Science practitioner. Apparently there was a lot of humming and hawing until at last my lady agreed to call a doctor who had once operated on her. He arrived, but he was the wrong kind of specialist. He knew nothing about spines. It was a considerable time before somebody came who had the necessary knowledge, and when he did her ladyship was against him treating Miss Wissie. Eventually she gave way. Now I'm not saying that Miss Wissie received any lasting damage, but I am sure that if the doctors had been left alone Miss Wissie would have suffered less hardship. As it was it took her a long time to recover. What was so irritating was that Lady Astor later pretended that Miss Wissie had had no medical help and put her recovery down to Christian Science. It comes to something when you have to lie to justify your religion!

Then it's always been my opinion that ordinary medical treatment might have spared his lordship a deal of suffering, and his life might well have been extended. On the various occasions when I was called upon to look after him I would so much have liked the benefit of working under the advice of a doctor. I felt as though I was groping around in the dark. Still, he was a man of principles and he held them to the end.

Another person whose death I believed to have been untimely was Lord Lothian. He was very popular with the staff at Cliveden and was regarded by them as part of the family. He and her ladyship were very close, but there could never be any suspicion that their relationship was anything other than a friendly and spiritual one. I sometimes wondered whether there was a deeper affection on his side for he remained a bachelor. They were in constant correspondence and I suppose he was our most frequent visitor. Both Mr Lee and Arthur Bushell liked him, though Arthur complained about him always singing in the bath in the morning. It wasn't his voice that Arthur was concerned with. He didn't think it decent that any man should be quite so cheerful so early. Lord Lothian died in America, where he was British Ambassador at the end of 1940. People put his death down to strain and overwork but I don't think anyone ever died of that, they can make a sickness worse but they don't kill on their own. His death was a great shock to my lady. It would have been greater, but it came at a time when she was frantically busy and when the death even of those nearest and dearest is somehow more easy to accept.

I have already said that during the last few years of her life my lady relaxed in her religious practices. I suppose it can be said that she did the same over drink, though she didn't know it. We heard that Mrs Lancaster, when she was a visitor at Haseley, had given her a little Dubonnet pretending that it wasn't alcoholic. She told Charles Dean and me that she thought it did her good. It was her ladyship's custom to drink a glass of Ribena every morning at eleven and every afternoon at four, so from that time on if ever Charles thought she looked a bit down in the dumps he would put a thimbleful of Dubonnet in her glass. As it was of the same colour she couldn't detect it. It was Charles's belief that it brightened her up. I am not sure it wasn't wishful thinking on his part.

Although I have never been a drinker myself it was her attitude towards drink that irritated me most about her. I tried to make her see the comfort it could be to the working man or woman. She refused to. That was her trouble – she could only ever see one side. It was black or white with my lady. When she'd been on about it in Parliament it always hit the headlines. 'Don't you see,' I said, 'this is all you let them know about what you do. If only you'd leave it alone people might hear about some of the good things.' It was like talking to a brick wall.

Frank Copcutt, eventually head gardener at Cliveden, who lived in a cottage on the estate near to The Feathers Inn, tells a nice story with an ironic twist. The inn stood in the estate of Dropmore and was a Free House, which meant that it was not owned or leased by a brewery, but was let direct to the publican. When the incumbent died, the owners decided to sell it, because licensed premises fetched a good price. Generally such places were bought by local brewers since few individuals could afford them. It was put on the market and the brewers duly put in their bid. Frank is not quite sure whether it was actually offered to the Astors, but the agents who were selling saw to it that the brewery was given to believe that it had been, so, knowing that if they bought it the Astors would close the place, the brewers upped their bid way beyond the market price. In that way the ill wind of temperance blew somebody some good.

Her ladyship tried always to recruit staff who didn't drink. Both the housekeeper and Mr Lee had their orders on this, but as Mr Lee said, 'When you're interviewing somebody he's hardly likely to admit he's an alcoholic. In my experience and that of many of the butlers to whom I've spoken, it was the men who swore they were teetotallers when they were interviewed that turned out to be the hardened drinkers.'

Mr Lee was also instructed never to engage a Catholic. 'It's not a pleasant thing, Miss Harrison, to have to ask a man about his religious beliefs, but I had to do it. I very much admired one man who replied, "What does Lady Astor want, a footman or a bloody parson?" She once converted a footman to Science. He didn't last long; in service I mean. Once my lady mistook Gordon Grimmett for him and asked how his Bible-reading was going. Gordon looked at her startled. "Oh," she said, "I didn't know it was you, Gordon, I wouldn't ask you that question: you're too far gone for redemption." '

Some of her secretaries were Scientists but it was impossible to recruit household staff who were. As I have said, it's not a religion for the working class.

Apart from making rosettes at election time politics was something I kept out of. My lady used to rattle on at me about it, but I refused to get drawn. As I've explained earlier she was mostly concerned where politics affected individuals or groups of people. She was all for women's rights, but was never a suffragette. I think she believed that if she got labelled as one it would lessen her chances of getting done the things she wanted doing.

There was a time when I became politically interested and so did many of the staff. It was when our house gave its name to a political group, the 'Cliveden Set'. I'm sure it's been given many more profound definitions, but the way I understood it was that my two were members of a band of people who believed in what Hitler was doing in Germany, wanted to keep on terms with him whatever he did and were plotting to bring about an Anglo-German alliance. I know a great deal has been written by historians and some of it I tried to understand. I could have saved myself the trouble, it didn't alter my judgement; if anything it made me more certain that the whole idea was poppycock.

By reason of my job I knew my lord and lady intimately. I didn't perhaps know a lot about them politically or intellectually, but I knew what by their natures they were capable of doing and not doing. I expect I shall be accused of over-simplifying, but if what I have written about my lady could permit anyone to believe that she was the kind of woman who would have been able to plot with a foreign power, or indeed the kind that any foreign power would plot with, then I haven't presented her as I should have. It just wasn't in her nature. She was too open. She didn't like anything or anybody that was underhand. She wouldn't have cheated her own political party; she went against them from time to time but she always let them know why.

Then who in his right mind in Germany would have plotted with her? They weren't a bunch of fools, they were a clever and formidable nation and must have done some research on her character. She could never have kept a secret. She was too changeable, too liable to blow hot then cold. She was too much an individual. I'm not saying she couldn't be devious. What woman can't? But when she was it was as a person not as a member of a team.

Then there was his lordship. Straight as a pit-prop. More British than the British. A conventional man if ever there was one. Always trying to persuade my lady to go through the proper channels. Clever people may try to make a meal and earn a coin or two out of the Cliveden myth but anyone who really knew either of them can only treat the idea with scorn.

Arthur Bushell laughed it off but he resented its implications. 'A pack of lies, Rose, whoever invented them ought to come and work here for a week as a housemaid. They'd find no Nazis under Cliveden beds.'

Mr Lee was of the same opinion. 'They write about Herr

Ribbentrop as if he was a crony of the Astors'. He's been to lunch once at St James's Square, never at Cliveden. Most other ambassadors in London would consider this a pretty poor score.'

Later he said to me, 'I suppose all servants become sensitive to atmosphere, it goes with their job. My men and I would have been bound to have had a scent of what was happening while it was supposed to be going on, so would you. Then if it had been true and we hadn't, we should have noticed some kind of serious reaction when the Press came out with the story. There was only laughter. It was all balderdash, Miss Harrison!'

If it needed anything else to convince me that the story was false it was her ladyship's attitude when I spoke to her about it, both at the time and later. She went all airy-fairy. Would neither confirm it nor deny it. It suited her to wallow in the notoriety. She got a kick out of it. She was, as I've said, one hundred per cent woman!

Apart from the Cliveden smear people were saying around that time and indeed since that my two were friendly with Hitler. This again is laughable. If either his lordship or my lady had even been in the same room with him she would never have stopped talking about it. There's nothing wrong with having looked the devil in the eyes. If my lady had met Mephistopheles she'd have boasted about it.

My only other political encounter was more personal and amusing. It didn't happen until after my lady had retired from Parliament. She was speaking on the West Hoe at Plymouth in support of Colonel Grand who was standing as Conservative candidate for her old division. Florrie Manning, the housekeeper at Elliot Terrace, suggested to me that we went to the meeting to hear my lady. It was held in the open air and we had a grandstand view of the platform from a bank at the back of the crowd. It all seemed to be going well, her ladyship was making all her points loud and clear as she always did with me. Then she started talking about her love of Plymouth and how proud she was of the way they'd behaved there during the blitz. At this some women behind me started making nasty audible comments about her. 'What would she know about how we behaved during the blitz? She wasn't here.'

I felt my hackles rising, but tried to restrain myself. Then when my lady was referring to the part the men of the city had played during the war, they began again. 'Men at war. Her husband had it cushy, so did her sons, I'll be bound.'

That was too much for me, I turned on them. 'You want to get your facts straight before you start saying things like that,' I said. 'I served Lady Astor during the war and I'll tell you some of the things she did for the likes of you. And I'll tell you about her sons.'

I went at them hammer and tongs and within seconds had quite a crowd around me. They egged me on. Then Florrie joined in. Our opponents gave way before the attack and fled. Things settled down for a bit but our feathers were still ruffled, so when some man started shouting about how Russia had won the war we waded into him. 'If it's such a marvellous place why don't you go there? We don't want the likes of you enjoying our freedom and then running the country down.'

He was more formidable than the other two and things got a bit ugly. 'You're a couple of capitalist cows,' he shouted at us, which was probably just as well because a policeman came up and told him he was using insulting language, and moved him away. The rest of the meeting passed off quietly enough.

As I dressed my lady that evening she suddenly said out of the blue: 'I've wasted your talents over the years, Rose.'

'What do you mean, my lady?'

'I saw you and Florrie this afternoon taking on the hecklers. In future you must come to all my meetings.'

'Not for all the tea in China,' I replied. 'I was lucky to

come away unharmed. I'll never risk my life like that again.'

I was as good as my word. Opening her rude letters was enough for me.

Politics and religion I'm told on good authority are the two subjects most likely to cause trouble, and publicans advise their customers to keep off them. I have tried to be brief, but since they were two of the most important things in Lady Astor's life, I couldn't ignore them altogether. I know I must have given offence to some and I apologize, but since I have learnt from my Yorkshire childhood to 'speak as I find', I have done just that.

There is one last thought while we're on the subject. There was something to be said for having a mistress who was a Christian Scientist. I never had to worry about packing pills or medicines.

Some two years before the war Lady Astor had said to me, 'Promise you'll never leave me, Rose.'

'That, my lady, is a stupid thing to ask me to do,' I replied. 'How do either of us know what the future holds? I've no intention of going at the moment so let's just leave it at that.'

It was during one of her emotional outbursts. She had them from time to time if she felt that someone had let her down. She wanted the assurance of my loyalty to compensate. I suppose if she'd asked me the same question after the war I would have been able to give my promise. Our lives were now it seemed irrevocably tied together.

One of the extraordinary things about the British is that after a catastrophe like a war with the social changes it brings, we expect to go back and start again where we left off. I know I did, so I think did my lady. She felt she'd been stripped unnecessarily of her Parliamentary duties, but I think felt that she could get back some of her old glory by entertaining again at St James's Square. This was not to be allowed her either. It had been bombed and his lordship decided to sell it to the government. A smaller establishment at 35 Hill Street, was bought, but it could never equal the glamour of our old town house. The size of the staff is an indication. There was only a butler and one footman, a housekeeper and one housemaid, a chef and a kitchenmaid, a chauffeur, William, the odd man and myself. The working hours were now much shorter so dailies were employed to compensate, but the old feeling of unity in the house was gone and would never return.

At Cliveden some servants had returned and more staff were recruited in the house and gardens. Mr Lee got some semblance of the pre-war service, but he was forever sighing about his staff, and he and I would wistfully recall the good old days and the good old faces. 'Change and decay in all around we saw.' Luckily in my job I was a loner. Nevertheless, despite Mr Lee's seeming pessimism he very soon had a good working team.

As I've indicated earlier much of our time now was spent travelling. When we were in England we were more at Rest Harrow where my lady took her frustrations out on the little golf ball. She just couldn't seem to settle. She continued to bear a grudge against his lordship for removing her from politics. I think that both he and I hoped that she would find some social work, the kind of thing she'd proved so good at organizing during the war, to occupy her mind. But work without the political power to back it was no consolation to her. She seemed to avoid his lordship's company at Cliveden. Fortunately he had his interests, the horses and the gardens. Frank Copcutt, the head gardener, and he were very near to each other, and he still worked on the reconstruction of Plymouth. During the next few years his health began to fail and he had to take to a wheelchair. I'm glad to say that by this time my lady's heart had relented towards him and she was able to be a deal of comfort to him until his death in 1952. Although expected, it came as a shock to her. She missed him more than she thought possible. He was her rock. Now she had no one to dance round. Even though they were so often away from each other his image had been there. She looked to others for consolation, but I don't think she ever found it. She thought she could compensate for her lack of attention to his lordship by nourishing Mr Bernard Shaw in his old age, but he later resented her attentions and a friendship of years nearly went sour on her.

With his lordship's death the title and Cliveden passed to Mr Billy. He had infinite thought for her ladyship. He remembered Lord Astor's last words to him: 'Look after your mother.' Thinking that the loss of Cliveden six years after losing St James's Square would be more than she could bear, he immediately told her that she could run it for as long as she wanted. She tried for a short time, but soon realized it was too much for her. Hill Street and Rest Harrow from then on were our only two real homes.

Let me not though become too introspective on her behalf. She still had plenty of spirit and fun in her and she remained a formidable lady to serve. She and I continued to battle on together. She didn't give up trying to outdo and better me till the end. I have a letter she wrote me only three years before her death in which, after giving me a bit of praise and urging me to return before the end of my holiday, she went on to say, 'There's one thing I feel I must ask you, Rose, and that is not to interrupt me before I've finished speaking. It's a very bad habit of yours, you know.' That after thirty-two years of my doing it!

Although as I've said we were out of public life my lady had a few memorable occasions of which probably the Royal Wedding of Princess Elizabeth and Prince Philip was the first in the post-war period. She went with her son, his lordship. A Royal Wedding is a testing-time for a lady's maid. The slightest thing wrong and it reflects on you. It's like getting a horse ready for the big race: there are a lot of things to be considered. First there's the style of the outfit. While that is decided between a lady and her dressmaker (in Lady Astor's case Madame Rémond of Beauchamp Place), a maid's opinion may be asked for. Although this can cause trouble, it must be honestly given. Some dressmakers go for an effect for their own sakes and don't always fully consider what suits the customer. Such occurrences were rare with my lady since she knew what she wanted, and said it. Anyway our tastes seemed always to tally, except for the occasional outrageous hat that I think she sometimes bought just to spite me.

My lady's outfit was plain, neat and smart and very effective. She wore a black velvet suit, to which were pinned her medals; her black sable stole, black patent shoes and a black hat with pink ostrich feathers and of course some of her most precious jewels. She was easy to dress. We had a trial run the day before so there was no question of last-minute panics like buttons coming off or zips going wrong. Then, unlike some other ladies, she always got to the course in the pink of condition. She took it easy a day or two before, early nights so that her skin was at its best. There were no tantrums about 'Where have these wrinkles come from?' that some ladies' maids had to endure and couldn't answer truthfully, 'The gin bottle and late nights on the tiles, my lady.' So she enjoyed these occasions and graced them because she looked good and felt good. Many people think that ladies like Lady Astor buy clothes for things like weddings and receptions and never wear them again. This in all my experience is untrue. I know that that velvet suit was worn so many times that eventually I had to pronounce it unfit for further service. It was the same with most of my lady's things.

One of the last large-scale parties that my lady gave was at Hill Street. It was for Davina Bowes-Lyon, a niece of the Queen Mother, who later married the Earl of Stair. It was for about seven hundred people. The house itself was of course too small, so at Mr Lee's suggestion a marquee was erected in the garden, linked to the ballroom. It really was a triumph of organization and the supper party and ball went with a swing. It turned sour on poor Mr Lee though. About half-way through the proceedings, while he was serving soft drinks to the guests (her ladyship had made this a stipulation when offering to give the party), Mr Bowes-Lyon, who was with a circle of people talking to the Queen, turned to Mr Lee and asked for a large whisky and soda. 'I'm sorry, sir,' he replied, 'that would be going against her ladyship's orders. If you get her permission I'll gladly fetch you one.'

'Don't be a fool, Lee, I don't need her permission, go and get me one.'

'I'm sorry, sir, I'm only a servant here and I have one mistress to whom I'm responsible. I must refuse.' And Mr Lee moved away.

It was obvious to my lady from Mr Bowes-Lyon's expression that something had gone wrong. She questioned Mr Lee, who told her what had happened. 'You should have told him to go out and buy himself one,' she said, indignantly. 'Never mind, I'll do it.' And she did.

'It didn't end there,' he told me. 'After this party Mrs Bowes-Lyon gave me five pounds for the servants. Naturally I thought it was for the menservants and divided it out accordingly. It wasn't much in all conscience for the hours and work they'd put in: it came to about one pound each. Mrs Hawkins, the housekeeper, heard that there had been some form of hand-out and was indignant that the maidservants had not had anything. She spoke to Lady Astor who in turn spoke to me about it. I explained the situation to her ladyship and when I mentioned the amount I'd been given she nearly exploded. I offered to share it round further, but she refused to allow me to do so. "Leave everything to me, Lee," she said, and stalked off. It was really all a storm in a teacup, Miss Harrison, but it had unfortunate consequences. She must have had words with Mr and Mrs Bowes-Lyon because from then on they were both always ill-at-ease in my presence.'

I have already mentioned our hasty return from America for the Coronation. It caught me unawares, as had the Queen Mother's invitation, and there was a lot to do in a little time. My lady's robes had been in a tin trunk since before the war and needed a deal doing to them: cleaning, restyling and refitting. All right, some peeresses didn't bother much, robes were robes and there was little you could do about them except to get the smell of mothballs out. This was not Lady Astor's attitude; she had to look just so, and I'm glad that she did, otherwise I could have had little pride in my job.

Then the jewels had to be selected and the Astor tiara cleaned. I must say my lady looked an absolutely perfect picture. She understood how to carry costume and how to move in it. It was the actress in her. She practised too, not leaving anything to chance. It has always astonished me how few peers ever managed to look anything in robes. They're supposed to add dignity to the occasion, but more often than not they do the opposite. Men seem to approach wearing robes selfconsciously, as if they are convinced they're going to look foolish, and so do end up looking like idiots. If any footman had the same attitude towards his livery he wouldn't have lasted two minutes with Mr Lee.

Ten days before the Coronation came the news that contrary to my expectations I had to visit Rhodesia with her ladyship, and that I was to travel on the afternoon of the Coronation. I remember it as one of the days of my life. Up at five, dressing my lady, getting her away on time – she had to be in her seat in the Abbey by eight-thirty – seeing that all her luggage was packed for a three-month tour, then putting my bits together. No wonder I needed a large brandy when I finally got on that Comet.

One thing I had missed in my life in service was a visit to a royal palace in Britain. I was anxious to see at first-hand how the staff were treated. One of the housekeepers from Cliveden had left us to go to Buckingham Palace, but she had been there before my time and though Mr Lee had remained friendly with her and had indeed visited the Palace on several occasions, I didn't just want to take his word about conditions there. I was therefore delighted when in May 1957 my lady had an invitation to stay at Holyroodhouse, Her Majesty's Edinburgh home. My lady's room was everything I expected it would be, but my own left much to be desired. It was a tiny place at the top of the palace with an iron bedstead, an old washstand and a nasty brown jug of cold water standing on it, a rush-bottom chair which I dared not trust myself on and a threadbare mat on the linoleum floor.

The servants' hall was little better. If there was a Pugs' Parlour I wasn't invited into it. There was no one to welcome me, the food was of the 'cookhouse door' kind, and served like it. There was one pat of margarine per person to be spread on a doorstep slice of bread. 'If this is life inside a fairy-tale palace I want none of it,' I thought as I pushed my plate away. When I dressed my lady I spared her none of the details. She was attending a banquet there so it was the full treatment: sparklers, the lot. As I was getting her ready and explaining my discomfort I asked her if she thought the Queen knew of the servants' conditions. 'I don't suppose so, Rose,' my lady said in that resigned voice of hers that she put on when she was tired of a subject.

'Then I shall write and tell her,' I said. 'It's high time she did. I'm sure she'll be glad to know so that things can be put right.'

This jolted my lady out of her complacency. 'You'll do nothing of the sort, Rose,' she declared indignantly. We spent the next quarter of an hour having a battle royal!

I must say that before my lady went down to the banquet she looked particularly beautiful in a wonderful pale lavender taffeta dress which her diamond tiara and earrings shone over like glistening stars. It was as if she was a delicate piece of china. As I looked at her my mood changed to one of sweet sadness and I felt the tears behind my eyes. For the first time I realized that she'd grown old. It had at last become noticeable to me. When later I heard the pipers playing outside the palace their plaintive notes matched my feelings. 'I shall remember Holyrood for more reasons than the discomfort,' I thought.

When on my return I told Mr Lee about the conditions

that I'd found there he was not surprised. 'Service with the Royals,' he said, 'is on too big a scale so it becomes less personal. It's like the factory floor, you have your particular duties to do, you rarely go outside them, it's a narrow sort of life. I once employed a footman from the Palace, but he had to go. He'd been used to set duties and resented doing anything that he thought was outside them. No initiative and no real interest in the purpose of the job.'

By 1958 it had become obvious that the house at Hill Street was an unnecessary responsibility. We were no longer entertaining on any scale and were only ever there for a few months in the year. It was sold and we leased a flat at 100 Eaton Square, part of the Duke of Westminster's estate. It was spacious enough, on the first floor and running the length of four converted houses. We had an excellent staff of the old school. Charles Dean, one-time footman, valet and under-butler at Cliveden, was now butler, Mrs Hawkins the housekeeper, the old and trusted William, odd man, an Austrian chef, Otto Dangl, who came to us from Lord Allendale and was to prove a wizard in the kitchen, and myself. There were of course under-servants, two in each department, a chauffeur who lived with his Rolls in Belgrave Mews and dailies to do the rough work.

So with Lord Billy's instructions that her ladyship was to want for nothing, we lived well and happily. We were now reaping the rewards for our years of service. The greatest of these was the complete trust shown in us by the Astor children. It's easy to say we deserved it, so had many others in our position who never got it from the families they'd served. It was something quite exceptional and something I shall remember until my dying day. It was given in the same manner by each of the children, even by Mr Bobbie Shaw who hadn't quite the same 'tribal feeling' as the others.

Apart from the frailty that I had first noticed at Holyroodhouse there were now other signs that my lady was growing old. Her memory, on which she'd so prided herself, began noticeably to fail on occasions and this made her tetchy. I also realized that my own attitude towards her had changed. I was more tolerant in a patronizing, 'there-there', sort of way, like a mother with a petulant baby. Not all the time of course, she would in some moods have resented it, but I found it was creeping in. She now became resentful if I was away from her. My mother had died and I'd now taken possession of the bungalow I had bought for her, and enjoyed spending some time there working on it, getting it the way I wanted it to be. My lady didn't like it. On my return I would be cross-examined as to where I'd been and what I'd done, and I'd be accused of neglecting her.

The other servants suffered too with her constant inquiries: 'Where's Rose? What time is she coming back? Why has she gone and left me?'

Perhaps as I write it it seems I was conceited and that I considered myself indispensable; believe me it wasn't that. I got so that I couldn't enjoy myself on my time off. I wondered what she would be getting up to and how the other servants were coping with her. Eventually I decided that for everybody's peace of mind it would be better if I confined my visits home to the Wednesday of each week from one-fifteen to nine p.m. It wasn't unselfishness on my part. It made life easier and for a greater happiness all round.

Now too I had to see my lady into bed. She was quite capable of attending to herself, but she developed the habit of getting half undressed, then thinking of something else she wanted to do and either getting into a dressing-gown or dressing again and busying herself around the flat. I couldn't sleep while she was doing this so I got into the way of being with her until she was in bed, tucking her up and putting her light out. Once again just as one would with a child. Unfortunately it was always past midnight before she could be persuaded into her room, so it was late nights for all of us, since neither Charles nor Otto would go to bed until I had. We got to enjoy our chats over hot drinks when my lady was safely stowed. It seemed the one time of day we could safely relax.

Our travels hadn't ceased, indeed it seemed we were away somewhere every weekend. When I put my lady's things out for packing I used to feel like saying to them, 'Now you all know where to go so why don't you just pop in.' Another sign of my lady's age was her sudden change of attitude towards money. She began to imagine she was poor. 'We must be careful, Rose,' she'd say, 'I've now only got four thousand a year to live on.'

This was a nonsense of course, it was nearer forty thousand, but it became quite an obsession with her. It didn't cure her foolish generosity towards others. I now had another duty; mistress of my lady's purse. We had found, and so had some of the scroungers who haunted Eaton Square, that she was still an easy touch and would often go out with a purse full of money and come back with it empty and nothing to show for it. It was obvious where it was going. At first when I took control she was allowed five pounds to take with her, but I later cut it to two pounds. Her cheque book was also taken from her when it became obvious that the scroungers were not all of one class.

There were two great events which regaled my lady's last years: her eightieth birthday party and the bestowing on her of the freedom of the City of Plymouth. Why the citizens had waited so long to give her this was something none of us could understand, but then in my experience city councillors are a rum, self-seeking and self-important lot. They even make me feel snobbish. Not quite out of the top drawer, many of them, and going out of their way to make this apparent. Some members showed how they felt about democracy by refusing to attend. It was one of the early symptoms of a disease which has now become wide-spread. However my lady managed brilliantly without their presence. She rose to any such occasion and gave a glimpse of her old energy and spirit. She also gave the city a splendid present, her diamond and sapphire necklace, to grace the bosoms of future mayoresses. I hope they've found some at least half as worthy of it as she was.

Naturally our visit there was not without incident. On the way to the dinner in her honour (she was wearing the necklace at the time), she lost part of it, a pear-shaped diamond drop with two shamrock shapes, valued then at five hundred pounds. She had to apologize that it was incomplete, but since it was insured she was able to promise them that it would eventually be made whole. She also announced that anyone finding it would receive ten per cent of its value.

When she returned from the ceremony she told me about the loss. I searched everywhere and eventually discovered it in the gutter outside 3 Elliot Terrace. My efforts were applauded, but needless to say when I mentioned my right to the reward it fell upon deaf ears.

My lady's eightieth birthday party was organized by the children. It was a gathering of the tribe given in the style that could be expected. My lady was honoured by her family. They were all there, and so were her immediate friends and relations, and the people like myself who had served her. She was given a solitaire diamond ring by the children, a real beauty it was. It delighted her. In a way I felt a little responsible for the choice since for years it had been the habit of Miss Wissie and the boys to ask me what I thought their mother would like for Christmas or for her birthdays and I'd always suggested a diamond ring, and afterwards given alternatives. It had become a sort of family joke. This time she got it. Diamonds were her favourite jewels. I remember once when she was dressed up to the nines for some function, she turned to me and said, 'What do I look like, Rose?' Quick as a flash it came to me: 'Cartier's, my lady.'

The last years passed, I won't say easily but without much incident, and with only one illness, the quinsy which I have described earlier. Physically and mentally she grew weaker but there were never any signs of senility. She was in possession of all her faculties, and was a handful to the last. Death in old age when it approaches is so often pathetic. It's like a tree falling. It cannot be raised, the leaves gradually wither and die. It was like this with my lady. In the middle of April 1964 I went home to Walton-on-Thames for the weekend, knowing that while I was there her ladyship would be with Miss Wissie at her home, Grimsthorpe.

On the Saturday she had a slight stroke while sitting in the drawing-room and was put to bed. On the Monday morning a car arrived for me at Walton and I was driven to Grimsthorpe. I was not shocked by her appearance when I saw her. Her speech was generally slower than it had been, but there were periods when there were flashes of her old spirit. I think she knew she was dying but she didn't give up, nor did she struggle against death. She had a doctor and eventually a day and night nurse. She didn't resent them but she wanted people around her whom she knew.

After about a week she drifted into a coma. She was conscious of what was going on and she knew that I was with her. I held her hand all the time that we were together and by the changing pressures we seemed to be able to say something to each other, and when I kissed her goodnight her grip seemed to tighten. As she grew thinner I would put a hand under her hip-bone to give her some relief from the pressure on it. She hated having to be turned by the nurses and would call out, 'Don't let them do it, Rose.' The coma became deeper. Now I felt powerless to help in any way; I could only be with her and watch her slipping away. On the Friday evening of the first of May I heard her speak her last word. She lifted up her hands and called out, 'Waldorf.' I left her at eight o'clock.

The next morning at seven Miss Wissie woke me to tell me that she was dead. I think perhaps she thought I would break down. 'Don't make it harder for me, Rose,' she said. But it wasn't really news and I was ready to withstand the shock. There was nothing more I could do at Grimsthorpe. I packed my belongings. I was going home. There was only one other thing I wanted while I was there, a last glimpse of my lady. 'Shall I come in with you, Rose?' Miss Wissie asked when I told her.

'No thank you,' I replied.

'But aren't you afraid?'

'No, Miss Wissie,' I said, 'death is nothing to be afraid of.'

I went into the bedroom. She looked so beautiful, and so very peaceful. She had suffered so little. It was a good picture to take away with me. I had one other thing to take as well, a link with the past, 'Madam', my lady's dog. Together we slipped quietly out of the house.

This then was the end of my life in service. During the next weeks I had time to take stock of myself. I was not dissatisfied as I looked back over my life. If complacency is necessarily a fault then I was guilty of it. I had given her my best and I had got a lot back from doing it. I'd fulfilled my ambition, I'd travelled the world, met interesting people, made many friends and most important of all become a member of a wonderful family. These were the big blessings I could count and there were many more.

Of course I missed my lady, particularly to begin with. There was a great sense of loss that had not been immediately apparent on her death. But if this book does nothing else it must show the many memories that I had of her, and which I could recall over the years ahead of me. And the family were still there and have been to this day. 'You will never want for anything, Rose,' her ladyship often said to me. The children have seen to it that their mother's word has been honoured. I was given a pension and instructed to ask for help if ever I wanted it. I think they will agree that I have made few demands on them. There is something else they have given me which has made my retirement the richer: their continued affection and interest. I visit them, they visit me. I am still one of the tribe.

Index

Figures in **bold type** indicate whole chapters or sections. For places visited, *see* 'travel'. *Abbreviations:* A – Astor, l.m. – lady's maid.

Aberconway, Lord, 32
Abercrombie, Lord, 194
Aberdeen, Marchioness of, 25
Aldfield village, Yorkshire, 1–14
Alexander, Frederick (under-butler), **141–2**
Alexandra, Princess, 30, 117
Americans in Britain, 181, 190, 200
Ancaster, Countess of (*formerly* Hon. Phyllis Astor, 'Miss Wissie', *q.v.*), 37, 173, 229, 259, 260
Anton, Count (of Hapsburg), 211
Appleby, Westmorland: Castle, 17, 20–3, 29, 166; Mayor of, 24
Apsley, Lady, 34
Ascot, Berkshire, 115; Week (racing), 29, 36, 135, **139–41**, 201
Ashton, (Sir) Frederick (choreographer), 138
Asquith, Margaret, Lady, 100
Astor, Miss Alice, 40, 55–6, 137–9
Astor, 'Billy', *see* Astor, Hon. William A.
Astor, Hon. David (2nd son of Lord and Lady A), 46, 167, 171, 172, 199, 233
Astor, Hon. Jacob ('Jakie', 4th son of Lord and Lady A), 46, 149, 158, 163, 167, 171, 172, 207
Astor, John Jacob (1763–1848), 40, 91
Astor, Lady, Viscountess Astor; Nancy Witcher, *née* Langhorne; (*sometime* Mrs Robert G. Shaw): personal characteristics, 37, 39, 44–6 p, 51–2, 54, 58, 62–7, 81–2, 88–103, 129, 135, 141, 158, 165, 192, 217, 222, 239, 245; her family, 44–5; birth and early life, 45; first marriage, 45, 89; first child, *see* Shaw, 'Bobbie'; a staunch teetotaller, 45, 124, 126–7, 181, 241, 242–3; second marriage, 45, 89–90; her Astor children, 46, **150–7**, 171, 238–9, 255, 258 (*see also under their names*); and 'Miss Wissie's' clothes, 52; her furs and jewellery, 52–3, 70–9, 141, 253;

and her l.m. (Rose), **63–80, 81–260**; and Christian Science, *q.v.*, 63, 64, 85, 145, 237–40; recreations, 49, 63, 64; daily routine, 63–4; and politics, 66, 243–7 (*see also* House of Commons); and Marks & Spencer, 67, 68; hats, 68–9, 139; and umbrellas, 69; and fans, 69–70; and lace, 70; and the Sancy diamond, 71–3; her pearls missing, 73–4; re-stringing her pearls, 77; and Lord Astor, 90, 96, 98–9, 145–6, 192, 204, 223, 249–50; and Mr Guy (Canadian), 90–1; and the two pictures, 91; 'an easy touch', 91–2, 257; and Rose's mother and family, 92–3, 101–3; and presents for the staff, 93–4; and Mrs Brand, *q.v.* 94–5; and Royalty, 96–7; and sex, 97–8; and T. E. Lawrence, 98–9; and Winston Churchill, 99, 191, 204; her annual children's party, 100–1; and reference to servants in their presence, 121, 122; and Copcutt (gardener), *q.v.*, 129–30; and table decorations, *q.v.*, 131–2; and literary and theatrical people, 136; and music, 136; and Ascot Week and the Royal Ball, 139, 141; and Alexander (under-butler), 142; after ceasing to be MP, 146, 203–4; her 'blitzes', 152; and Tarbert Lodge, 157–8; and a shooting at Rest Harrow, 162–3; her dogs, 167–70, 260; and cats, 170–1; knitting socks, 171–2; and her sons' wives, and son-in-law, 172, 173; and 'Miss Wissie's' dinner dress, 173–4; and 'Billy' A and the Profumo affair, 175–7; in World War II, **178–204**; MP for Plymouth, and Lady Mayoress, 179; and the unexpected, 182–3; in Plymouth air raids, **184–9**; and a French boy in hospital, 191; her hospitality to strangers, 199; and Americans in Britain, 200; at Bow Street Magistrates' Court,

202; public speaking in USA, 206–7; Continental visits, 207–13 (*see also* travel); and the Abdication, 214–15; outspoken at Savannah (USA), 216; on board SS *Eros*, 217–19; attacks Senator McCarthy, 223; and Lord A's death, 223, 249; and Sir Stewart Gore-Brown, 226; and King and Queen of Sweden, 296; and Mrs Dana Gibson, 226; and Mrs Hobson, at Nassau, 226; and Mrs Dudley Ward, 228; with Nancy Lancaster to Sweden, 230–1; and Rose's church attendance, 234; and Lord Lothian, 238, 241; and 'Miss Wissie's' spinal injury, 240; and Bernard Shaw, 241, 249; speaking for Col. Grand at Plymouth, 245; after the war, 249; her later memorable occasions, 250; her dressmaker, 250; and Princess Elizabeth's wedding, 250–1; one of her last large-scale parties, 251; and Mr Bowes-Lyon, 252; and the Coronation (1953), 223–4, 252–3; at Holyroodhouse, 253, 254; her last years, 254, 255–60; her death, 260; *other mentions*, xi, 36–40, 44, 47–50, 162; *see also* travel

Astor, Lord (Waldorf, 2nd Viscount Astor): personal details, 44, 89–90, 144–5, 173, 200, 241, 244; his valet (Bushell, *q.v.*), 31–2; his father, 40, 71; marriage, 41, 45; Rose's high opinion of, 44, 144–5, 173; and racing, 64–5, 146–7; and the Sancy diamond, 71–2; and Lady Astor, 90, 96, 98–9, 141, 145–6, 192, 204, 223, 249–50; a teetotaller and Christian Scientist, 124, 126–7, 237; his other interests, 139; and Ascot Royal Ball, 141; sets standard for family and household, 144; his social security service, 148; and his children, 148–9, 152, 156, 171; and games, 148; daily routine, 148–9; visiting Russia, 164; his dogs, 167; and 'Jakie's' wedding, 172; and World War II, 178; Lord Mayor of Plymouth, 179, 203; in Plymouth air raids, 183, 186, 188, 190–2; ill, goes to Cornwall, 192–4; and re-building of Plymouth, 194, 249; and Americans in Britain, 200; to Yugoslavia, 210–11; on board *Queen of Bermuda*, 214; to New York, in SS *Eros*, 218; at Hotel Astor (N.Y.), 219; at Tucson,

Arizona, 221; his later sufferings, 240–1; after the war, 249; failing health, 249; his death, 174, 223, 237; *other mentions*, 47, 49, 50, 58
Astor, Hon. Michael (3rd son of Lord and Lady A), 44, 46, 107, 158, 167, 171, 172
Astor, Hon. Phyllis, *see* 'Wissie, Miss'
Astor, Vincent, 59, 214
Astor, Lady Violet, 51
Astor, Hon. William ('Billy', eldest son of Lord and Lady A; *later* 3rd Viscount Astor), 39, 46, 55, 149, 154, 167, 171, 239, 249–50; his marriage, 172; and the Profumo affair, 174–7; inherits title and estates, 174, 223, 249; and his mother, 249–50, 255
Astor, William Waldorf (Lord Astor's father, *later* 1st Viscount Astor), 40, 71
Astors, the, 29, 31, 36, 39–62, 234; family history, 40–7; estates and houses, 47–50; the family, 144–77; the children, 150–7, 238–9, 255, 258 (*see also under their names*)

Balsan, Lt-Colonel and Madame Jacques, 30
Baron, Lady (of Sawley Hall), 7
Bell, Sir Alan, 25
Belloc, Hilaire, 238
Bessie (l.m.), 27, 28
Bickham, Dartmoor, Devon, 196
Bouverie, Mrs, 40, 139, 201
Bowes-Lyon, Davina (*later* Countess of Stair), 251–2
Bowes-Lyon, Mr, 251–2
Brand, Jim (Lady A's nephew), 182, 185
Brand, Mrs (Lady A's sister), 57, 94–5, 214
Bray House, Cornwall, 170, 196
Brooks, Peter and 'Winkie' (Lady A's nephews), 57
Buccleuch, Duke of, 53
Buckingham Palace, 119, 253
Bullitt, William (US Ambassador in Paris), 220
Bushell, Arthur (Lord A's valet): his high opinion of Lord A, 178; in Plymouth air raids, 185, 186, 188; to Ivybridge, 190; and incendiary bombs, 197–8; foreign travel, 210–21; *other mentions*, 31–2, 60, 88, 99, 122, 128, 141, 147, 149, 150–1, 164, 210, 241, 244
Byles, Miss (l.m.), 60
Byng, Lord and Lady, 212–13

Cambridge, Lady Mary, 24
Camm, Mr (head gardener), 129
Campbell, Lady Illona, 24
Campbell-Gray, Mrs (Lady A's companion), 175
Canadian soldiers, Lord Astor's hospital for, 90
Carcano, Mr (Argentine Ambassador), 112
Cartier (London jewellers), 76, 259
Casa Maury, Marquesa de (*formerly* Mrs Dudley Ward), 227, 228
Cavendish, Miss Alex, 32
Cavendish, Lady Moyra, 27
Cecil (Gascoyne-Cecil), Hon. Michael, Richard and Robert, 28
Chanel, Madame (couturière), 32
'Chiquita' (married Hon. Jacob A), 172
Christian Science, and C. Scientists, 63, 64, 85, 145, 146, 154, 194, 237–41, 243, 247
Churchill, (Sir) Winston S., PC, MP, 99, 191, 113–14, 204
Clay, Mrs Spender (Lord A's sister), 161, 162
Cliveden (the Astors' estate near Taplow, Buckinghamshire) described, 47–9; the staff, 48–9; burglary at, 74; Military Hospital, 90, 179, 240; Club (for staff), 104; summer and Christmas parties (for staff), 104–6; entertaining at, 108–43; silver ware (polishing), 109–12; staff liveries, 114, 118–19; chefs and kitchens, 119–20; receptions, and the police, 122–4; announcing the guests, 124; 'decorator' at, 128–9; in Ascot Week, 135–6, 139–40; Stud Farm, 146; Cricket Club, 148; *other mentions*, 29, 30, 36, 39–41, 47, 48, 59–63, 79, 92, 96, 115, 149, 154, 157, 174, 176, 179, 180, 200, 223, 241, 244, 248–9, 250, 253, 255
'Cliveden Set' (political group), 135, 148, 243–4
clothes, 2, 12–13, 32–3, 48, 49, 52, 64–6, 173–4, 250
colour problem: in Rhodesia, 225; in USA, 56–7, 221
Colville, Lady Cynthia, 216
Cooper, Lady Diana (*née* Manners), in *The Miracle*, 138
Copcutt, Frank ('decorator', *later* head gardener, at Cliveden), 65, 66, 128–35, 149, 249; his flower arrangements, 129–30, 140; on Lord and Lady A, 148

Coppins, Iver, Bucks., 201
Cranborne, Lady, 27–38, 165–6, 234
Cranborne, Lord (*later* Marquess of Salisbury), 27, 29, 33, 166, 234
Cranborne Manor, Dorset, 27, 29
Craven, Earl of, 17

Dangl, Otto (chef), 255, 257
Dean, Charles (butler), 40, 55, 117–18, 137, 138–9, 174, 175–6, 201, 241, 242, 257
Dean, Sir Patrick and Lady, 117–18
Derby, Earl of, 119, 147
Derby, the, 147
Devonshire, Duke of, 140
Dillon, Clarence, 219
Dorothy, Miss, of Bertha Hammonds (ladies' hair stylists), 83–4

Eaton Square, No. 100 (flat): 40, 170, 174, 175, 230, 231, 255, 257
Edward VII, King, 201
Edward VIII, King, 212, 214, 215
Elizabeth, Princess, 101, 250
Elizabeth, Queen, 101, 183–4, 223, 224
Elizabeth II, Queen: her Coronation (1953), 223–4, 252–3
Elliot Terrace, Plymouth, No. 3: 47, 50, 73, 170, 178, 183, 192, 200, 258
Emms, Miss (Lady Tufton's personal maid), 17–18, 20, 21, 22
Eros, SS, 217–19, 227
Eton College, 18, 28, 154–5, 239
Eydon Hall, 94–5

'Feathers, The' (inn, near Cliveden), 242
Florrie (housemaid), 186, 193
Flynn, Mrs (Lady A's sister), 222
footmen, 118; as valets, 137
Fortescue, Lady, 216
Fountains, Yorkshire, 12; Abbey, 1–2
French lessons, 15, 16

Gandhi, Mahatma, 113
George V, King, 122, 126
George VI, King, 183–4
Gibbons, Nanny (Astors' children's nurse), 101–2, 149–52, 154, 172
Gibson, Mrs Dana (Irene, Lady A's sister), 45, 56–9, 94, 226
Gilbert, Monsieur (chef), 119, 120
Gladys (second parlourmaid), 24
Glasheen, Mr (head gardener), 129
Glentanar, Lord and Lady, 24
Gore-Brown, Sir Stewart, 226

Grace (second housemaid), 24
Granard, Lady, 59
Green, Sir Raymond, 216
Grenfell, Joyce, 70, 161
Grimmett, Gordon (footman), 112, 149, 243; joining the Astors, 114–17; and Eton College, 154–5; on romance at Rest Harrow, 159–61
Grimsthorpe (Lady Ancaster's home), 259, 260
Gustav, King (of Sweden), 96, 226, 230
Gustavus Adolphus (Crown Prince of Sweden), 159
Guy, Mr (a Canadian soldier), 90–1

Hall, John (Duke of Kent's valet and batman), 201
Harrison, Francis William (Author's brother), 2
Harrison, Mr (Author's father), 1–14, 26, 35, 82
Harrison, Mrs (Author's mother), 1–16, 20, 26, 35, 82, 120; and Lady A, 92–3, 101–2; and Queen Mary, 101; her bungalow at Walton-on-Thames, 102, 217, 226, 256, 259; her death, 256
Harrison, Olive (Author's sister), 2, 13, 103, 120, 137
Harrison, Rosina (the Author, 'Rose', 'Ena'): birth, parentage, family, education and early life, 1–14; her ambition to travel, see travel; 1st job (with Lady Tufton), 15–26; 2nd job (with Lady Cranborne), 27–36; 3rd job (with Hon. Phyllis Astor, 'Miss Wissie'), 37–62; 4th job (with Lady Astor), 60–260; and Mr Lee (butler), 40–7 (see also Lee); to USA and back, 53–9; her 'ten little nigger boys', 56; on treatment of Negroes in USA, 56–7; and Mrs Vidler's departure, 60; becomes Lady A's l.m., 60–2; 'My Lady and My Duties', 63–80; and Lady A's jewellery, 52–3, 70–7; and the safe, 74–5; and Russian sable tie, 78–9; and police and porters, 79; and tipping, 79–80, 195–6; 'Coming to Terms with My Job', 81–103; her 'love-life', 81; professional competence, 81–2; relationship with Lady A, 81–107, 178, 185, et passim; a psychological or spiritual change, 82–5; her social life, 103–7; at Cliveden fancy dress dance, 104–7; other dances and balls, 106–7; her sense of 'belonging', 107; and 'Bobbie' Shaw, q.v., 165–6; and Lady A's dogs, 167–70, 260; and the Profumo affair, 174–7; on MPs, 177; her philosophy of life, 177; on 'Lord Billy' (3rd Viscount A), 177; and rats, 183; in Plymouth air raids, 184–9; to Ivybridge, 190; and Lord A at Rock, Cornwall, 193–6; at Bickham, Dartmoor, 196; her 'maternity smock', 196–7; and incendiary bombs, 197–8; and changes in employer/staff relations, 203; and bugs in USA, 206; and Queen Mary, 216; her life insurance, 217; and a bungalow for her mother, 217; on board SS Eros, 217–19; and the Coronation (1953), 223–4, 252–3; gives a scarf to Lady Tredgold, 225; and a Fair Isle jumper to a Rhodesian chieftain's son, 226; and Lady A's jewellery at Miami, 227; her 'fondest wish', 232; religious experiences, 233–6; and church attendance, 234; and the war-work tribunal, 236; on Christian Science, 194, 237–41, 243; and politics, 243; defends Lord and Lady A at Plymouth, 246; and Lady A's last years, and death, 250–60; and royal weddings, 250–1; at Holyroodhouse, 253–5; her mother's death, and bungalow, 256; on City councillors, 257–8; and Lady A's death, 260; end of her life in service, 260–1
Harrison, Suzanne ('Ann', Author's sister), 2, 86
Hatfield House, Herts., 27, 28, 152
Hawkins, Mrs (housekeeper at Eaton Square), 231, 255
Hawkins of Plymouth, 124–5
Helpmann, (Sir) Robert, 138–9
Henley Regatta, 239
Hetheringtons of Ripon, 16
Hill Street, London, No. 35: 248, 250, 251, 255
Hitler, Adolf, 196, 243, 245
Hobson, Mr and Mrs, of Richmond, Va, 58, 226–7
Hofmannstahl, Hugo and Raymond von, 138
Holyroodhouse, Edinburgh, 253–5
Hopkins, Mr (Lady A's chauffeur), 99, 106
Hopkins Jones (jewellers), 77

Hothfield Place, Kent, 17–18, 22, 28
House of Commons, 64, 65, 66, 73, 86, 96, 99, 115, 132, 136, 179, 202

Ingrid, Queen (of Denmark), 230
Ileana, Princess (of Hapsburg), 211
Irvine, Miss (Lady A's secretary), 93, 103
Ivybridge, near Plymouth, 190

Jacqmar, 68
'Jakie', see Astor, Hon. Jacob
James, Mrs Willie, 201
Jeffries, Bert (second chauffeur), 154, 155
Jenkins, Miss (Lady A's secretary), 74
Jessie (Tuftons' head housemaid), 17
Jones, Miss (Lord A's secretary), 71

Keene, Nancy Witcher, see Langhorne, Nancy Witcher
Kennedy, Sir John and Lady, 224
Kent, Duchess of (Princess Marina), 30, 200–1, 210, 211
Kent, Duke of, 200–1, 210, 211
Kindersley, Miss (Lady A's head secretary), 37, 113

Ladies' maids, 15–16, 22, 35; see also young ladies' maids
Lamé, Monsieur (chef), 189
Lamont, Thomas and Mrs, 206, 220
Lancaster, Mrs Nancy (Lady A's niece), 169, 230–1, 241
Langhorne, Chiswell Dabney (Lady A's father), 44
Langhorne, Nancy Witcher, née Keene (Lady A's mother), 45, 89
Langhornes, the, 44, 45, 57
Lansdowne, Lady, 216
Lanvin, Jeanne (couturière), 32
laundry work: at home, 7–8; in service, 48, 49
Lawrence, T. E., 98–9
Lee, Edwin ('Mr Lee', butler at Cliveden): personal details, 144, 179; his account of the Astor family, 40–7; his 'standards', 44; and the Sancy diamond, 72–3; and Lady A's pearls missing, 73–5; and beggars, 91; timing the arrival of Royalty, 96–7; and 'confidences', 97; his 'guest-book', 108–9; and functions at Cliveden, 109, 113; and his silver, 109–12; 'nearly left the Astors', 112; and guests' criticism, 114; his livery, 114; and additional staff, 117; and 'odd

men', q.v., 121; his kindly discipline, 121; and receptions, 122–3; and police, 122–3; as an 'announcer', 124; at dinner parties, 125; and 'best vintage claret', and other wines and liqueurs, 125–6; on Royalty, 127, 255; and Lady A and table decorations, 132–3; on conversation with guests, 136–7; and Freddy Alexander, 141–2; and Lord Astor, 144, 148–9; and the Derby, 147; and an idle chauffeur, 160; and a honeymoon at Rest Harrow, 159–61; on homosexuality, 163–4; and the Profumo affair, 174–5; on tipping, 195–6; ran Cliveden in wartime, 202; on Lady A's religion, 238; on teetotalism, 124–5, 242–3; and Catholics, 243; on the Astors' politics, 244–5; after the war, 248–9; and the Bowes-Lyons, 251–2; other mentions, 40, 48, 61, 62, 71, 72, 91, 98, 103, 114–16, 118–19, 127–8, 147–50, 154, 155, 159–61, 174, 179, 180, 241, 251, 253, 254
Lillico, Robert (tailor), 116–17
Lister, Mr and Mrs (school teachers), 3, 4
liveries, men-servants', 114, 118–19
Lloyd George, David, 41
London (see also Eaton Square, Hill Street and St James's Square), 16, 17, 22, 79, 157, 165, 166; Season, 29; air raids on, 180; locations: Aeolian Hall, 19; Albert Hall, 106; Babmaes Street, 180, 181; Café Royal, 76; Carlton House Terrace, 51; Guards Chapel, 234; Hammersmith Bridge, 34; Jermyn Street, 180–1; Regent Street, 49; Savile Row, 33; West End, 22; Westminster Abbey, 234; Wharncliffe Rooms, 106
Lothian, Lord (Philip Kerr), 237, 238, 241
Lyttelton, Dame Edith, 207–10

MacIntyre, Mr and Mrs (at Tarbert Lodge, q.v.), 50, 157
McMillan, Margaret, 136
Magnier, Mademoiselle, 29–30
Malcolm, Lady, her Servants' Ball, 106–7
Manning, Florrie (housekeeper), 245, 246
Margaret, Princess, 101, 224
Marie, Queen (of Rumania), 211
Marie, Queen (of Yugoslavia), 101, 210, 211

Marks & Spencer's, 67, 68
Marlborough, Duchess of, 30
Marshall, General George C., 222
Mary, Queen, 77, 94, 101, 102, 122, 126, 216
Masseys of Baker Street (domestic agency), 27
Menzies, Sir Robert (PM of Australia), 186
Metcalfe, David, 67
Metcalfe, Major (Equerry to Prince of Wales), 127
Mildmay of Flete, Lord, 216
Mirador, Greenwood, Va., (Langhornes' estate in USA), 45, 57-8
Mollie (Princess Obolensky's maid), 55, 56
Moore, Lottie (housekeeper), 166
Mount Edgcumbe, Lord, 216
Mountbatten, Lady Louise, 159-61
Munnings, Sir Alfred, RA, 148
Mussolini, Benito, 31

'Nannies', 101-2, 149-50; see also Gibbons
Newborough, Lord, 126
Nicholas, Prince (of Greece), 211
Norman, Miss (Lady Cavendish's maid), 32
Norman, Montagu (Governor of Bank of England), 114
nurseries and nurserymaids, 151-2

Obolensky, Prince, 55-6, 137-8
Obolensky, Princess (formerly Alice Astor, q.v.), 55-6, 137
Observer, The, 164
O'Casey, Sean and Mrs, 136, 238
'odd men', domestic, 120-1; see also 'Sailor' and William
Olga, Princess (of Yugoslavia), 211

Papillion, Monsieur (chef), 119
Paul, Prince (of Yugoslavia), 211
Phipps, Nora (Lady A's sister), 72
Phipps, Tommy (Lady A's nephew), 161, 162
Pinet (Paris ladies' shoe shop), 33
Plunkett-Ernle-Erle-Drax, Admiral and Lady, 216
Plymouth (see also Elliot Terrace), 165, 179, 180, 183-92, 240, 245-6; air raids on, 184-9, 195, 199; rebuilding, 194, 249; in 1941 and 1942, 200-1; Lady A given 'Freedom of the City', 257-8
politics, 66, 243-7; see also House of Commons

Pooley, Mr (W. W. Astor's butler), 41
Prince of Wales (later Edward VIII, q.v.), 76, 127, 133, 134
Profumo affair, 174-7
Profumo, Mr and Mrs, 175

Rasputin (1871-1916), 138
receptions at Cliveden and St James's Square, 122-5; 'dry', 124
recreations, 3-4, 13, 49, 63, 64
religion, 233-43; see also Christian Science
Rémond, Madame, of Beauchamp Place, 250
Rest Harrow, Sandwich, Kent, 47, 49-50, 87, 157, 159-61, 178, 249-50
Ribbentrop, Herr, 244-5
Ripon, Marquess and Marchioness of, 1, 2, 7, 10
Ripon, Yorkshire, 13, 16
Robertson, Ben (American journalist), 184-5
Rock, Cornwall, 170, 192-6
Rood's (London jewellers), 76
Rothschilds, the, 129
Royal Weddings, 250-1
Royalty, 96-7; and domestic staff, 102, 255; and punctuality, 127

'Sailor' ('odd man'), 121, 128
St James's Square, London, No. 4: 47, 49, 67, 79, 91, 101, 106, 114, 129, 131, 132, 180-3, 244, 248; entertaining at, 108-43 p; police on duty at, 122-3; in air raid, 180; domestic details at Cliveden, q.v., also apply here.
Salisbury, Marquess of, 27
Samson, Miss (one of Lady A's former l.m's.), 73-4
Sancy diamond, Lady Astor's, 71-3
Sandwich, Kent (see also Rest Harrow), 158-9, 167, 168
Sargent, John: his portrait of Lady Astor, 91
Sawley Hall (Lady Baron's home), 7
Sellars, Miss, of Bond Street (domestic agency), 27
servants' halls, 23-4
Seymour, Sir Reginald, 216
Shaw, 'Bobbie' (Lady A's first son, by her first marriage), 46, 57, 163-5, 171, 176, 232, 255; and his mother, 163-5; his misfortunes, 166, 180; his dogs, 166, 167
Shaw, George Bernard, 83, 136, 164, 238, 249

Shaw, Robert Gould (Lady A's first husband), 45, 89
Sinn Feiners, 25
Southampton: Customs office, 68–9
Stairs, Earl and Countess of, 251–2
Studley Park, Yorkshire, 5, 10
Studley Royal, Yorkshire, 1, 2; Church, 1, 6; dairy, 12
Sweden, King and Queen of, 226, 230

Tarbert Lodge, Jura, 47, 50, 157–9
Trafford, Sir Humphrey and Lady de, 227
Tranby Croft, 2
travel, foreign: Author's ambition achieved, 24–5, 53–9, 205–32, 260; *places mentioned*: Belgrade, 210, 211; Bermuda, 213–14; Biarritz, 32, 212; Boston, Mass., 58; Budapest, 211; Bulawayo, 224; Carolina, South, 220; Casablanca, 229; Charlottesville, Va, 45, 57; Copenhagen, 216; Danville, Va, 45; Denmark, 216, 226; Des Moines, Iowa, 222; Dublin, 25; Eire (Ireland), 25; Eze (French Riviera), 30; Florida, 215, 219–20, 227; France, South of, 30; Garmisch Partenkirchen, Bavaria, 234, 235; Ireland (Eire), 25; Istanbul, 207–10; Italy, 30–2; Marrakesh, 229; Miami, Fla, 227; Monte Carlo, 30; Munich, 234, 235; Nassau, Bahamas, 226, 227–8; New York, 40, 56, 58, 68, 89, 213, 218–20 (Hotel Astor, 219; Ritz Carlton Hotel, 219; Waldorf Astoria Hotel, 213; Westbury Hotel, 206); Palm Beach, Fla, 215; Paris, 32, 208, 212, 229, 231 (British Embassy, 208; George V Hotel, 212; Hôtel du Rhin, 32; Place Vendôme, 32; The Ritz, 32, 229); Rhinebeck, NY, 59; Rhodesia, 223–6, 253; Richmond, Va, 45, 58; Rome, 30–2; Russia, 164; St Jean de Luz, Biarritz, 32; Salisbury (Rhodesia), 225; Savannah, Ga, 216; Sweden, 226, 230–1; Tucson, Arizona, 221–2; USA, 53–9, 213, 215, 216, 218–23, 226, 227; Vienna, 211–12; Vimy Ridge, 212–13; Virginia, USA, 44, 45, 57, 58, 226; Washington, DC, 220, 223 (British Embassy, 40, 117; Canadian Embassy, 58); Yugoslavia, 210–11
Trebetherick, Rock, Cornwall, 196
Tredgold, Sir Robert and Lady, 225

Tribal Feeling (by Michael Astor), 44, 107
Tufton, Ann, 16–18, 20, 21
Tufton, Hon. Harry, 18, 25
Tufton, Lady Ierne, 16, 17, 21, 25, 26, 37
Tufton, Major, 22
Tufton, Patricia, 16–21, 23, 25, 29
Tufton, Peter, 18
Tuftons, the, 19, 29, 234; Author's service with, 15–26; their town house, 17; domestic staff, 17–24; their dogs, 166

Vidler, Mrs (Lady A's previous l.m.), 36, 37, 50, 53–4, 60
Vimy Ridge, 212
Virginia, USA, 44, 45, 57, 58, 226; Blue Ridge Mountains, 45, 57; Governor of, 58

Walton-on-Thames, Surrey, 102, 217, 226, 256, 259
Ward, Dr Stephen, 174
Welham, Miss (milliner), 69
Werner, Sir Harold, 148
White, Miss (manageress of Mirador, *q.v.*), 57
Wilkinson, Ellen, MP, 191
William ('odd man'), 170, 181–2, 248, 255
Wimborne, Lord, 34
Windsor Castle, Berkshire, 96, 141
Winn, Elizabeth (Lady A's grand-niece), 220
Winn, Mrs (Lady A's niece), 51, 228
Wintringham, Mrs, MP, 142
'Wissie, Miss' (Hon. Phyllis Astor, only daughter of Lord and Lady A; *later* Countess of Ancaster, *q.v.*): personal details, 50–3; to USA and back, 53–9; her dog, 167; and Lady A, 172–3; her marriage, 173; injured while hunting, 240; and Lady A's death, 260; *other mentions*, 37, 39, 46–55, 61, 103, 105, 146–7, 207, 224, 225, 229, 240, 258, 259
'Women's lib', below stairs, 22
Woodman, Nanny (Cranbornes'), 28
Wynn, Freddie (butler), 126

Xenia, Grand Duchess (of Russia), 91

York, Duke and Duchess of, 215
Yorkshire, 1–14, 16; accent, 26, 85–6; high tea, 230; pudding, 6
young ladies' maids, 16; duties, 17–22, 29; wages, 25, 37